THE ABSENT STATE

Insurgency as an Excuse for Misgovernance

NEELESH MISRA & RAHUL PANDITA

hachette
INDIA

First published in 2010 by Hachette India
(Registered name: Hachette Book Publishing India Pvt. Ltd)
An Hachette UK company
www.hachetteindia.com

This edition published in 2016

SRD

ISBN 978-93-5195-106-3

Hachette Book Publishing India Pvt. Ltd
4th & 5th Floors, Corporate Centre
Plot No. 94, Sector 44,
Gurgaon 122003, India

Typeset in ITC Giovanni Std 10/14
by InoSoft Systems, Noida

Printed and bound in India by
Manipal Technologies Limited, Manipal

MIX
Paper | Supporting responsible forestry
FSC™ C043100
FSC www.fsc.org

THE ABSENT STATE

Neelesh Misra is the author of three books – *173 Hours in Captivity: The Hijacking of IC-814* (HarperCollins), *End of the Line: The Story of the Killing of the Royals in Nepal* (Penguin India) and a novel, *Once Upon a Timezone* (HarperCollins). He has also co-edited *India Yatra* and *Inspired India: Ideas to Transform a Nation*. His stories on insurgency have won him the Ramnath Goenka Award for Excellence in Journalism and the K.C. Kulish Memorial Award. Neelesh is an amateur photographer, and writes lyrics and scripts for Bollywood.

Rahul Pandita is a journalist and author. He has previously worked with the Indian Express Group, *The Hindu*, *Open*, Aaj Tak and Zee News, and is a former NEMEP and Sarai-CSDS fellow. A chronicler of conflicts, Rahul has reported extensively on Iraq, Sri Lanka, Kashmir, India's Northeast and Naxal-affected areas. He is the author of *Hello, Bastar: The Untold Story of India's Maoist Movement* and *Our Moon Has Blood Clots: The Exodus of Kashmiri Pandits*.

Praise for *The Absent State*

'This book is highly recommended for its sincerity towards the voice of the muted, for the inner foul that shrouds our peripheral glory, for the bravado of the authors who took the nerve-whacking journey and turned it into a directory of India's other existence. One piece of advice that would come handy while reading the book: Keep the brain and the heart in their respective places. A merger would prove costly for perception.' – *IBN Live*

'There is no doubt about the importance of the issue [that *The Absent State*] deals with. It is a compilation of the dispatches by two journalists working with national dailies, who have "travelled thousands of kilometres for close to three years into some of India's remotest corners" in these three regions.' – *The Hindu*

Neelesh's parents, Nirmala and S.B. Misra
Rahul's parents, Shanta and P.N. Pandita

Who let their sons disagree on a thousand things.
Who taught them that it is better to have a label on the forehead than blinkers on the eyes.

Contents

Foreword

INDIA, AT WAR WITH ITSELF

'If we could read the secret history of our enemies, we should find in each man's life sorrow and suffering enough to disarm all hostility.'

—Henry Wadsworth Longfellow

Seventeenth of May, 2010. Delhi is burning. It's almost 48 degrees Celsius outside. I step out of the plush air-conditioned chamber of the finance minister of India along with my colleagues from the film industry. We are here to prevail upon the minister to spare the film industry from any extra tax burdens since – contrary to the image that is being portrayed in the media – Bollywood is in the throes of death.

As I get into the car and begin making my way to the airport I notice almost a dozen OB Vans parked outside the home minister's office in North Block. 'What's going on?' I ask my friend Ajay Kanchan, with whom I had made a documentary on the Naga insurgency in Nagaland. 'The Maoists have struck again, sir. Thirty-one people have been killed in Dantewada. It looks like India is haemorrhaging. We have violence in Kashmir, trouble in the Northeast and now Dantewada has become the war theatre,' he says dismally.

His words hurl me back into memory land. I am reminded of my visit to the enchanted forests of Bastar.

The year was 2003. I was tired of manufacturing illusions for the dream factories of Bollywood and I was pining to get a glimpse of 'real life'. So it was hardly surprising that when a friend put forward an idea of filming a documentary on the tribal life of Chhattisgarh, I embraced the offer right away. Little did I know then that there, in the dense jungles of Bastar where the Naxalites operate, I would come face to face with a handsome boatman who would give me a taste of the real India.

Here is a replay of the conversation that took place by the side of a turbulent river, at the crack of dawn:

MB: From where did you get this ancient boat?

Tribal: *(Wiping the sweat from his body)* It is our family boat. It belonged to my grandfather. He gave it to my father who then passed it on to me. This boat and this river have fed us for years.

MB: How much money do you make by carrying people across the river every day?

Tribal: Two rupees per person is what I charge one way. I don't charge money for children and very old people.

MB: *(Pointing in the direction of a construction site at a distance)* Aren't you afraid that this bridge which is being built by the government will rob you of your livelihood? Once the bridge is made, people will no longer need your boat to go across this river. What will happen to you and your family then? How will you survive? Aren't you worried?

Tribal: *(After a long pause)* Whatever has to happen to us will happen. But this bridge will certainly help the people of this region. They will no longer have to pay me money to cross the river every day. Isn't that good?

The heartbreaking generosity and the selflessness of that man moved me to tears. His words still resonate within me. I wonder often if that boatman has now become a militant. Because if he has then 'we' as a nation are wholly and solely responsible for it. It must have taken a lot for 'innocence' to pick up the gun. And it is hard to live off that innocence and wisdom for long, isn't it?

In large parts of India tribals are being pushed to the fringes in crueller ways than before, as the so-called New India tramples over their lands to reach out to its imagined tomorrows.

A friend of mine once told me, 'Humiliation gives birth to desperation and desperation gives birth to uncontrollable rage.' I realize now how true that statement is. Maoist leaders have effectively harnessed the rage of the tribals and are now using it against the state. This vicious cycle of atrocities between the Maoists and the state will not stop unless the civil society of India sheds its apathy and partners with sane forces to bring about a peaceful resolution to this blood feud.

The bigoted nationalists of our country who are asking the government to take military action against our own people must be reminded that this Naxal violence will raise its head over and over again because at its heart is the deeper structural violence that our democratic republic has refused to address. The truth is that sixty-three years after Independence 77 per cent of Indians live on less than twenty rupees a day while a minuscule 5 per cent enjoy what borders on an obscene surplus. It is the humiliation of the desperately poor which fuels these outbursts of violence and that is the very lifeblood of the various insurgencies that are endangering the sovereignty of India.

Democracy does not come from the top – it comes from the bottom. The need of the hour is to recognize and appreciate the drive of the people in these 'troubled zones' for self-affirmation and self-assertion. A young cop who drove me through the Naxal-affected region of Bastar told me: a society which is able to assert itself socially is seldom vicious; it is the weak that are most likely to stab themselves in the back.

In the year 2001, I was in Nagaland shooting a documentary. While I was in the quaint village of Khanoma, I visited a school to talk to the children there. I asked them on camera what their dream was. I distinctly remember a young Naga boy who fearlessly went up to the blackboard and wrote; almost violently, 'My dream is to free Nagaland.' When the young boy realized that he wasn't being reprimanded for stating this fact so plainly, and when he eventually saw himself being given a place in the documentary, he ended up forming a very warm friendship with me. I realized then that when alienated and humiliated societies aren't allowed to truthfully express their rage and let go of it through their words, they express it through guns and bombs.

In this book, Neelesh Misra and Rahul Pandita give you an intimate view of the world's biggest communist insurgency which is currently raging right here in India. These two young men have dared to take an unflinching and honest look at the real truth behind the insurgencies in northeast India and Kashmir. They have reframed the existing narratives and myths and they have brought us the truth from the bottom up by engaging with those who are in the eye of the storm.

In an India where the rift between reality and reporting has reached its end and where the mainstream corporate media has failed to bring us the truth as it exists, this book is an invaluable gift. It is angry and hopeful; it has both passion and authority. Bertrand Russell once said: 'You can either go mad with the truth or stay sane with lies.' I am so glad someone decided to voice the unspeakable. I am so glad someone refused to participate in a lie. Just when I was beginning to believe that god's in his heaven and everything is well with my country, along comes a book of extraordinary courage that dares me to see what I have never been told. The writers go about their reporting with the precision of surgeons who peel off lies and lay bare the truth. Do you have the courage to take it? Because it is the truth which will free us.

I have just concluded writing this Foreword. My blackberry beeps. The words 'breaking news' flash on the screen: thirteen coaches of a Mumbai-bound passenger train were derailed and then hit by a speeding goods train in West Bengal. The Maoist-backed People's Committee against Police Atrocities (PCAPA) has claimed responsibility for the derailment of the Kurla-bound Gyaneshwari Express, which killed sixty-five people and wounded two hundred. Posters demanding immediate withdrawal of the joint forces from the area were found on the railway tracks.

My daughter Pooja, reacting to this news, explodes, 'If they are going to target trains and kill civilians in their fight for self-assertion, then the nation needs to oppose them. They can't get away with this.'

So many truths, so many views are colliding. Mark my words, they are all true. That is the magic of this nation – that a million differing views abide here in an uneasy coexistence.

But when it comes to insurgencies, New Delhi has been quick to brand rebels as 'the other', forgetting that their back stories are not stories of people who have picked up guns to oppose the nation; combined, they give us the story of the nation itself.

Mahesh Bhatt
Mumbai, 2010

Authors' Glossary

God is in the semantics. The meaning and loose usage of the word 'terrorist' is a matter of debate all over the world. The authors have used the following logic:

> An armed rebel who attacks an armed soldier is a militant not a terrorist.
>
> An armed rebel who lobs a grenade at a moving military vehicle in a busy market, knowing full well that it could miss its target and kill or wound civilians, is a terrorist.
>
> An armed rebel who kills an unarmed man either on suspicion of being an informer or for extortion is a terrorist.
>
> Regardless of what the media might tell you, every person arrested on charges of being a militant is not a terrorist. A large number is actually completely innocent.

Prologue

The world's largest communist insurgency. The world's oldest-running ethnic insurgency. One of the world's most complex Islamic insurgencies. Welcome to India, the toast of the world, where one in every five citizens lives under the shadow of the threat of armed rebellion.

India might be one of the fastest-growing economies in the world, a nation assiduously wooed by global powers, but in many rural areas the Indian state simply does not exist. The country, it seems, is offering an example for other regions of the world that are being ripped apart by armed conflict – from Iraq to Afghanistan, to Peru and Colombia, to Chechnya, Sudan and Nigeria, to the Philippines and Spain – of how *not* to deal with armed rebels. For it has made insurgency a convenient excuse for misgovernance.

It's not that the government hasn't pumped development funds into these areas. In fact, the premise for this book began with those very numbers. Around 11 per cent of the budget of the Ministry of Rural Development in recent years has been allocated to insurgency-affected districts, across Kashmir, areas under Naxalite influence and in the Northeast, but the central government does little to monitor its use. In 2006–07, when we first began our three-year investigation into development funds in the insurgency-affected areas of India, we found that Rs 5,800 crore had been disbursed to some one hundred and fifty-two districts across twelve of India's twenty-nine states. But, out of that, at least Rs 2,700 crore had not been used. In 2009–10, around Rs 6,900 crore had been earmarked for development projects in India's Naxalite-affected areas. These funds were allocated to states for the construction and upkeep of schools, homes, roads and jobs, measures that could help ease the seething discontentment. It remains to be seen if the money will be effectively utilized.

In many of the country's militancy-wracked regions, the state and its symbols have long been invisible; functional schools, medical facilities, even police stations do not exist. In the Northeast, underground groups often decide and influence administrators on how taxpayer's money should be spent, or prop up their own contractors to build infrastructure, and much of the development funds are routed through them. This is true also of Naxalite-affected areas, where taxpayer's funds routinely reach the rebels in the form of 'levies'. In many areas, where justice has failed the common people, they approach militants and not the courts of law when rapes, murders and abductions take place.

When you assemble the pieces of the jigsaw – social discontent, unemployment, poverty, ethnic and tribal rivalries, forced recruitment by rebels, the high-handedness of the security forces, and the promise of thrill and power for the 'adventurous' – they complete a picture of a hundred rebellions eating away at the country. With rebel presence in about two hundred of the country's six hundred-plus districts, albeit less in some areas than in others, the everyday lives of some 25 crore Indians are shaped by insurgents. Every fourth Indian who lives in an area of rebel influence has to think twice before stepping out for an evening wedding or a religious ceremony or a trip to the market. The decision, in some states, to arm the common man to fight militants and protect himself without any provision for adequate training and guidance from the security forces, has added to the disaster by making the villagers even more vulnerable to gruesome revenge attacks by militants.

It is a crisis spiralling across the country. It might not yet be putting a complete dampener on India's success story, but it is certain that insurgency is set to become the ball and chain shackling a country that is poised to fly high and dream big.

To tell this story, we travelled over thousands of kilometres for close to three years into some of India's remotest corners. In many of these areas, villagers mistook us for government officials who had never been anywhere close. They wanted their complaints heard. They wanted their names written down in notebooks. They wanted to be assured that the troubles of their lives had been documented somewhere on some piece of paper that would become a part of government files.

During our journey into the heart of India's battle zones, we came across some well-known and little-known truths.

We found the first casualty of war: a sense of perspective. It's easy to be labelled traitors, or spies, or terrorists in the war zones. The police readily put anyone behind bars, at times even for offering food to insurgents under duress. The insurgents tag anyone talking to the police – even if they do so out of fear – as informers and punish them. For the NGOs and activists, whose presence is often more prominent than government officials in these areas, any point of agreement with the state, or any positive action or reaction connected to it, however rational, is unacceptable. It seems that often India's so-called civil society movement, built on the edifice of dissent, can't handle an iota of dissent when someone disagrees with it.

We found the absent state. Government officials have not administered many of these areas in any real sense for decades. The last time revenue officials mapped villages in what is known as the Abujhmaad forest in Bastar, Chhattisgarh, was more than four hundred years ago, during the reign of the Mughal emperor, Akbar! In many places it is the insurgents who set benchmarks for rural administration by applying innovative measures that few elected governments think of when it comes to grass-roots India.

We found policemen fighting an impossible battle for their own survival in a land of cruel geography, where even ferrying rations is like participating in a war. In addition is the little recognition of the tough conditions they work in: 50 degrees Celsius heat, with no reinforcements at hand, little communication or operational support in unfamiliar surroundings where local insurgents can ambush and kill them and vanish without a trace.

Here is what this means: In a country that has 32 lakh elected representatives – the largest number in any democracy in the world – lakhs of people have been pushed out of the democratic process. In regions hit by insurgency, in particular, all symbols of democracy appear to be fading rapidly: village councils are nearly defunct, politicians and administrators are conspicuous by their absence, elections have poor turnouts amid rebel calls for boycotts.

Even as India presses forward a major offensive against insurgency, it is clear to most that military solutions will not help. 'This is not a law and order problem. It is simply a question of governance,' Ramesh Saran, an economist at Ranchi University who has closely studied the Naxalite movement, told us. According to him, crushing the rebels with force would boomerang. 'It is like a strong headache. You will pop an aspirin, push it aside and pretend it is gone. But it is there. And it will return.'

The Naxalite surge makes up a major portion of the book. Simply, it is India's biggest internal security challenge as of now, although, until recently, governments have shied away from recognizing it as such. Compared to Kashmir, which has always been seen as the 'sexy' insurgency, the one that got the international headlines since it involved India and Pakistan and occasionally other nations, the Naxalite was seen as the poor rebel, fighting a faraway battle in

India's forgotten lands. But behind our backs it has grown into a crisis that questions all that modern India seemingly stands for. Most importantly, economic progress, spiralling development and failed delivery of justice. Our stories focus more on Jharkhand than on Chhattisgarh, another hub of the Naxal surge, because our book is not about rebels, but rather about people and governance, and Jharkhand is representative, by far, of the larger picture of insurgency-as-an-excuse across a dozen-odd states.

In Kashmir, until the most recent upheaval in 2010, violence was at a minimal level compared to earlier years. Tragically, this was seen, as it often is, as the primary barometer of 'normalcy' in a state governed by very cruel mathematics. While the de-escalation of violence eased the lives of Kashmir's residents, the rush of development that the improved situation should have ensured did not follow. The snapshots we encountered showed that Kashmir was on autopilot, with little accountability in governance and limited efforts being made to decrease the military presence that was clearly not needed at such overwhelming levels.

From there on to the Northeast, a classic case of how insurgency has become so deeply entrenched in the system that it resembles the system itself. We have told this story through Manipur, which highlights this crisis like no other region. The insurgent is a part of the everyday life here for citizens, and the effects of the insurgency and the 'taxes' charged by the rebels permeate into everything from the price of milk powder to parking-lot contracts. New Delhi has mostly looked the other way, content that there is a government in place at all.

But, as you will discover in the pages that follow, across India's troubled regions, there isn't.

Part One

The Naxalite Surge

'EVERY FIRE STARTS IN THE BELLY'

1

We do not know what Turia Munda looked like. He did not leave behind a picture. But if one was to guess the appearance of the dead father from the face of his eldest son, the forty-year-old farmer had perhaps been lean and short, with puffed cheeks, dark, slightly wrinkled skin burnt by the oppressive Indian sun, and had probably worn broken slippers, just like his child.

Who knows what was going through Munda's mind as he awoke on that February night in his small, rectangular mud-and-thatch hut in Gitildi village in Jharkhand? Munda walked past his four children sleeping on the mud-caked floor and picked up a sari worn by his wife until a few months ago, when she died. In the silence of the night, he stepped out into a little clearing outside his house and walked across a narrow path that ran along a row of bushes behind the house. He stood before a huge berry tree looming above him under the clear night sky. He climbed it - it was one of the first skills he had learnt as a child - and then tied one end of the sari to a branch and the other to his neck. Who knows if he gasped, or muttered something, or had second thoughts? He let go and leaped, the impact of the brutal jerk breaking his neck and wrenching the life out of him. With that single action, the angry farmer, who had been dismissed by government officials throughout his squalor-ridden, wretched life, became tragically famous in his death. He was the first man to die because he had not received wages under the National Rural Employment Guarantee Scheme (NREGS), purported to be the world's largest social security set-up.

Behind that single moment of desperation – and defeat – lies a story.

Seventeen years ago, on the morning on which Turiya Munda's body was discovered hanging lifeless from the berry tree, things were happening in other parts of the world.

It was 24 July 1991. On the other side of the globe, in Room 118 at the office of the Texas Water Commission, government officials were squabbling over petty sewage issues. In another part of the state, a man called George W. Bush, son of the then president of the United States, had just bought a larger stake in the Texas Rangers baseball club, amidst swirling rumours that he was set for a career in politics. That scary situation – which would soon begin to impact ordinary, unknown people like Turia Munda in faraway countries across the world – was some time away, but for another political newcomer it was already the big day.

In India, wearing the light blue turban that would become his fashion statement in the years to follow, Finance Minister Dr Manmohan Singh was getting ready to make his speech in the high-ceilinged, colonial-era building that houses the Indian Parliament, a speech in which he would present the national budget to a gloomy, despairing nation.

In 1991, India was in ruins, on the verge of bankruptcy. For a country that was once so rich that it was called 'the golden bird', it was a moment of shame and a stunning indictment of the people who had governed it. While the country was still recovering from the brutal assassination two months ago of former prime minister Rajiv Gandhi, some 20 tonnes of gold had been transported in jetliners to Switzerland and sold to prevent an economic collapse. Another 46 tonnes had been shipped to London as collateral for a loan from the Bank of Japan. India was smarting with humiliation, and anger.

For a whole week before the finance minister was to make his crucial announcement, employees of the press where the budget papers were being printed had been cloistered in their office, a tradition that had been followed for years to maintain confidentiality. They couldn't make calls, they couldn't step out. That year, they were prisoners trying to unshackle the nation from impending economic doom.

Ancient fans whirred listlessly from the towering ceiling of Parliament's lower house. The hum of lawmakers slowly died down. When his turn came, Manmohan Singh stunned the nation by slashing away the cobwebs of a socialist-style economy. He quoted before a disbelieving audience his favourite phrase, the words of Victor Hugo: 'No power on earth can stop an idea whose time has come ... I suggest to this august House that the emergence of India as a major economic power in the world happens to be one such idea.'

It was no ordinary day. It was no ordinary budget. Manmohan Singh had laid the foundations of what would, in less than a decade, become the buzzword of the world: the New India.

At about the same time, around 1,000 kilometres east of the British-era hall, a group of young men, some with crude guns slung over their shoulders, were making their daily journey towards a village in Bihar, one of the country's poorest states. They were Naxalites – communist rebels – who had made their first appearance with arms in the village that very month. That year, 1991, was when the communist militants would take the most dramatic step of their decades-old movement, emerging with guns in places of their choosing in the vast Indian countryside, seeking out support and entrenching themselves in strongholds.

Three years after that day in 1991, Dr Manmohan Singh tabled his second budget. By this time, the Indian middle class, living in bustling, chaotic metropolises and teeming million-plus cities, had begun to feel the effects of economic liberalization. You didn't have to bribe government officials any longer to get telephone or cooking-gas connections. It had become possible to get a two-wheeler ahead of the mandatory waiting period. Consumer durables such as tape recorders and cameras could be bought at affordable prices. People could now take loans to purchase anything, from an apartment in a high-rise building to a washing machine. New wheels were invented for a smooth, if indebted, life: In fifteen years, there would be 2.5 crore credit card users in India.

Yet, in large swathes of rural India, the 1991 budget had had little impact. Years of exploitation of land and resources, years of forgotten promises of rehabilitation and development would give rise to further discontent and lead to these remote areas becoming susceptible to the influence of insurgents and to widespread insurgency.

In the late 1960s, two men, Charu Majumdar and Kanu Sanyal, had started a tiny revolution in a small village in West Bengal which would give a movement its name. They were among a handful of men who believed it was fruitless to try to change the social order by peaceful means and they spread their message quite effectively among discontented land labourers. Led by the new rebels and armed with indigenous weapons such as bows and arrows, local tribals swooped down on landowners, forcibly occupying their land. The sickle with which they had slaved away in the fields became a potent weapon against oppression.

It was not the first time that peasants in the region had risen against hunger and oppression. Before India became independent in 1947, Bengal had been witness to a movement started by peasants to press for a better crop share for themselves. Around the same time as the movement was launched in Naxalbari in Bengal, Andhra Pradesh saw a similar uprising taking shape in Srikakulam, where the local hill people, known as Girijans, revolted against exploitation at the hands of landlords. Yet, Naxalbari became the masthead of the red rebellion. China, the land of Mao, hailed the developments in Naxalbari as 'a peal of spring thunder'.

As expected, violence was met with violence as armed peasants clashed with their erstwhile masters. After mulling over it for days, the West Bengal government finally ordered the police machinery to tame the revolutionaries. And so they did, supposedly, official records tell us, within fifty-two days. But by then the fire had spread. Young men and women who were living in insulated centres such as Delhi and Bombay, fed on a heady dose of idealism, left cushy career prospects and joined the rebellion. Hostel rooms at India's premier institutes of higher education, from St Stephen's College in Delhi to Presidency College in Calcutta, emptied out.

Between 1970 and 1971, the Naxal movement touched its zenith and spread to other states, including Bihar, Uttar Pradesh, Punjab, Orissa and Kerala. Eventually, the government of India decided it was time for action.

In 1970, India was ruled by Prime Minister Indira Gandhi, the daughter of India's first prime minister, Jawaharlal Nehru. Fourteen years later she would be shot dead by her own bodyguards looking to avenge a botched-up military operation she had ordered on a Sikh shrine. But in 1970, nothing she did was wrong for the people. As a sycophant in her party so famously said, Indira was India.

Four days before the country was to celebrate its twenty-seventh Independence Day, Indira Gandhi addressed the upper house of the Indian Parliament, delivering an iron-fist message that went well with her reputation: The government would fight the Naxalites with all the strength at its command. 'These elements will be fought to the finish,' she announced. True to her words, the Indian state cracked down on the rebels with all its might. Most of its top leaders were either eliminated or arrested.

Maoist ideologues believe that the period of Emergency declared by Indira Gandhi in 1975 was not due to any political crisis; it was aimed at bringing the Naxalite leadership to its knees. Although such a claim seems a bit far-fetched, it is true that the Naxalite leadership, released from prisons after the Emergency, used the last three years of the 1970s to regroup and plan new strategies. By 1980, the Naxalites had become active again, mainly in Andhra Pradesh and Bihar. In Andhra Pradesh, the People's War Group (PWG) is said to have redistributed close to 2,020 square kilometres of land across the state to landless farmers right through the 1980s. By 1990, it had become a major rebel group, launching deadly attacks against the police and paramilitary forces in its areas of influence. In Bihar, the Maoist Communist Centre (MCC) was formed in 1975, as an afterthought to a string of stirrings – very much on the lines of the Naxalbari movement – against upper-caste landlords.

By 1992, when Manmohan Singh had already ushered in a new era of liberalization, these two groups had started thinking along the lines of merging in order to extend their power to larger territories. It was in this year that the PWG and the MCC organized many mass movements together. In 2004, the two merged to form the Communist Party of India (Maoist) [CPI (Maoist)], and became, according to a Maoist ideologue, 'as big as the Congress or the Bharatiya Janata Party (BJP)', India's two main political parties at the time.

That might or might not be true, but over the past ten years the Naxalites have certainly become the biggest adversaries of New India, aided by a collapse of lower-level governance in vast areas of the country. The country is now a theatre staging the world's largest communist insurgency, dramatic in its sweep and influence and yet blissfully wished away by India's blinkered policymakers.

'Every year, the Andhra Pradesh government comes up with exact figures of Maoists active in the state,' a Maoist ideologue tells us in Delhi. 'For example, in December 2007, they said there were nine hundred and ninety-three Maoists in Andhra Pradesh.' He looks at us, lights a small Gold Flake cigarette, and mutters, 'I personally know that in the last fifteen years they have killed around five thousand men, including over two hundred rebel leaders in the state.'

He quotes home ministry reports that say that there are around thirty thousand Maoists active in some fourteen states. 'But I tell you, this number should be much larger,' he says, fiddling with his cellphone, taking a puff of his cigarette and blowing the smoke into the warm Delhi air. 'They are where the government does not even suspect them to be.'

The heart attack came at the most unexpected moment. Ranjan Roy was working on his computer at his home in New Delhi, when he collapsed. Roy was a widower, who lived with a servant to cater to the daily chores. He had seen less lonely days. The sixty-nine-year-old was a former chief of the Research and Analysis Wing (RAW), India's external intelligence agency. As his former colleague, B. Raman, now India's leading security analyst, put it, he was 'one of the heroes of Indian intelligence'.

Months before his death, Roy had expressed a desire: He wanted to go to Jharkhand to meet a relative and to visit some of the state's famous sites. First, he planned to travel to Palamau district to visit the Betla National Park, home to the Palamau Tiger Reserve, the state's most popular tourist destination. The national park has 1,000 square kilometres of dense sal and bamboo forests, with nearly a thousand different kinds of plants and hundreds of species of birds and animals. Roy would stay in a 'tree house' – actually a house on wooden props beside a tree, not on top of one – for Rs 160. Then he would travel 120 kilometres to Netarhat, a charming, forested plateau overlooking the Koel river in the valley below.

There was just one slight problem. Much of the area Roy wished to visit was under the control of Naxalites and it was impossible to travel there without the fear of being seized or attacked by them, especially if the traveller was one of India's legendary spymasters. Their intricate network of informants would ensure that every detail of the traveller's identity and his itinerary was accessible to them. The remaining area was frequently under attack from dacoits, who waylaid, beat up and robbed highway travellers. It was a well-known fact that in the complete absence of policing and accountability in the areas, the bandits operated through an arrangement with the police – an amount was fixed as a commission for the police for every bus looted. As a bus driver on the route told us, both the police and the bandits were known to follow the rules strictly. On several occasions, the bandits had forced a bus to stop, thrashed the passengers and robbed them. Then they had followed the bus and made it halt again, got in and returned the money at gunpoint, forcing the confused passengers to take everything back. Such incidents occurred when the bandits counted the money they had looted and realized that it was less than the commission they would have to pay the police. Rather than suffer a loss, they returned the money forcibly so that this particular bus loot would be excluded from the deal.

Not one to be deterred by such circumstances, Roy called his cousin in Ranchi, a top bureaucrat in the Jharkhand administration. The bureaucrat, in turn, called a local functionary who said he would pass on the message to a Naxalite area commander believed to be in charge of the stretch through which Roy wanted to travel. The word got through, and the Naxal commander sent a reply to the top bureaucrat soon enough. 'We can control our men, but we cannot take any responsibility for the local criminals,' the commander said. 'But we can still offer him safe passage.' The rebel commander suggested that if Roy agreed to travel in one of two air-conditioned Boleros which carried Naxalites down the road, he would be safe. Both the local gangs and the police knew that the SUVs belonged to the Naxalites and, even amidst turf wars, their safe passage was an unstated agreement that was honoured. India's legendary spymaster, the former chief of one of the world's leading intelligence agencies, was being offered safe passage by communist rebels.

It is not known whether Roy considered it, but he chose not to take up the offer.

But in Gitildi village, where Turia Munda killed himself, and across the regions where the Naxalites have now gained ground, common people have little to choose from. Munda's life is a tragic snapshot of the lives of millions living in insurgency-affected India, a nation within a nation, where governance has collapsed and life is on autopilot. Sixteen years after Manmohan Singh announced its arrival, there seems to be no sight of the New India anywhere close to villages such as Gitildi.

There is amazement when we arrive at the village, where practically no one comes from the outside world. People rush to offer plastic chairs. Someone scrambles to make tea, without milk. The elders settle down on a cot made of jute ropes. Bare-bodied children run around, chasing nothing in particular. Women in colourful but faded saris peep from a distance, standing on their toes at their doorsteps.

We are sitting near Munda's home, not too far from the tree where he hanged himself. Munda had not sought much in life. He had a wife, Itwari Devi, and five sons. In a country fascinated with sons, where female foeticide is outlawed but rampant, that could have been something of a jackpot, but Munda had little to feed his crown jewels.

One of them died of malaria in 2006. This is not unusual in these parts. The mosquito is a socialist – it bites the villagers, the police and the Naxalite rebels with equal intensity. The Naxal guerrillas pop quinine tablets as part of their war drill. But Munda's family, and the rest of his village, does not have access to the tablets that cost a few rupees for a strip. There is no health centre in the village of a thousand people. The nearest hospital is almost 13 kilometres away, and the road that leads to it non-existent. The doctor has passed on his tasks to an assistant. The assistant has, in turn, passed them on to a woman in the village who visits once a week, on a Thursday – that is when she visits at all.

Apparently, life in Gitildi does not follow socialist dogma. There is no electricity or provision for drinking water. The villagers, like those in all other villages they know, bathe in the river that flows past, which is also the source for their drinking water. During summer even that runs dry. Some hand pumps, seven in all, were installed a few years back, but they pump out muddy water, which is worse than what is drawn from the river. A year after Munda's son passed away, in 2007, the bad water, the harsh living conditions and the location of the health centre conspired to rain yet another blow on his family. Munda's wife, Itwari Devi, unexpectedly – or perhaps not so unexpectedly – came down with diarrhoea. Munda had no money to have her treated; their neighbours pitched in with local herbs. When her condition worsened, Munda borrowed money and hired a jeep to take his wife to the health centre beyond a bumpy, wretched road. She was too frail to walk – two people had to lift her and place her in the jeep. The pain of the journey by road was unbearable, and Itwari Devi died soon after. Munda did not have the money to organize even the ritual *bhoj* (community lunch) after her death, a fact that troubled him for months.

Munda was now left with four children – the youngest, two years old; the eldest, twelve – and he had to be both mother and father to them. Within his means, he was doing well enough. Three of them went to school, a big achievement in the village. But there was no money for much else, not to organize the ritual lunch, not even to support the family.

Then a ray of hope appeared. The village headman announced that a pond was to be dug nearby under the NREGS, which promised a hundred days of employment every year to every adult who asked for it. The programme seemed like manna from heaven, the perfect solution to the rural poverty that forced hundreds of people to flee their villages every year in states such as Bihar and seek work in faraway metropolises. Like many others in his village, Turia Munda signed up under the NREGS. He worked for forty-eight days, digging a pond a kilometre away from the village. He then waited for months for his money, Rs 3,360. Finally, one day, he gave up. They found his body the next morning, hanging from the berry tree.

Munda's sons dropped out of school. The younger three were taken away by their uncle. The oldest, Jholu Munda, stayed back in the village, sleeping all alone in the hut where he had last seen his father alive. Wearing his broken pink plastic slippers held together with a thin wire, he now sat outside his hut swinging his legs and listening to everyone else recounting the story of his father's last days.

The little clearing in the village became an enduring image of the defeated citizens of India, the dispossessed who populated the places where governments had stopped functioning out of fear of rebel terror. For the shadows of the rebels have indeed passed through Gitildi; in fact, the Naxalites came here often, looking for support, asking the villagers to join their overground outfits. The villagers have risked their lives and politely turned down the requests so far. They share the same yearning – to study or get their children educated, to get ahead in life and improve their lot.

Still, Gitildi continues to exist in a vacuum of governance. 'In this village, there is nothing. We want to educate our children – that is all we want,' says Guruwa Munda, who used to be Turia Munda's classmate. 'Earlier, in our time, the local primary school had three teachers. Now we have one. We had one teacher for forty students. Now, one teacher teaches a hundred and thirty students.'

Arun Munda is seventeen years old, studying in the eleventh standard. He likes to dream big. He also knows he is the guy with the best aim in the village with the *gulel* (sling), which he carries with him at all times. 'My aim is good. I can hit a target at ten feet. I want to join the army, and if they don't want to give me a gun I always have my *gulel*!' he chuckles, wearing a T-shirt with the words 'Goa at its Grandest' printed on it.

He loves watching television – anything he can get through a dish antenna – the news, soaps and cricket. The few people here who have TV sets run them on batteries. Some whose family members are able to go to the cities and work also have cheap DVDs and a few CDs that they watch over and over again. Through cable TV and the few better-off people in their midst, the youth of the village get a window into the dazzle of urban life but as inhabitants of Gitildi they are untouched by modern India. Only a few boys are aware of the hairstyle and batting prowess of India's star cricketer Mahendra Singh Dhoni, who hails from the state's capital.

'When I go to Ranchi, I also wish I was staying in a place like that. But I don't like the way many girls dress there – they are too modern by my standards,' says Arun Munda. When he returns to reality, he goes out to the forest, cuts wood and makes Rs 50 a day.

Down the mud path from Arun Munda's hut lives the man who is considered one of the VIPs in the village – Ravindra Munda, who owns a motorcycle. When a villager falls seriously ill, the family has only one desperate hope – that Ravindra Munda has not gone anywhere. The patient lumbers on to his motorcycle, if he or she is able to, and is taken to the nearby town of Bundu for access to proper healthcare.

'My motorcycle is known as the village ambulance,' Ravindra Munda says.

The 'ambulance' is often very busy – after all, there are seasons of diseases in Gitildi. In the months of July and August, diarrhoea strikes. In November and December, it is malaria. The rest of the year, it could be anything, really. During the monsoon, the road is submerged and the sick person has to be transported either on a bicycle or on somebody's back.

Children die. Women die. And so do able-bodied men.

Samla Munda points towards a small, two-room structure near the entrance to the village. It looks ravaged by years of disuse. 'This was supposed to be a health centre, but no doctor has come here for almost two years now,' he says. The means of prevention and precaution are also not at hand. A mosquito net costs Rs 60, and not everyone can afford one.

When minor ailments afflict them, the residents of Gitildi walk a few dozen feet from Turia Munda's hut, then turn right, and walk another five minutes to a larger hut on the left. This is the home of Draupadi Devi, the 'nurse' of the village. She unofficially stands in for the government nurse, who is herself a stand-in for the government doctor. 'If you come in November or December, you will find every family has a malaria patient,' Draupadi says, holding one end of her cream sari wrapped tightly around her. 'But government officials tell us we cannot come here because it is an MCC area,' she says.

The government will not recognize her as an employee, but Draupadi is a very important woman in the village. After all, when children have a cold or a tummy upset it is she who decides what medicine to give them. She has no medical training, just a piece of paper the government-appointed nurse has prepared for her, which tells her what to do in minor crises. But Draupadi has some credentials on her biodata to qualify as a stand-in nurse. She is the only woman in the village who is set to graduate from a college in three years.

'I am thirty years old, but only on paper. My real age is twenty-six,' she says, blushing. Her infant son is in her lap as she sits on the floor. He gurgles and giggles. He wears nothing but a thick black thread around his waist – a trick Indians have used for centuries to ward off the evil eye, hopefully with some success. In her hut is an old TV set mounted on a table, a transistor radio, a few framed images of Hindu gods on the walls. A few packs of Paracetamol and some antibiotics are arranged on a stool in a corner. The radio is playing the hit Kishore Kumar song, '*Pyaar kar liya to kya*'.

Love is a luxury for Draupadi. Her husband works at a school in another district and they meet once in several weeks. She grew up 16 kilometres away in Tirildi village with three brothers and two sisters. 'My father could not go to school – he was a farmer – but he wanted his sons and daughters to study,' she says. So they did. The three brothers graduated from college, and a younger sister finished the tenth standard with similar aspirations. Then, one night in 2001, Draupadi's family was ripped apart. Armed MCC cadres stormed into the village and attacked them, accusing them of being police informers. Within minutes, her father and three brothers lay dead on the ground.

The quiver in her voice betrays Draupadi's emotions for a second, and then she looks out of the hut, as if plunging her face straight into the sunlight.

'Earlier, I used to dream a lot. When I was studying, I wanted to have a job like modern women, I wanted to work and bring some money home for my father's well-being. I wanted to look after him,' she says. 'Now I just want to manage my household, take care of my family.' She pauses, and then says, 'Maybe I will be able to do something good in life, but I don't want to dream about it.'

Every week, the rebels visit the village, she says. Every week, they get to hear the same answer from the villagers. 'We are very united in our village. We are not swayed by them. Some days ago, they said again, "You all become members of our party." They asked the youth to join them. We ignored them. They tried to pressurize us. They held meetings, no one went. We decided not to go.

'We told the *dasta* (the squad), we don't want to join you,' she says. 'But the government does not want to do anything for us, the government officials just take the name of the Naxalites all the time and say they will do nothing for us – no roads, no water, no electricity. So, let us see how long we can hold out ...'

As the villagers despair near the mosquito-ridden swamps of Gitildi, mosquito repellents work overtime in the imposing corridors and swanky rooms of New Delhi's North Block, where the attitude has changed little since the days of the British Raj. The powers that be at New Delhi continue to harp on Naxalism being solely a security problem, ignoring its socio-economic connect.

In December 2007, while addressing the Chief Ministers' Conference on Internal Security, Prime Minister Manmohan Singh said, 'Left-wing extremism is probably [the] single biggest security challenge to the Indian state. It continues to be so and we cannot rest in peace until we have eliminated this virus. They are certainly targeting all aspects of economic activity. They are targeting vital economic infrastructure so as to cripple transport and logistics capabilities and to also slow down any development activity,' he said. 'We need to cripple the hold of Naxalite forces with all the means at our command.'

But it was too late. Naxalite influence had by then extended to well over fourteen states in India, including Orissa, which is the poorest state in India with close to 40 per cent of its population earning less than Rs 12 a day. Jharkhand, where Gitildi is located, and its neighbouring state of Bihar appear second and third, respectively, after Orissa on poverty's wall of shame.

The government's own numbers are a stunning indictment of the state of affairs in the country. Some 77 per cent of Indians – around 84 crore people – live on less than Rs 20 a day. 'This is the other world which can be characterized as the India of the Common People, constituting more than three-fourths of the population and consisting of all those whom the growth has, by and large, bypassed,' a national commission said in a report. 'Such a sordid picture coexists uneasily with a shining India that has successfully confronted the challenge of globalization powered by economic competition both within the country and across the world,' the report says. It goes on to state that 26 per cent of India's population lives on less than Rs 12 per day. Some 92 per cent of the country's total workforce of 45.7 crore people is employed as agricultural labourers and farmers, or in odd jobs such as working in brick kilns or quarries. It is a truth the world – and India – has not been told enough: In stark contrast to the sheen of the new India, a majority of Indians lead a lacklustre life, struggling with hunger and disease.

As we found during months of travel through the Naxal heartland, the Naxalite movement is hardly the biggest threat to India. It has, in fact, become the biggest *opportunity*, at least for thousands in the government and for contractors working on taxpayer-financed government projects in those regions. Taxpayer money meant to build schools, health centres and roads has not been spent for these purposes. Rural health centres have not seen doctors for more than fifteen years. Teachers do not go to teach. Policemen do not go on patrol. Officials in the third tier of the government, such as block development officers, have stopped going to their offices. These officials complain that they cannot do any work because they face a security threat.

Arun Kumar Sinha, Jharkhand's state secretary for roads, put it this way, 'This is a chicken-and-egg story. Our functionaries, under the garb of such disturbances, do not reach out to remote areas. They do not stay in block headquarters. For those carrying out these projects, it has become an excuse to file an FIR with the police and say, "We are feeling insecure, we cannot go there." But we have seen that wherever people [contractors and officials] are present at the site and doing good work, people [locals] are supporting us.'

Another official says cynically, 'We keep hearing how India is the next world tiger. Well, in huge parts of India where there is insurgency, the India I see and deal with every day, that India is just a paper tiger. Officials do not go to inspect village projects, so roads are built on paper, schools run on paper, and doctors examine malaria patients on paper,' he says, declining to be named. 'Despite such an atmosphere, our politicians are not worried – and maybe they are getting assistance from these fellows [rebels].'

A senior IAS officer sounds even more bitter and defeated. 'We are abandoning the countryside, abandoning the blocks. No one checks daily attendance in the field any more. There is a complete vacuum of governance. And there is no intelligence about the Naxalites either – because the police do not move around,' he says, sipping his third coffee of the day at his apartment in Ranchi, the capital of Jharkhand.

'Ranchi is like a piece of butter with fire all around it – it is melting. We are totally at the mercy of these bums,' the officer says of the Naxalites. 'I have no control over anyone. My minister takes money directly from everyone in illegal mining and deforestation. Ministers in Jharkhand charge a higher percentage than Naxalites. People are not worried about corruption. People are worried about corruption within corruption.'

'This is a nice place,' he continues with a straight face as he puts down his coffee cup. 'An Alice in Wonderland kind of joint.'

'Twenty years ago, life was better. We could get food more easily; we were young and would roam in the jungles and collect berries. But now, that is no longer possible. We are getting mowed down by elephants, wild pigs and Naxalites – in that order.' On the Jharkhand–West Bengal border, an old man reading a local newspaper offers us his take on the 'situation'.

We are in Jharkhand's East Singhbhum district, on the narrow, dusty road that leads to the twin villages of Narsinghpur and

Mirgitand, the last habitations within the state on that road. Beyond these villages, a narrow road runs through a jungle and connects to West Bengal's Purulia district. After sustained operations against the Naxalites in the jungles of the Rani Jharna hills that surround the area, many of the rebels are believed to have shifted to this part of Jharkhand.

There are tell-tale signs everywhere. Hand-written messages cover government hoardings, warning villagers against venturing into the forest to collect firewood. Right at the border, the West Bengal government's forest guest house lies desolate after the Naxalites blew it up with dynamite, punching huge holes into its concrete walls. A weary-looking man rests on a small mound in front of the shattered building, next to his bicycle, which is fitted with a pink plastic rose. He is among the many villagers from the twin villages who have to set out at least once every two days to do odd jobs such as collecting firewood. Like fifteen-year-old Jhumri, who collects firewood and then walks barefoot on a stone-strewn path to Galudi town, 16 kilometres away. If she is lucky, she gets up to Rs 25 by selling the wood to a local hotel. Then she walks back to the village after buying rice with the money. If she fails to sell the firewood, her family has to go hungry.

But haven't the villagers here benefited from schemes such as the NREGS, the jobs-guarantee scheme under which Turia Munda worked?

'The NREGS is for the rich, not for the poor like us,' a villager, who is waiting for a bus, laughs when we ask him. 'We have gone to the government officials for work so many times. They tell us that the scheme is yet to reach these parts.'

Like most of the villages in Jharkhand, there is no electricity in Narsinghpur or Mirgitand. A single well serves a population of around nine hundred people. There is supposed to be a sub-health centre a few kilometres away in Kesarpur, but, as another villager tells us, 'this too exists only on paper'.

'If a villager here has to do anything – say, get a birth certificate – he has to go to Ghatsila block, which is more than twenty-two kilometres away,' says a villager. 'If someone leaves for Ghatsila, he has to head back by 3.00 p.m.' Their fear runs both ways – those who are out after sunset can be questioned by both the police and the Naxalites.

In Ranchi district of Jharkhand, where Gitildi is located, a survey of twenty-eight NREGS worksites was conducted in May 2007 by the Delhi School of Economics. The survey found that 96 per cent of the labourers did not know how to apply for work. In 54 per cent of the cases, as happened with Munda, the wages were not paid within fifteen days as required under the NREGA, causing enormous hardship to the workers. Around 14 per cent of the labourers did not even know that they could expect their wages within a fortnight. Some 71 per cent of the labourers complained about wage payments, including underpayment and fraud.

The most sordid picture of what ails the NREGS is the gruesome murder of social activist Lalit Mehta in the Palamau district of Jharkhand. According to reports, Mehta was in possession of a CD of the social audit of a pond project allotted under the NREGS. Two days before his body was found on 16 May 2008, a number of people had approached him, complaining against the officials and contractors involved in the scheme.

After the murder, Mehta's colleague, development economist Jean Dréze, who is one of the architects of the NREGS, said, 'There is too much corruption and if this is not contained, it will be very difficult for the scheme to really take off.' In January 2009, the police recovered the body of Raju Singh, a prime accused in Mehta's murder. A pamphlet found near his body said that CPI [Maoist] cadres has shot him dead.

In Chhattisgarh's Naxal-affected Kanker district, investigations have brought to the fore a multi-crore rupee scam in the implementation of the NREGS. It was revealed that agricultural instruments, fertilizers and pesticides worth Rs 6 crore were purchased under the NREGS and distributed among labourers. Further inquiries revealed that the pesticides had been bought at ten times the actual price. All this material was procured using 60 per cent of the funds meant to be spent as labourers' wages. A local leader alleged that he had complained to the collector many months ago, but the collector chose not to act. 'I suppose the collector is also involved in the case,' said Sanjay Parate, coordinator of the Kisan Sabha, or farmers' council.

In Orissa's Kalahandi district, often described as the hunger capital of India, a team from the Delhi-based Centre for Environment and Food Security [CEFS] reached out to villagers who had worked on three road projects between June and August 2006 and in January 2007. Tragic stories turned up of how virtually every labourer had been cheated of a few thousand rupees that often means the difference between life and death for an Indian farm labourer.

Like Turia Munda in next-door Jharkhand, Rupa Majhi worked on a road project in Kalahandi. Going by the daily wage rate of Rs 55, Majhi should have received Rs 1,155 for his twenty-one days of work, but he was paid only Rs 600. On top of this, his job card said he had worked for not twenty-one but three hundred and thirty-six days. On searching the NREGS government website, it was found that Majhi should have been paid Rs 6,310. He had been robbed of more than 90 per cent of his wages.

In a survey carried out in a hundred villages of the Kalahandi-Bolangir-Koraput (KBK) region in Orissa, the CEFS found that out of the Rs 733 crore spent under the NREGS in 2006–07, more than Rs 500 crore had been siphoned off and misappropriated by government officials. The report, after preparing a list of five thousand villages in the nineteen districts in the region, says that more than 75 per cent of the NREGS funds spent during 2006 have vanished. It says that it is absolutely certain that there are thousands of villages in Orissa where the scale of misappropriation of funds touches 90 per cent.

'We have reason to believe that the entire state administration is party to this loot,' said Parshuram Rai of the CEFS. In an open letter to Prime Minister Manmohan Singh, he stated, 'It is not the epidemic of cholera, but the cancer of corruption that is killing hundreds of adivasis. On the Human Development Index, many sub-Saharan villages would fare better than most of [these] villages.'

For thousands of villagers in these states, dinner is often just gruel of dried mango kernels. When, thousands of kilometres away, in the final days of his tenure, United States President George W. Bush blamed the better nutrition and better eating habits of Indians for the increase in world food prices, here is what no one told him, or the Indian government, for that matter: The eating habits of one-third of India, reeling under insurgency, could not actually cause a food crisis. Just the world's largest armed communist rebellion.

Corruption has, in fact, become such a fine art in India that officials have even started innovating on time-honed methods. A block development officer in the Hussainabad block of Jharkhand's Palamau district wrote down the registration number of a truck in which he was supposed to transport sixty-seven quintals of food grain. Nobody suspected anything till a team from the Comptroller and Auditor General (CAG) carried out a random check of fifty-six of the six hundred and sixty-seven consignments of food grain.

The truck registration number the block development officer in Hussainabad had written turned out to be that of a Vespa scooter. The registration number of trucks as shown in six consignments were those of smaller vehicles like jeeps in which such large quantities could not have been carried. Clearly, the food grain, meant to be distributed among the poor under the central government's Sampoorna Grameen Rozgar Yojana, was being diverted elsewhere, most probably for sale in the open market. No inquiry was instituted. Monitoring agencies such as the CAG hardly have the mandate to perform open checks in any particular area. They can only look for the loopholes that exist in the paper records submitted by various government agencies.

Another CAG report says that the Jharkhand government failed to provide safe drinking water to its rural population under the central government sponsored Accelerated Rural Supply Programme. A performance audit on the implementation of the programme during 2002–07 reports that more than 13 lakh people in rural Jharkhand have no access to adequate drinking water.

No action plan was prepared for the implementation of the programme. As a result, the state was deprived of central assistance worth Rs 58.40 crore. Nearly Rs 7 crore meant for providing drinking water facilities to around four thousand schools in Jharkhand was not utilized. Excess fluoride, iron and arsenic were detected in the water in twenty-two districts and, as the CAG report makes clear, no significant effort was made to carry out remedial measures.

So, what does the Jharkhand government spend its money on? It spends its money on Bijendra Goel.

Goel is the resident commissioner of the Jharkhand government and works out of a rented building in New Delhi's diplomats' enclave, Chanakyapuri. His job in the national capital, as he describes it, is to act as a proxy for the chief minister in a few official meetings and occasionally inspect Jharkhand Bhavan, which is currently under construction. By his own admission, he does no other work. For the duties mentioned above, he and his staff was paid around Rs 50 lakh between 2002 and 2007. Since Goel enjoys the status of a state minister, he is entitled to a chauffeur-driven car, a stenographer, a private secretary and a peon. To help him avoid the inconvenience of travelling to office through Delhi's chaotic traffic, a house has been allotted to him in the same area, where rents run into lakhs of rupees.

Stories such as these reverberate across insurgency-affected areas in India. With no monitoring of development programmes, corruption has reached levels far higher than in the rest of the already corruption-ridden country, and the discontentment among villagers is fertile ground for the surge of the Naxalite movement and the rebels' recruitment drives.

2

If you were to go strictly by the law, then a vast stretch of the Amazon-like forest in Jharkhand is still a part of Britain. The remote, mineral-rich region of Kolhan was directly administered by London under a colonial law and apparently fell through the cracks when India became independent in 1947 and more than six hundred feudal kingdoms were united to form a disparate nation. According to all available evidence, Kolhan is still not a part of India – due to its traditional, village-based administration, there was no king who could have signed the Instrument of Accession that would make it a part of the newly independent nation.

When the captains of the communist rebellion walked in here in 2000, they, too, were determined that they had nothing to do with India. They had arrived in a land that was home to natural wealth worth countless fortunes, wealth that had somehow eluded the people living there.

Far away in the cities, that wealth continues to change lives, running industries and propping up towering buildings that are the signposts of New India. These signposts are expensive, to say the least. Today, a mere square foot of space in an apartment in the suburbs of New Delhi or Bengaluru costs a whopping Rs 8,000 – US$200, 120 Euro, 1,100 Chinese Yuan. Every day, newspapers are flooded with advertisements for luxury condominiums and upmarket stores selling expensive consumer durables. Despite the global economic meltdown, urban India has become a hungry demon-child that has to be fed constantly with the soft pap of materialism. New roads and highways are meandering through the country; air conditioners and plasma TV sets are flying off the shelves. The gleaming high-rises are dwarfed only by the ambitions of the neo-rich.

To feed that beast, New India digs into the Other India. To raise those buildings and keep raising them, the country needs to double its steel production capacity from 600 lakh tonnes to 1,100 lakh tonnes a year. And, for that, New India looks to the faraway expanses of Chhattisgarh and Jharkhand – major suppliers of coal, superior-quality iron ore, as well as limestone, copper, bauxite, graphite and asbestos.

There is inevitably, the other side of this coin. At least 30 lakh people have been displaced by reckless and poorly planned mining in mineral-rich lands across India, tens of thousands of square kilometres of forestland in these stretches have been diverted. Yet, not even a quarter of the population has been rehabilitated, let alone given a share of the earnings. Even the forests, a crucial source of livelihood for the people, have vanished. It doesn't come as a surprise then that the thirteen mining districts in these states are among the fifty most backward of India's six hundred-plus districts, as also the hub of the biggest-ever armed rebellion against the Indian state.

In a small interrogation room in Jharkhand, Sushil Roy, a sixty-six-year-old former engineer, a top Naxalite leader now in custody, put it eloquently. It was as simple as mathematics, he told his interrogators: 'Forests mean minerals, minerals mean money, money means guns, guns mean power.' Roy is a member of the politburo, the core body of the rebels, and a contemporary of Charu Majumdar and Kanu Sanyal.

The Saranda forest, deep in the heart of Kolhan, knows the story intimately.

We travel to the West Singhbhum district of Jharkhand, to the 820-square kilometre forest – a sprawling, rocky expanse of hills draped kilometre after kilometre in sal, mango, jamun and jackfruit trees. Sunlight rarely cuts through the dense umbrella formed by the thick, high branches, which shields the tranquil villages of the Ho tribe, formerly animists and now mostly Christian converts. Wild elephants roam about at night, blocking the roads and often hurling with fury a lone cyclist who dares to venture out in the dark. Sambhar and cheetal deer saunter around in the upper reaches, and occasionally the villagers may run into a leopard or tiger.

Saranda – which literally means 'a hundred hills' – was once one of the largest forests in Asia. It was so vast that during British rule in India sal wood was transported from here to Burma (now Myanmar) to build the railway there. Until the mid-1980s, local police officers say, there was hardly a day when sal trunks as thick as a car were not sawed down and lugged away to be crafted into furniture for the homes of senior officials in the administration and the police.

All the while, the events that changed the tenor of Saranda's – and the Naxalite movement's – tranquil, slow-moving saga were happening thousands of kilometres away. It was 1995. Demand for iron ore was soaring globally, and India, the country with the fifth-largest iron-ore reserves in the world, after Ukraine, Russia, China and Australia, was reaching out to global markets. Jharkhand – then part of undivided Bihar – was the instrument that would help India realize its ambitions. The huge global demand meant there was big money to be made. Realizing this, India's top steel companies as well as the Naxalites began to mobilize themselves, inching slowly towards Saranda.

'There is just one primary source of resources that runs the Naxalite movement all over India – Jharkhand,' Sushil Roy, the arrested Maoist leader, had told his interrogators. While the rebels enlarged their sphere of influence to touch and then overrun the great forest, two of India's steel giants, the privately owned Tata Iron and Steel Company (TISCO) and the state-run Steel Authority of India Limited (SAIL), were making their presence felt in the area. They had begun mining iron ore in the forest to feed the huge global demands. While the Naxalites looked upon the companies as intruders, they entered the forest themselves and established their first bases. In 2000 they issued an unexpected invitation, by word of mouth, to people living within a 200 kilometre radius to come to Saranda, clear patches of forest and live there.

'Meanwhile, Naxalites and white-collar Naxalites – the politicians – both flourished,' says a police official who had served in the area for years and often travelled incognito deep into Saranda. 'In this country, after all, there is neither socialism nor communism – there is just opportunism.'

Mine owners paid off the Naxalites and their representatives in New Delhi, Kolkata and Ranchi. Commissions were decided upon for development projects. For projects of up to Rs 2.5 lakh, the rebels were to be paid 8 per cent of the worth of the project, and for projects worth more than that it was 11 per cent and upwards, going up to 25 per cent in some cases. The rebels also said that if it was proved that there was no corruption in a government project, no commission would be charged. Forest department officials who have served in Saranda confirm that this was indeed so.

The levies system was meteoric and arbitrary, a bit like the fees charged by film stars in Bollywood. One day in the middle of May 2007, the rebels summoned forty small mine owners and said that their levies were being raised from Rs 5 lakh a month to Rs 10 lakh. Some of the mine owners begged them to show mercy. One of them said his ailing father would not be able to take the blow. The rebels did not relent. And why would they? Saranda had now become their unquestioned stronghold. They had to secure it.

Saranda was the venue for the most crucial turn in the Maoist movement when, in September 2004, a three-month unification conference was held deep inside the forest. The two main Naxalite insurgent groups, the MCC and the PWG, united to form the CPI (Maoist). Participating in the conference were invitees from twenty-one countries, including Germany, Bulgaria, Portugal, Peru, Venezuela, Nepal, Bangladesh and Burma. Inside the forest, they found the rebels functioning with sophisticated logistical support, including extremely powerful 25 KVA generators and laptops. Evidently, they had reached areas where no government official had gone before. It was a journey as adventurous as that in *Star Trek,* except that this was in the heart of the real India, not in the realm of science fiction. It was clear that they had stepped into a huge hole in governance – a land where there were no signs of the India that India had left behind.

The rebels had come to the stronghold of the 'Kolhan Tiger', former rebel, ageing patriarch, and beloved of all in the region. Few would have remembered the name of the sixty-nine-year-old Krishna Chandra Hembrom, at one time the undisputed Robin Hood of Kolhan. There was a time when journalists and politicians sent secret messages to meet Hembrom and had to wait weeks, even months, until they were granted an audience in a remote location where he would be guarded by up to twenty men armed with bows and poisoned arrows. Now the retired revolutionary is a chubby grandfather residing in the tiny town of Chaibasa in the Kolhan region. Children born after his time often pass the tea shop, where he sits quietly soaking in the afternoon sun, unaware of the drama and adventures of his life.

In his time, Hembrom lived in the treacherous forests of Saranda, ate red ants to survive, launched a massive movement to save his mineral-rich land with an army of archers, disguised himself in many roles including that of a beggar and a burqa-clad Muslim woman, and stood up to both the Naxalites and the corporate giants.

All three protagonists – the corporate giants, the Kolhan Tiger and the Naxalites – had risen in Kolhan over the question of the people's control over the one treasure that could change the game – the region's seemingly unending mineral wealth.

Saranda is sparsely populated. Officially, on the revenue maps, only nine villages were recognized by the British authorities in 1909 as revenue-generating villages, mainly to help control the frequently raging forest fires. That still remains the official number, although, in truth, more than two hundred and fifty villages have been thriving there for years.

There are few things that make the simple villagers of Saranda angry, but there was one wrong that had not been corrected since the time of Jagannath Mishra, the former chief minister of undivided Bihar, which truly affected them. Mishra had ordered that the monthly stipend given to the villagers since 1909 for safeguarding the forest from fires be discontinued. More than a decade had passed and even the arrears were not cleared.

The villagers were upset. Saranda was pumping out iron ore; other big finds like manganese and dolomite were also being extracted from the region. The forest department did little to protect the vast swathes of forest were that being cut down illegally. In many cases, with little power, no weapons and no authority to use them anyway, forest officials were incapable of providing protection. The villagers who inhabited the land had no right to it, and no means of earning wages.

In such dire circumstances, the Naxalites held out a tantalizing bait to the residents – they would help the villagers to become the owners of the forest. Frustrated with the lack of initiative on the part of the government towards any developmental activity in the area, thousands of villagers moved into the forests, creating a buffer zone for the Naxalites, a first line of defence against any interference in rebel activities from the state, and providing the rebels with a vast recruitment pool. By January 2000, the rebels began holding informal discussions with the heads of the villages, marking the beginning of recruitment drives that would intensify over the coming months.

For the villages, the cause was not a new one. Thousands in Saranda had fought a relentless bow-and-arrow war through the 1980s against the government and all outsiders to protect their land and seek ownership of its natural resources. At that time, the battle had been led by Krishna Chandra Hembrom, the Kolhan Tiger, one of the most famous leaders of the Ho tribal community.

The Ho, who speak a language of the same name, live near rivers and springs, and engage in farming and manual labour in the mines that dot the region. They follow an ancient system of governance. The head of the village, known as the *manki*, takes decisions for the community and must get consent for all resolutions from each member of the village before implementing them. *Manki*s and *munda*s, also village leaders, have traditionally respected judicial rights and usually settle local disputes with punishments ranging from a penalty of ten hens to some kilos of grain.

The tribal residents of what is now known as Jharkhand are simple people whose naivety has been the stuff of folklore, but they are also known to have fought fierce battles through the eighteenth and nineteenth centuries against the British colonial rulers. The first-known Ho tribal was a warrior called Tilka Manjhi, who led the Santhals against the local landlords and the British in 1771, seeking to wrest the land of his ancestors from the colonialists. The British crushed the uprising, but it was followed by protest movements by the Bhumij tribes in 1779, the Chero tribes in 1800, the Oraons in 1807 and the Mundas in 1811 and 1813. The Hos in Singhbhum rose in revolt against exploitation by the British in 1820 and battled their adversaries for two years. Two fiercer rebellions followed – by the Kols in 1832 and the Santhals in 1855, under the leadership of the brothers Sidhu and Kanhu, whose statues can be found everywhere in the Singhbhum region, symbolizing dissent even today. And, finally, between 1895 and 1900, came the bloodiest and most celebrated uprising of them all, led by twenty-five-year-old Birsa Munda, which endures through folk songs and legends.

The thread of unstated rage had run deep across the peaceful region till, on a September afternoon in 1980, it exploded. In the southern mining town of Gua, men from the Bihar Military Police fired at a gathering, killing at least three people and wounding dozens of others. The next morning the police raided a hospital, killing eight villagers. They were sick and wounded and waiting for their turn to meet the doctors.

Months of police terror followed. Villagers were beaten, raped and terrorized; they would hide in the Saranda forest the moment they saw a police jeep approaching. Among them was Hembrom, who vanished from his timber cooperative one day, full of violent rage. Hembrom went on to set up a massive underground movement that earned him the name 'Kolhan Tiger'. He set up a force of villagers armed with bows and arrows, which dug itself deep inside the forest, guarding hideouts, preparing for war. A massive street movement was launched demanding the creation of a new state, Jharkhand, with a simple slogan that united thousands of people: 'This land is ours, this water is ours.' The police began to raid the forest. In one confrontation, the villagers gored nine policemen with arrows, killing all of them; in turn, the police killed nine tribals.

'I was accused of murder,' Hembrom says, basking in the afternoon sun at the Chaibasa tea shop.

So he raised the stakes, saying that Kolhan was not a part of Bihar at all, but an independent region. 'I said "Bihar laws will not run in Kolhan. The police cannot enter here without permission. We will go to London and Geneva to investigate whether or not Kolhan merged with India at the time of independence,"' Hembrom tells us, the tea-seller nodding his head in agreement.

Ten minutes later, we are in a room where Hembrom pulls out bundles of paper to support his claim. Yellowing copies of British laws in small typewriter print. Some smudges. Some notations with a pen. He runs his fingers over a 1913 British document that talks of a 'Kolhan government'. He pulls out Section 7 (C) of the Independence Act 1947, which, according to him, leaves the Kolhan government untouched among all former British territories, with the secretary of state for India in council as the owner of the territory. These are the documents that have sustained years of discontent and feelings of separatism in this region, and eventually fed Naxalite activity in Saranda. 'When we wanted to find out the paperwork necessary for a visa to the UK, the high commission told us that you don't need a visa – you are part of the UK,' Hembrom said. As incredible as that sounds, the British High Commission in New Delhi did not dismiss Hembrom's claim outright when we called them for clarification, and reverted after a couple of weeks to say that the issue was unclear because the records in question were dated too far back. Nevertheless, a small team of Hembrom's men did make it to London in 1982 to present their case; they returned after meeting some officials. On their return, they were promptly arrested.

In 1984, Hembrom was offered the opportunity to transform his army into an armed militia along the lines of the Naxalites, when a powerful tribal leader, once his confidant, came with an offer.

'He said, "We have arms, we will help your campaign." I refused. I said we have our bows and arrows,' said Hembrom. He remained underground for seventeen years, from 1982 to 1999, leading the villagers' movement and living the life of a fugitive as hundreds of policemen searched relentlessly for him.

'I used to hold meetings at night and sleep during the day. Twenty people with bows and arrows protected me at all times. I used to walk a lot, sometimes all night. I have walked up to fifty kilometres. If there was the rustling sound of leaves, we ran and hid,' he remembered. 'When a stranger approached us, they sounded the *dugdugi* [handheld drum] and surrounded the person. When I whistled thrice, he was allowed passage. I slept in caves. There would be bears there. My attendant went for his puja one day, and the moment he lit an incense stick, a bear bit him.'

Hundreds of policemen raided possible hideouts, looking for Hembrom. If he had to walk through public areas, he wore dirty clothes and dressed as a beggar. Once, he was on a train, pretending to be a Muslim woman in a burqa, when a policeman sat next to him, and told him during the conversation: 'You must be careful, there is a very dangerous man on the loose, he is called the Kolhan Tiger.'

Towards the close of the 1990s, a turn in political fortunes saw the criminal cases against Hembrom being withdrawn and politicians seeking his support in elections. Soon after he emerged from hiding in 1999, the battle for Saranda got a new, decisive twist. The Naxalites arrived to make it their operational base and they wanted to collaborate with him.

'I told the Naxalites, you are in hiding, I don't fight like you. I might have been underground, but my fights are in the open. I will not hide,' Hembrom said. 'I have people in every village.'

Indeed, every village contained raw material for rebellion. For decades, governments had ignored Saranda and left vast regions of the forested land virtually ungoverned, and now the protests that were erupting as a result of that misgovernance had become the alibi for more misgovernance.

'There is no food, no health facilities. Nothing. Villagers live by selling trees and leaves. The youth go hungry; they take tablets to kill hunger, hormone tablets,' says Hembrom. 'So the Naxalites lured them. They said, "We will give you three thousand rupees per month, plus education and medical treatment, plus some ten or twenty thousand rupees as allowance per year." The Naxalites have become a nice excuse for the government to not spend money on anything for the people and for officials to not do their jobs. There are schools inside the forest, but teachers never go there. If they did, do you think we would be in this state?'

A tribal youth picks up a stone from the ground, mounts it on a sling, takes aim and brings down a bird soaring above him. He does not know that the stone is precious it could have earned his family food for a year or more. That is the enduring contrast of Singhbhum's natural wealth: The villagers who live there have no stake in the riches of the land and often have no idea of the unimaginable wealth on which they sit. Some are trying to change that.

A young man with a cheerful face and a hint of a paunch sits in the doctor's room at a newly built nursing home in Chaibasa town. Thirty-two-year-old Mukesh Birua is not a doctor – he just owns the nursing home. He is one of the well-known faces among the seven lakh Ho tribals who live in the mineral-rich Singhbhum district.

'This is our wealth and the government and everyone else is exploiting it. The stones here are very valuable, but we use them to kill birds or to threaten bulls. We never treat them as something valuable and we never realized we were sitting on something so precious until the companies began making money from them,' says Birua.

It is estimated that, every day, iron ore worth Rs 50 crore – more than US$12 million – leaves the Saranda forest and its nearby Naxalite-affected areas from the Jamda, Noamundi, Kiriburu, Gua and Chidia mines. Yet, valuable gemstones are often known to be sold for as little as Rs 10 a kilogram by ignorant villagers. To try and claim a stake in the region's mining enterprises, the Ho tribals have now formed the Adivasi Khadan, a cooperative society that aims to mine the area, possibly in technical collaboration with large mineral companies and according to the tribals' traditional *manki* system of governance.

'So far, our hands have been tied. We have seen this dream. Let us see how far it takes us.' The quiet confidence in Birua's voice is cause for hope.

As of now there are few takers for an idea that could serve as a template for sharing resources between tribals and corporate interests. Enough motivation will be required from both sides to transform Birua's dream into reality.

Nayagarh, Orissa. On 15 February 2008, more than three hundred armed guerrillas, including a group of women, swooped down upon the town, entering in small groups. Eyewitnesses say they saw strangers moving around in the market square after sunset. Some of them were seen eating dinner in the hotels around the town's main bus stand. A few were said to have entered the town as part of a marriage procession.

Late in the night, at around 10.30 p.m., the rebels began what they had named Operation 22. Entering Nayagarh from various directions on motorcycles and in stolen trucks and buses, they cut off the town's power supply and disconnected all its communication lines. Squads comprising some seventy highly trained men and women blocked the entry points to Nayagarh and fanned across the town, making announcements on loudspeakers, urging them to stay indoors. They laid siege to the offices of the two highest-ranking government officials in the district, the collector and the superintendent of police.

Afterwards, the Naxalites carried out synchronized attacks on the police armoury, the police training school, three police stations and one police outpost. Inside one of the police barracks, several policemen were playing cards in the recreation centre when the

Naxalites struck. The policemen got no chance to escape. The Naxalites fired indiscriminately and even hurled bombs at the fleeing policemen. Fourteen police personnel and a civilian were killed in the well-planned attacks. The rebels took away a huge cache of arms, including five hundred .303 rifles, four hundred INSAS rifles, twenty AK-47 rifles, seventy self-loading rifles and three machine guns. They also looted a hundred thousand bullets. Two hours later, after roaming through the town at leisure, the rebels escaped, retreating into the nearby jungle in separate groups.

A day after the attack, India's then union home minister, Shivraj Patil, said in a television interview that Naxalism was not the single biggest threat to the country. Patil's statement made instant headlines and caused much embarrassment within the government. The home minister's statement came just a day after a massive attack on the might of the Indian state and barely seven weeks after India's prime minister, Manmohan Singh, had termed left-wing extremism as the single biggest threat to the country.

'How can he speak like this?' reacted an activist working in Orissa. 'Has he ever felt the pangs of hunger? Does he know what it means to eat rice gruel in Kalahandi? Does he know where the Naxalite cadre comes from?'

A journalist, who had gone to Kalahandi district in Orissa many years ago to file a report on starvation deaths, was speaking to a man who had recently lost his son.

'So, how did he die?' the journalist asked the man.

'He was suffering from a disease,' the man said.

'Which disease?' the journalist asked.

'The disease of hunger,' was the matter-of-fact reply.

Ironically, Kalahandi has the highest number of rice mills in Orissa, roughly around a hundred and fifty, and yet the people there have little to eat. It has been a long journey. In 1942, when a massive famine hit Bengal, the first shipload of rice that reached there went from Kalahandi. In 2007, activists surveying the district found that people in Kalahandi had had no rice to eat for nine months. Some of the families were seen boiling the bark of bamboo trees for food. Around the same time, hundreds of people in the region were reported to be dying of cholera. Aid workers blamed this on years of neglect, but the Orissa government and the Indian government were reluctant to accept that people were still dying of hunger.

Rice is just one of Kalahandi's many resources. The entire region is, in fact, filthy rich in minerals. In August 2008, India's Supreme Court approved a proposal from British mining giant Vedanta Resources to mine bauxite in the area. Vedanta Resources is investing Rs 4,500 crore to set up a refinery in Kalahandi district along with the Orissa Mining Corporation. It will mine bauxite in the Niyamgiri hills, a place that is sacred to a local tribe called the Dongria Kondh. In 2007, the same court had ruled against granting permission for Vedanta's mining operations, but it had left an option open. It would allow Vedanta's Indian subsidiary, Sterlite, to reapply if it promised to put 5 per cent of its profits into conservation and development. And that is what the conglomerate did.

The company plans to mine 30 lakh tonnes of bauxite every year and feed it to its Rs 2845-crore refinery. As the inhabitants of these hills, such as the Dongria tribe, struggle with increasing food shortages, the aluminium extracted from the ground beneath them will be used for making Coca-Cola cans.

The government of Orissa is reported to have signed mining agreements worth more than Rs 7,157,672 crore since 2006. Even as the government planned more such agreements, the state's chief minister, Naveen Patnaik, seemed oblivious to the damage these agreements were causing to the livelihood and sustainability of his people. 'No one – I repeat no one – will be allowed to stand in the way of Orissa's industrial development and the people's progress,' Patnaik said. Meanwhile, the price of Vedanta's shares has multiplied five-fold in five years.

Another mining company, Jindal, which has mining interests in Orissa, is drawing water from borewells in its area of operation. According to one report, Jindal uses a truck to sprinkle 10 kilolitres of water three times a day in the mining area. That is 30,000 litres of water a day just for sprinkling. Down the road from the Jindal mines, people say their streams are drying up, the water table has fallen and the soil has lost its fertility in the six years since the company began its operations. 'The crops have died, there is no place to graze cattle, the people cannot collect firewood in the project area and the hand pumps yield foul, yellowish water,' a local community leader informed us.

A mining proposal from South Korea's Posco, Asia's third-largest steelmaker, has also been cleared in Orissa. The project is estimated to bring in US$12 billion in foreign direct investment. Posco requires around 4,000 acres of land for its 120-lakh-tonne steel plant, of which it already possesses a quarter. The Supreme Court has now given Posco a green signal for acquiring the remaining 3,000 acres of land.

For three years now, the site where Posco plans to build its factory has been witnessing a series of agitations by the local people, backed by anti-mining activists, who say that the company will rob the region of its natural resources. From 2008 onwards, a large contingent of police has been deployed to thwart any resistance to the project – eighteen battalions have occupied government school buildings in the region and keep a close watch on the locals for any signs of protest.

The Indian government could perhaps take a lesson from other countries on how to safeguard the country's natural wealth from exploitation. Towards the end of 2007, the government of Norway withdrew all investments in Vedanta after it was concluded that the company 'has caused serious damage to people and to the environment as a result of its economic activities'. Norway's state pension fund is believed to have withdrawn US$13 million from Vedanta's projects. Yet, while other countries are becoming increasingly intolerant of environmental and ecological violations, New Delhi and India's state governments continue to lay out red carpets for such companies. Mining companies such as Vedanta are allowed almost free use of some of the nation's resources, such as groundwater. Other resources such as coal are provided at cheap rates.

Meanwhile, back in Niyamgiri, a village elder from the Dongria tribe rues the damage done to the hills that have been their home for centuries. He says that already big animals like the tiger and the bear can no longer be seen there and anticipates the further losses local inhabitants will have to cope with in the days to come.

What if the mining consortium were to offer them proper houses, electricity, schools, health centres and running water, even motorbikes or cars, would that not be a fair exchange for their sacred mountain, the Dongria elder is asked.

'Vedanta can give us a helicopter each but we won't give up our hills,' he said. 'We'll fight. What choice do we have? If we give up the hills, we'll die anyway.'

3

As in the mineral-rich regions of neighbouring states, Bastar too has seen steel giants such as Tata and Essar invest Rs 30,000 crore in steel and power. The official website of the Chhattisgarh government says that the state is the richest in India in terms of mineral wealth, with twenty-eight major minerals, and diamonds, found here. But this mineral wealth does not translate into enough jobs for the poor of this area. Thirty-nine per cent of the people live below the poverty line and it is not just jobs that are at stake. The industry predicts that Bastar could become a primary industrial zone by 2011. But would this also mean something for the people of Chhattisgarh?

Dandakaranya is the sprawling 'liberated zone', now administered by the Maoists, extending over 1,00,000 square kilometres and incorporating parts of the states of Chhattisgarh, Orissa and Andhra Pradesh. It has a population of more than 2 crore. Along with the rest of Dandakaranya, Abujhmaad, the thickly forested area stretching across 40,000 square kilometres in Chhattisgarh's remote south, appeared to have escaped India's memory post the reign of Emperor Akbar. Until the day a few men who had recently been freed from prisons began invoking its name. These men were the soldiers of Mao and wanted, as their revolutionary ideologue had asked of them, to first seize power in the most backward regions and then prepare for the big war. Today, in most of Dandakaranya, and even outside it, in some specific areas of Jharkhand and West

Bengal, Maoists run the show. The void created by the absence of the elected government has been filled by them.

The Dandakaranya area is rich in mineral and forest wealth and many rivers flow through here, but the local population remains deprived of water and irrigation facilities. In this impoverished expanse, lives are wrapped in supreme irony. From one market alone in Bastar, business worth millions of rupees is done per annum from forest produce such as tamarind and gum, but the people living here remain untouched by this wealth. Until two decades ago, less than 2 per cent of the land here was under irrigation and more than 90 per cent of the population was illiterate. People had no idea about basic agricultural practices such as the use of fertilizers or weeding. There was no concept of sowing crops. The region had remained so backward that people in many villages did not use the plough on the land because they thought of the earth as their mother. There was no trace of modern medicine. The villagers were steeped in superstition and the local *vadde*, the witch doctor, dictated their lives. No welfare scheme, no Nehruvian five-year-plan ever came within whistling distance of it.

The members of the Gond, Govari, Koya and Kondu tribes, among others, were the worst sufferers. Leaning upon a series of illogical forest acts that deprived the tribals of the use of forest land, local oppressors – especially businessmen, in connivance with government officials and politicians – exploited the original inhabitants of the land. Forest officials would demand that the tribals give them grain, chicken, goats and their local liquor in exchange for permission to collect a few branches of trees for firewood or other such trivial use. Traders routinely duped them in simple calculations of prices and payments because the tribals were illiterate.

Then came the mines. By 1981, activists claim, bauxite was being mined across a hundred and fifty villages. While the people in these villages received no compensation, hundreds of square kilometres of fertile agricultural land were destroyed. In the region around Bailadila, from where iron ore was exported mainly to Japan, all the rivers were polluted and thousands suffered from unknown diseases. Many young men, with no prospects of jobs or any benefits from these projects, turned into thieves. Young girls were forced into prostitution.

Meanwhile, with the growth of the Naxalite movement in the neighbouring Karimnagar and Adilabad districts of Andhra Pradesh, the PWG decided to spread its movement to Dandakaranya in 1980. Three guerrilla squads of six members each entered this area from Andhra Pradesh. They surveyed the area, looking for class contradictions and assessing the socio-economic condition of the people. And, gradually, they began establishing contact with the masses.

Alerted by their colleagues in Andhra Pradesh, the police in Maharashtra and Madhya Pradesh (of which Chhattisgarh was then a part) took action, killing a prominent Maoist functionary sent into the Gadchiroli area. But by then it was too late. The local people were angry and ready to revolt, and slowly the Naxalites became a part of their lives. Forest officials were thrashed publicly by the rebels and asked not to enter any villages.

Gradually, the handful of Maoists became the face of resistance in this area. The poor people of this region, who by now had nothing more to lose, were attracted to these men and women in shabby camouflage. The first mass mobilization for militant action happened soon afterwards, with a campaign to ensure higher rates of payment for workers cutting down bamboo trees and picking tendu leaves, used for making hand-rolled beedis. For years, the locals had been paid a pittance for these jobs. After the guerrillas intervened, their wages increased almost four times. Many businessmen who were reluctant to toe the Maoist line suffered losses as their depots were burnt. This was followed by a sweeping push to occupy land.

Mass organizations were formed, those for peasants and for women among them.

By the time the police intervened and arrested and killed a number of guerrillas, the movement had caught the imagination of many in the area. With the formation of village-level self-defence units, the Gram Rakshak Dals, there was a large influx of locals into the guerrilla squads.

To train people – most of them illiterate – in their ideology, the Maoists began organizing crash courses in Marxism and current affairs. In the military camps, men and women were taught how to use guns and put through military drills. Local issues were handled by what came to be known as the *praja* courts, or people's courts, which adopted excessive and often cruel ways of meting out justice but nevertheless filled in the vacuum created by a defunct judicial system.

Then the Naxalites set out to provide a model of village governance that could well have been emulated by the state government. By the early 1990s, the Maoists formed committees to undertake development projects. In July 1994, the Gram Rajya Committees were formed. The Maoists used these committees to undertake the work the government should have got done through the village panchayats or village councils.

The first priority for the Maoists in garnering the people's support was to take care of their hunger. For that, it was vital to rescue agriculture and the Maoists began to concentrate on the availability, conservation and usage of water. Almost 50 per cent of the population does not have access to drinking water at home. According to the Centre for Science and Environment, iron-ore mining alone used up 770 lakh tonnes of water in 2005–06 – water, which, it says, is enough to meet the daily needs of more than 30 lakh people. In the Basaguda township, for example, a dam that would supply water to around ten villages was breached by floods during the monsoon in the early 1980s. Despite repeated pleas to government officials, no government agency responded. Years passed. In 1998, the Maoists finally galvanized the people of the affected villages to form a tank-building committee. For a month, four hundred people worked to construct a bund with the help of a seed fund released by the rebel leadership. Those who worked on the project were given a kilogram of rice per day. One of the Maoist leaders who supervised this work claims that after the rebels undertook this project, the government panicked and released Rs 20 lakh for the project – sudden generosity which the local community rejected. By 1997–98, more than a hundred tanks had been constructed in Dandakaranya under the guidance of Maoist groups.

Ironically, the communist guerrillas had found something in common with Narendra Modi, the Hindu nationalist chief minister of the state of Gujarat hundreds of kilometres to the west. Both had come to realize the importance of check dams and had initiated the construction of thousands of them in their respective turfs. In the Naxal heartland of Dandakaranya, numerous check dams have reportedly been built under the supervision of the Maoists. Diesel-run pump sets, which were unheard of in the interiors of Chhattisgarh, have been introduced. These are used to transport water to the fields. Hundreds of wells to provide drinking water have been dug with the help of experienced masons brought in from cities.

The Maoists also encouraged the cultivation of vegetables for which seeds were procured and distributed among villagers in more than two hundred and fifty villages. The rebels encouraged people to grow legumes and oilseeds so that they could earn some money by selling a portion of their produce. Mango and guava plantations were introduced in more than a hundred villages.

A number of cooperatives were started once it was found that the crop yield turned out to be much better when people worked in larger groups beyond their immediate families. The villagers were offered technical advice on topics of immediate concern such as crops, soil variety and crop disease. 'We have banned the use of chemical fertilizers. We have taught people how to make organic fertilizers instead,' said a Maoist ideologue.

The Maoists also destroyed the monopoly of rich landlords over fish rearing. The masses were introduced to pisciculture and, according to a Maoist leader, 'The fish reared in Dandakaranya is marketed in Delhi and Kolkata.'

In the months when there is no agricultural work, adult education classes are held. In areas where there are government schools, villagers have built huts for teachers, with the permission of the Maoists, to encourage them to stay on. 'In many places we give salaries to government school teachers,' claimed a Maoist leader. To discourage tribal youth from drinking and gambling at rooster fights, games such as carrom and volleyball have been introduced.

Death is common in this region. Every year, hundreds of people die here because of diseases such as diarrhoea, cholera and malaria. Over the years, the Maoists have built clinics where a few chosen tribal youth trained at medical camps provide basic medical treatment to the people. These youth are trained to identify common diseases, their symptoms and even give injections. The party's central fund provides the seed funds for these clinics.

In the mid-1970s a young educated man became a member of one of the squads sent by a senior Naxal ideologue into Dandakaranya. Over time, he acquired in-depth knowledge of traditional medicine and began treating minor ailments among the local tribals. This dabbling in medicine earned him the nickname 'Doctor' from his comrades. Many years later, when he was no longer underground, Doctor came down with a high fever that he suspected was a fallout of malaria. He went to a clinic, where a young doctor advised some blood tests. While Doctor was trying to follow the instructions, he noticed that the young man was looking at him intensely. 'What is your name?' the young doctor asked. Though he wouldn't have known Doctor's real name, some memories were aroused at the mention of it. The young doctor smiled at Doctor. 'You wouldn't recognize me, but I know you. When I was a child, you came to my village and treated me for scabies,' he said.

A Maoist-run clinic seems like a tempting alternative in a state where ten out of sixteen districts do not have a hospital. A primary health centre caters to an average of forty thousand people. This is because the state chooses to spend only 4.45 per cent of its budget on healthcare in remote areas. Government officials point their fingers at Naxalites when confronted with such statistics, but it is they who stop individuals and agencies from taking healthcare to the villages in the state. It is widely known that the Chhattisgarh government asked Médecins Sans Frontières, an international agency, to stop its humanitarian and medical aid in the villages. It was alleged that the organization had been providing medical help to the Maoists.

On a November evening, dozens of villagers – all men – are squatting outside the Bedanji village in Chhattisgarh's Jagdalpur district, and we wonder what's going on as we pass by. It is a mourning ceremony for an elder who has died, we are told. The men sit in total silence, until the visitors walk up. Within minutes, the conversation turns to something else they are mourning, a matter of far greater import, a matter of life and death.

'We will not give our land to Tata,' says sixty-year-old Sankar Das, a skinny dhoti-clad Hindu priest. Bedanji is part of the land in which Tata Steel plans to invest Rs 19,500 crores towards a steel plant spread across 21 square kilometres. It is projected to produce 55 lakh tonnes of steel per year. In all, ten villages have to be vacated and the land sold to the private-sector company.

Das pokes around in his bag and produces a frayed piece of paper. 'The Kakatiya kings brought and settled us here from Warangal twenty-two generations ago to worship the goddess and supervise sacrifices on Dussehra,' says the letter, handwritten by Bedanji residents in Hindi to the administrator of Jagdalpur. 'We shall not move.' The Kakatiyas were medieval kings who ruled what is now Andhra Pradesh. This, though, is the story of modern India – an infrastructure-hungry nation needs energy and steel and other ingredients to grow, so big businesses head to the heartland of resources to set up power plants and mine iron ore and other minerals. But local farmers are determined to fight for their land.

A government commission headed by the then Rural Development Minister Raghuvansh Prasad Singh said in late 2009 that companies like Tata and Essar had undertaken a corporate takeover in the hinterland of Chhattisgarh and warned of 'the biggest grab of tribal lands after Columbus'. It was an indictment that stunned even the most steadfast opponents of the government. 'This openly declared war will go down as the biggest land grab ever, if it plays out as per the script,' said the report. 'The drama [is] being scripted by Tata Steel and Essar Steel who wanted seven villages or thereabouts each, to mine the richest lode of iron ore available in India.'

Both companies strongly rejected the allegations.

'This is ridiculous ... there is a formal Memorandum of Understanding, the land was allocated, and the whole process was done in a legal manner. There is no land grab,' said Tata Steel spokesman Sanjay Chowdhary.

'It is completely incorrect and baseless,' an unnamed Essar spokesman said in a statement to the *Hindustan Times*. 'Biased and one-sided reports like this only contribute towards vitiating the atmosphere.'

Prime Minister Manmohan Singh acknowledged recently that the country was now having to face the repercussions of widespread exploitation of India's tribal population – an apparent reference to the rapid growth of the Naxalite movement. Tribal people, after all, make up only 9 per cent of the country's population, but more than 40 per cent of the land used to build development projects has been theirs, according to government estimates. 'There has been a systemic failure in giving tribals a stake in the modern economic system ... the alienation built over decades is taking a dangerous toll,' he said. 'The systemic exploitation of our tribal communities ... can no longer be tolerated.'

Still, there seem to be few checks and balances, and Maoists are using the discontentment to gain support, telling people that they do not own the huge natural wealth beneath their feet which rightfully belongs to them. Government officials aren't helping either. On 12 October 2009, in Jagdalpur district, the collector held a public hearing as required under law before any acquisition of village land. It was hardly a 'public meeting', held in a hall that could accommodate just about three hundred people, some 30 kilometres away from the homes of the villagers whose lives were being decided upon.

Officials had refused to travel to the villages, saying there was a Naxalite threat. They pointed to the killing in June 2009 of Vimal Meshram, forty-two, a staunch supporter of the Tata project and an influential tribal leader. A small group of rebels had walked up to him at a weekly market in Lohandiguda village, 340 kilometres south of Raipur, shot him at close range in full public view and walked off.

On the day of the public hearing, when villagers started to travel towards the collector's office in large numbers to express their disapproval of the land deal, barricades were built on the roads and their entry was restricted. Back at the hall, many people in the gathering described as villagers were accused of being government employees pretending to be farmers by those villagers who had somehow made it. The meeting was deemed to have resulted in public approval of the project and cheques were quickly distributed in the days and weeks that followed. Many villagers complained that compensation cheques had been given away to the wrong people impersonating landowners. When the number of complaints increased, several criminal cases were registered. Yet, Collector Manohar Singh Paraste said all was above board and that support for the project had been unanimous. He asserted that there was no need for a public hearing to be held among the people who would be most affected. 'This is how it has been done in the past, and this is how we will do it,' he said.

Travelling through rural Bihar in 1975, when Naxalism had made inroads into vast expanses of the state, socialist leader Jai Prakash Narain had urged people to shun violence and work, instead, for 'total revolution'. 'If within five years, nothing changes, I will not ask you to give up Naxalism,' he had promised them.

Five years passed. Then another thirty. Little changed. The Naxalite movement cascaded through the country, riding on the back of independent India's worst disaster - poor governance.

A report drawn up by the Planning Commission of India in 2008 admitted many truths that successive governments have pushed under the carpet and acknowledged facts that authorities have long labelled as Naxal propaganda.

'There is no denying that what goes in the name of "Naxalism" is to a large extent a product of collective failure to assure to different segments of society their basic entitlements under the Constitution and other protective legislation,' the report said in its epilogue. It conceded that the Naxalites have been able to put an effective end to the exploitation of tendu-leaf pickers - after the Naxalites' intervention, remuneration for tendu-leaf pickers has increased by up to 50 per cent. 'It is therefore necessary,' the report advised, 'for the state to provide for a minimum support price for all types of minerals and forest produce.'

It spoke about Naxalite influence in administrative and judicial matters. 'In the matter of resolution of disputes among the people and finding redressal, the contribution of the Naxalite movement has been significant.' It also acknowledged that the Naxalite movement has 'given confidence to the oppressed to assert their equality and demand respect and dignity from the dominant castes and classes'. 'The fact that the cadre and most local leaders of the Naxalite organizations consist of poor villagers of castes looked upon as lowly has endowed the oppressed with much strength. A sense of powerlessness is a characteristic of the psychological make-up of oppressed classes. The typical Naxalite cadre, however, is a confident teenager from those very classes. To see young boys and girls of their own villages and their own class or caste active in the Naxalite movement and wielding power over the "big" men of the village and the high and mighty *tehsildar* has given a sense of empowerment to the oppressed that has inestimable value,' the report said.

One man had lived through these truths. This was Misir Besra one of the highest-ranking Naxalite leaders.

Decades ago, not very far from where Jai Prakash Narain was making a promise to the people of Bihar, a young Santhal boy was receiving the customary brand on his wrist – the mark that was supposed to protect him from his 'enemies'.

While studying in a school in Giridih district of the then undivided Bihar, the boy became aware of who his 'enemies' were. As he would later recall, he witnessed a lot of discrimination against his fellow tribals in his youth. In 1985, Misir Besra joined a college for an honours degree in Hindi. He had a keen interest in political science and remembers reading with rapt attention the stories of revolutionaries such as Bhagat Singh and Khudiram Bose.

When he returned home, he realized that the discrimination against his tribe hadn't stopped; it had only worsened. 'One day, I took a pitcher of mahua to a shopkeeper. When I asked him for money, he asked me to run away before he thrashed me,' recalls Besra.

We were sitting before Besra, who was in police custody. He was feeling a bit cold, but wore a hint of a smile. The sear from being branded shone on his pale skin. He refused a cigarette, saying he had quit smoking. 'I had come to drink tea when the police came and picked me up,' said the man who had spent twenty-two years in the jungle, his teeth now chattering in the cold. When the police party approached the car in which Misir Besra was travelling, he did not run away. Until then his strategy had worked perfectly. Besra's photo had never appeared in police records, and from his face and physique, no one would suspect him of being a much-wanted Naxalite leader. But this time the police were not taking any chances. Besra was detained and his photo circulated among imprisoned Naxalites. His men identified him in no time. After all, Misir Besra, alias Commander Sunirmal, alias Bhaskar, was no ordinary foot soldier. As a member of the CPI (Maoist)'s politburo and their central military commission, Besra headed the eastern command, supervising the party's activities in Orissa, Chhattisgarh, Jharkhand, West Bengal and lower Assam. He was also in charge of the Naxalites' military intelligence wing and helped the party procure arms and ammunition.

His story had begun with a jackfruit tree. Soon after the shopkeeper had threatened to beat him up over payment for the mahua, an old jackfruit tree in his village was cut down by a few landlords. 'They took away the branches, but I decided that I would not let them take away the trunk,' said Besra. Besra and a handful of his friends guarded it. Even after the block development officer and the *tehsildar* tried to convince him to hand over the trunk to the landlords, he did not budge. The incident left an indelible mark on him, says Besra.

In October 1985, a left-wing song and dance troupe visited Besra's village. After listening to their revolutionary songs, Besra decided to join them. By that time he was also attending a post-graduation course, but decided to discontinue it. 'I slipped away with the troupe after their programme got over,' he said.

There was a time, Besra remembers, when the Naxalites possessed only a few double-barrel guns. 'Initially, we were treated like dacoits by the villagers,' he said. But things changed over time.

New recruits like Besra received training from the rebels of the PWG in Andhra Pradesh. During the ninth congress of the by then consolidated CPI (Maoist), held in Bhimbandh in Bihar for ten days, Misir Besra was in charge of security. On their way back, his company is believed to have raided a police picket in Lakhisarai district of Bihar, killing four police personnel. In 2004, Besra is said to have planned and executed an ambush in Baliba in Jharkhand's West Singhbhum district, in which twenty-nine police personnel were killed.

While in custody, Besra told the police that the budget for the Maoists' central military commission for two years (2007–09) is Rs 60 crore, of which around Rs 42 crore was to be spent on procuring arms and ammunition and other logistics and Rs 10 crore was reserved for the formation of the central technical committee, which works on the production of arms, among other things. Besra further revealed that the Maoist leadership had recently been looking to recruit a chemist and an electronics engineer. They were keen to hire computer professionals as well. Where does this money come from, we asked. Besra admitted that most of it comes from extortion of contractors and miners, and levies on government agencies and officials.

During the party congress, it was decided that two regional commands would be formed, each of which would maintain its own teams for action, intelligence, technology, medicine and communications, as well as its own supply mechanisms. The

Maoists now also have their own central instructors' team. It consists of nine members who are supposed to move around the states to impart training to Naxalite cadre. Some of them are already under arrest and at least one is believed to have died in Orissa while handling grenades.

Besra revealed that state committees of the CPI (Maoist) also exist in states such as Delhi, Haryana and Punjab, and that it was decided during the Naxal congress to maintain one urban combat team specifically to identify targets in Delhi and Haryana. 'Without the participation of the middle class, there will be no revolution,' he said.

An internal party document on urban warfare, released during the ninth congress, clearly states the CPI (Maoist)'s focus areas in urban India: 'The work in urban areas involves the task of unifying the working class, building worker–peasant solidarity and alliances, uniting with other classes in the cities, building fronts against the exploitation and oppression of imperialism and the comprador bureaucratic bourgeoisie, against their war designs and globalization, and against Hindu fascism, against state repression, Dalit and women's oppression, etc. This is a very important aspect of the work of the party in the cities.'

How much success have they achieved in urban areas such as Delhi? 'Not much,' Besra confessed, 'but our members are active there.' Besra's admission is confirmed by the fact that Maoist literature and CDs containing Maoist propaganda have recently been recovered from Haryana. An intelligence report by the home ministry maintains that the Maoists are trying to engineer caste conflicts as a part of their strategy in states such as Haryana and western Uttar Pradesh. After a clash between the police and the workers of a Honda factory in Gurgaon in 2005, a Honda showroom was attacked in Kaithal in Haryana. The attack is believed to have been led by a member of a left-wing organization.

In May 2009, three Naxalites were arrested in Delhi by a special cell of the Delhi Police after being tipped off by their Jharkhand counterparts. One of them, Yogendra, was a zonal commander of the Maoists in Jharkhand. He was being treated for a bullet injury he had received during a shootout with a rival group in Jharkhand. Senior Maoist leader Kobad Ghandy was arrested in Delhi in September 2009. In 2010, the police have arrested a number of suspected Maoist leaders who had set up base in the capital. Some of the protests that turned violent after four members of a Dalit family were lynched to death in Khairlanji in Maharashtra in 2006 are also believed to have been orchestrated by Naxalites.

According to Besra's interrogation report, the rebels had planned to target at least two police officers, H.J. Dora, former director general of the Andhra Pradesh Police, who lives in Delhi, and Anil Palta, an Indian Police Service officer who is responsible for many successful operations against the Naxalite cadre. Some of the political leaders on the Naxalite hit list include the former and current chief ministers of Jharkhand and Chhattisgarh. Among the places that serve as meeting points for the Naxalites are a number of railway stations, including some in Patna, Jamshedpur, Ranchi, Nagpur and Kochi.

The central government now says that it is taking the Naxal threat seriously. It cites the raising of another special force called Cobra (Commando Battalion for Resolute Action) as an example of New Delhi's commitment to 'wipe them out'. But it is becoming increasingly apparent that the answer does not lie in eliminating the Naxalites by force.

'Its [the Naxalite movement's] geographical spread is rooted in failure to remove the conditions which give rise to it,' the Planning Commission report of 2008 states. The report also questions New Delhi's stand on Naxal groups vis-à-vis other militant groups in the country. Pointing to the government's stated position of willingness to hold talks with any group that is prepared to come to the negotiating table, the report asks: 'Why a different approach to the Naxals?'

'*Datkar khao, datkar chalo* (Eat as much as you can, walk as much as you can).' That is the motto of the ordinary Naxalite worker. For him, revolution still means, to a large extent, freedom from hunger and the possession of a .303 rifle, which will act as a deterrent to the local oppressor. Tackling this internal security crisis requires governments to go back to what they were elected to do – work towards the welfare of the people, not wage gun battles.

Meanwhile, in prison, Misir Besra was passing his time by reading. 'I've just finished reading a novel by Agyey.'

Is he in touch with his comrades?

'No,' replied Besra in a matter-of-fact tone. 'Since I was put under arrest, they don't trust me any more.'

But they did trust him. On 23 June 2009, less than two years after he was arrested, Misir Besra was brought to a court in the Lakhisarai district of Bihar. It was a hot afternoon and, as a five-member police team escorted him out of the courtroom, some three dozen Maoists stormed in on motorcycles and started firing and hurling bombs. One policeman was killed. The Maoists grappled with the policemen, managed to free Besra and drove him away on one of the motorcycles. They also snatched some guns from the police for good measure.

4

Dear Comrade Kavita Didi,
I send you a lal salaam [red salute].
Kavita Didi I don't know how you are. You must be well.
Comrade, I was very sick for four months. I am fine now. I was then in the village, I was very upset. I didn't even know what disease I had, and if I hadn't recovered, I was considering going home.
But now I won't. Whatever hardships I face, I will not leave the party, I won't go home. I will keep fighting to protect the people.

The forty-two-year-old Maoist rebellion has created some of the grittiest insurgents in the world, making the battles in their heartland tougher to fight, some say, than in Afghanistan or Iraq.

The rebel's personal letter – which spoke only of war – was written in longhand in the Gondi language on a page torn from a school notebook used by students. It was signed by a guerrilla who identified himself as Comrade Kital of the Indrawati National Park *dalam* (military platoon). The letter, and others like it, was seized by the police on 3 July 2009 in a jungle raid that also yielded a scanner and photocopier from deep inside the inaccessible forest. Letters – a bonding mechanism between comrades-in-arms living in impossible conditions – are a rare seizure but are commonly used by the guerrillas in a monolithic set-up that thrives on written documents and manuals, including a military strategy doctrine, motivational literature and regular newsletters. They are the staple diet, as it were, of an organization with the most educated cadre of armed rebels in India. In fact, the senior Naxal leadership hardly uses phones and other modern devices for communication. This is to prevent the security agencies from getting to know their location, movements and plans. Messages are mostly delivered by human couriers, and letters or notes are referred to as 'biscuits'.

The rebels' military structure is complex, and largely invisible even within civilian populations. Its building block is the *sangam*, the Maoists' eyes and ears, operating from the ground out of every village. *Sangam* members are tasked with organizing public and private meetings of the rebel groups with villagers, and for arranging for food by telling villagers to cook for the squads. A rank above is the militia, whose members are armed with bows and arrows, some tipped with detonators meant to explode on hitting trees, as a signal to other guerrillas. This leads up to the Local Guerrilla Squad the strongest foundation of the rebels, merging into platoons and companies. In southern Chhattisgarh's Abujhmaad area. The rebels have now also created army-style divisions – one army division has some 10,000 soldiers. In most of the attacks, the modus operandi is the same: an improvised explosive device (IED) blast is triggered off and in the ensuing chaos, the security personnel are fired upon from vantage points. In some cases, bombs are set up in advance at points where it is anticipated the security personnel will take position. To teach new rebels guerilla tactics, regular classes are held by the Maoists' state and central military commissions. Just as in the government against which they are fighting, Naxalite rebels are transferred and promoted. There is career growth.

There are friendships made in the battlefield, as other letters indicate.

Dear Comrade Raju,

I am fine, I am working for the party with all my heart and soul. During the last assembly elections, the police had forced people of this area to vote. So our party workers have explained to the people that on the day of the Lok Sabha elections, no villager will remain in their village. A committee has been formed to hide the people.

Dear Comrade Somali,
Sukko of my village is also in the Maad dalam. To take forward the revolution, Comrade Supal is also in the Gadchiroli district, his name has been changed. He is now called Comrade Kishore. If you meet him, tell him Raju sent a red salute.

These foot soldiers of the Maoist rebellion are masters of jungle warfare. 'Their military company is well trained, like the police and paramilitary,' Vishwa Mohan, the director general of the Chhattisgarh Police, said candidly as he sat in his Raipur office, a huge room with walls covered in trophies, books and paintings. The chain-smoking Mohan, a painter and lover of music, is nothing short of a public enemy for Maoists and pro-Maoist human rights groups, who often engage him in media face-offs. Still, Mohan has a deep academic interest in communism and the Maoist insurgency, and has studied the subjects closely since his days as a college student in Kolkata, when he used to frequent the busy College Street to buy books. His collection includes a treasured possession – a banned thirty-two-book set of Mao's teachings.

Out in the field, his men, too, have grudging admiration for their adversary. 'The beauty is their structure. You can eliminate fighters, but it's very hard to kill the structure,' says a senior police officer. 'He [the Maoist] is very smart, very intelligent, very systematic, very methodical. Every operation could be preceded by months of preparation.'

The Maoists have a wide network of intelligence. In villages, people sympathetic to them act as their eyes and ears. It is through these people that the Maoists learn about the movement of security forces in a particular area. So, if a CRPF company is on the move on an area-domination exercise, the Maoist guerillas are tipped off in advance in most instances. That is how they get time to move away from that area, or, if they wish, to set up an ambush. In some cases, they are even known to have set up police informers against the police itself.

This is the level of preparation that went into the attack on Dhanaura village in the Nelnar area of Chhattisgarh on 5 June 2009, as a letter from Comrade Rita, dated 20 July 2009, reveals.

> *Dear Comrade Chaitu Dada,*
> *Policemen used to go for ablutions every day at 5.00 a.m., so our comrade was waiting in ambush in civil clothes, with a bow and arrow.*
> *They emerged like every day, and our comrade got one of them with the arrow. He was wounded but did not die. We ambushed again on the 8th in civil clothes from three places. One policeman died and another was wounded.*

Some letters contain accounts of operations that went wrong due to a range of reasons, like wrongly timed IEDs, or misinformation resulting in civilians getting killed instead of police targets.

'In the Pallamandi area, we carried out an explosion assuming they were policemen, but seven teachers died. In another incident, we ambushed and killed fifteen policemen and seized sixteen guns,' says a letter of 14 June 2009 from Comrade Raju of the Manpur division operating in the Bastar region. All these situations are discussed threadbare within the organization, and responsibility fixed by decision-making committees.

~

They gored him with a dozen sharp spears. In a second, the most nimble police guide in the advance party had plunged in the dark into the grave-sized hole camouflaged by grass and twigs. Six-feet-high sharp spikes planted by Naxalites in the soil had ripped through his right leg. Deep inside Naxal territory, the rebels had prepared meticulously for war. IED explosions did not take place here; few policemen or paramilitary soldiers ever ventured this deep. But the threat of a large-scale conflict was looming, and the defence was getting more aggressive and lethal.

The booby trap was a war tactic that Vietcong rebels had often used against American soldiers in the impossible jungles of Vietnam. It was the kind of trap that poachers laid to capture elephants. Here, in Chhattisgarh, it had become part of the strategy used by guerrillas to attack India's state forces when, in the winter of 2009, security personnel prepared to sweep through the forest. The central government seemed keen for the first time to help the states in their fight against communist insurgency and thousands of paramilitary soldiers, largely from the Central Reserve Police Force (CRPF), poured in from across the country, even from other strife-torn areas such as Kashmir.

On 23 October 2009, in the operation in the state's Bijapur district, the painful trap delayed the police by several crucial hours. The battle had started even before the first bullet was fired.

'Saheb, I need to go back,' the wounded police guide said as he writhed in pain. The entire team came to a halt.

'We gave him an injection but he began to faint,' recounts Sub-Inspector Naresh Chauhan, who commanded a hundred and sixty-eight men in the raid.

Two men helped the guide to his feet and assisted him as he slowly hobbled away into the dark with their help. New guides stepped in to take forward the battle in the middle of nowhere. The team knew well that dozens of pairs of eyes were watching them. 'As we began to walk ahead, we saw shadows chasing us – the Naxalites were keeping track of us on the flanks, armed with bows and arrows. No one said a word. We would fire a shot; they would disperse. But they came back again – like ghosts chasing us through the night.'

The shadows were just one of the many lines of defence set up by the rebels. They soon began to shoot arrows at the policemen, who took cover, fired back, then trudged ahead. There were more trenches with booby traps that were fortunately spotted and avoided. For hours, both sides played a cat-and-mouse game in the heart of the forest, stopping short of a full-blown confrontation.

The policemen were hungry. So the hundred and sixty-five men – three short of their original strength – stopped at a clearing, set up a protective cordon, pulled out stoves and bags of rice and pulses, and began to cook. No war can be fought on an empty stomach.

Right after their dinner – or an early breakfast – the gunfight began, from beyond a river across the clearing. It was as if the Naxals were daring their adversary, now that he was on a full stomach. Bullets pierced through the twilight. Two policemen were wounded and two Naxalites were killed before day broke, and the policemen began their tough walk back to the barracks, past the same trenches that would await them on another day.

Across the densely forested countryside, numerous such traps lie hidden under camouflage, dug during the nights since the autumn of 2009. There is no one to stop them – India's government does not exist here.

'This is many levels more difficult than Kashmir,' says Bijapur's twenty-nine-year-old Superintendent of Police Avinash Mohanty, who witnessed Kashmir operations. 'All operations are on foot. In the jungles there are no roads. You could have fifteen men surrounded by two hundred Naxalites in a forest with no reinforcements for hours. It's just you – on your own.'

'I know one thing,' he says, 'my men are true heroes.'

The rebel squads often employ simple but ingenious tactics to interrupt police action. During an operation on 23 October 2009, they pushed herds of cows in front of the soldiers, mostly Hindus who worship the animal and would not fire at cattle.

'They have small detonators fixed to arrows,' says Satwant Singh Yadav, an assistant commandant in the CRPF. 'Children grazing cattle aim them at trees and shoot – it creates a small explosion. A signal for others as we approach their positions. They also have poison-tipped arrows.'

The lean, Haryana-born Yadav has seen the Maoist rebels in action from close quarters. They nearly killed Yadav on 8 June 2009 in a deadly operation. He had led his men deep into a forest not far from Chhattisgarh's Bijapur town, acting on intelligence that a large group of Naxalites was present in the area. The policemen combed through a large expanse, but then came under heavy gunfire and Yadav acquired several gunshot wounds. He sent his men ahead of him as he sat against a rock, protected by a few guards, resting and waiting for the worst. Grievously wounded, he struggled to take out his mobile phone from his pocket, switched on to video mode and recorded dying instructions for his men.

Fortunately, they didn't need them.

The information was rock solid – '*ekdum* pukka', as the informant told the policeman: Naxalites had been spotted near a hillock in the Hazaribagh district of Jharkhand.

It was a hot May afternoon and a few men from the Jharkhand Police and the CRPF were applying mosquito repellent cream on their faces and necks. The men were about to leave for a joint long-range patrol. But now, with news of Naxalites having been spotted, a quick change of plans was in order.

'*Uda do saala lal chaddiyon ko* (Blow off those red knickered b—s),' a policeman said, as he lifted his sten gun. Clutching their weapons, the men patted each other's backs and climbed into an armoured truck. An hour or so later, a fierce gun battle took place in a remote hilly area. The police and the Naxalites were both heavily armed and out to gather heads. But the Naxalites had the advantage of altitude. Soon, two men at the foot of a hillock – a sub-inspector of the Jharkhand Police and a CRPF soldier – collapsed on the rocks with bullet injuries.

'Don't worry, you will be all right – we will get you airlifted in no time,' the commander of the police party comforted the wounded men as they struggled to breathe, the afternoon heat smouldering their faces.

As he sought the deputy inspector general over the crackling wireless and urgently requisitioned a helicopter, the commander assumed that within a short while he would hear the whirring of the helicopter's blades. After all, the Jharkhand government had spent Rs 35 crore on a flying machine so it could be of use during anti-Maoist operations. But his senior's instructions were crisp and heartbreaking – for both the superior and the commander. He was asked to try and evacuate the wounded men by road. The helicopter would not arrive. Its rotor blades had developed a snag.

The Naxalites soon disappeared into the thick of the jungle, and the two policemen died a slow death in the arms of their fellow soldiers.

'If the helicopter was meant for us, its control should have been with the police department,' said Ashok Pathak, vice-president of the Jharkhand Police Association.

'I lost a DCP in a similar encounter because we couldn't carry him to a hospital,' says Inspector General S.N. Pradhan, who is in charge of modernization of the Jharkhand Police. 'He bled to death while speaking to his wife over the phone.'

It was hardly a surprise that the helicopter was not in flying condition. It was a machine, after all, and had been used extensively. In the two months before the day the policemen watched two of their comrades die in front of their eyes, it had been flown for a hundred and sixty hours – nearly three hours a day – ferrying the chief minister of Jharkhand and his colleagues.

A white-clad waiter nervously serves tea at the sprawling colonial-era mansion of Jharkhand's director general of police, J. Mohapatra, as he begins to answer the first question posed to him on a muggy afternoon in Ranchi in July 2007. The families of the two dead policemen in Hazaribagh, the men who died waiting for a helicopter to rescue them, would have wanted to listen in.

'Two hundred and fifty of our men have died in the past seven years, but due to their own mistakes, because they were not professional,' says Mohapatra, speaking slowly as he leans back in his chair. 'They made tactical mistakes. Sheer foolishness.'

We recall an earlier meeting far away from Ranchi, in the Gudabanda region. A police officer sat in the ramshackle building of a primary school, converted into a police station for lack of better accommodation, saying bitterly, 'I am a man who is riding an elephant, but is being bitten by a dog. An officer who wants to work gets demoralized ... He thinks, "My department is totally corrupt, why should I give my life for it?"'

The officer sat in his undershirt on a jute-rope cot, bellowing to his men to bring tea for the visitors. On the table in front of him was a telephone that did not work, a lantern, a torch and a register with marks that looked like attendance records. Behind him, the blackboard was blank. There were sandbags outside the school building and barbed wire fencing. The police station had no advanced weapons, no bulletproof jackets and, truly, no will to wage a seemingly impossible battle. This was the only police station covering the constituencies of three members of the legislative assembly, over hundreds of square kilometres. Since the police had taken over the school building, the children of the area had not gone to school.

'I am paying the price because government officials do not do their jobs,' the officer said with acid in his voice. 'There is no doctor for fifty kilometres. All colleges are fifty kilometres away. Barely one or two out of a hundred students manage to go to college. For employment, the men grow paddy and the women pluck leaves – sal or tendu.'

In what used to be the school playground stood a huge metal hulk – a yellow generator in disuse, wrapped in a tarpaulin sheet. Electric bulbs did not light up here. The government had installed such generators a year ago, but had forgotten to earmark allowances for diesel, mechanics or sheds to shelter the generators. Some four hundred and fifty police stations across Jharkhand had these trophies sitting in their compounds for a year now, all bought with the taxpayer's money and all of which had not produced a watt of electricity between them.

Back in Ranchi, 2007, the tea is not over yet. Gardeners are busy at work, mowing the beautiful lawns outside the windows. DGP Mohapatra, is finally opening up. He knows the story of the generators, and the one about the computers, too.

'There is money for generators, but the government could not decide on the agency that would build the sheds. And the DIGs [deputy inspector generals] did not approve the diesel bills,' he says. 'We were planning to set up computers to connect all police stations through the Internet and share information ... we are purchasing computers, but there is no electricity.'

How can something as basic as fuel expenses be held up, we ask. How will the policemen work?

'That is the procedure. And that's not all. Even if one room has to be built, the director general has to pass the order. Money has not been dealt with in a practical way,' Mohapatra says candidly.

Hundreds of kilometres away, in Andhra Pradesh, taxpayer money has been misused in a similar manner. Expenditure is meant to be shared between the central and state governments, but between 2002 and 2006, according to the CAG, the Andhra Pradesh government has not pitched in with its share of almost Rs 100 crore. From the funds it got from the centre, it spent 13 to 38 per cent on different counts, which did not include the primary developmental activities for which the money had been apportioned.

In a state which has faced terrible Naxalite attacks in the past decade and been identified as the stronghold of the PWG, more than a thousand police stations – 63 per cent of the state's police stations – have not been provided jeeps. Where new jeeps have been supplied, there has been no real increase in police mobility because 58 per cent of the new vehicles have merely replaced battered, old ones. The authorities who planned the police budget had shown the policemen another dream. They had assured that a minimum of sixty patrolling parties would get SUVs fitted with geographical information system devices. The SUVs arrived, but minus the tracking devices. The police force was expected to walk into the jungles to fight the Naxalites, and when they came home they could as well sleep in the police stations and work in open fields because the construction of some 53 per cent of the staff quarters and 43 per cent of the non-residential buildings had not been completed by the government although sufficient funds were available.

When the policemen went on patrol, they were supposed to be armed with AK-47s, 7.62 mm self-loading rifles, 9 mm carbines and 5.56 mm INSAS rifles, or at least that is what the state officials had promised in their security projections in 2001. Money was sanctioned the following year. Some of the weapons were bought in 2005 and were then locked up like trophies in armouries at district headquarters across the state. On the field, the policemen fought crucial battles with primitive weapons such as .410 muskets and .303 rifles. The money meant for all these devices and weapons has been locked away for several years in fixed deposits with the Andhra Pradesh State Police Housing Corporation even as policemen worked and lost their lives in the worst working conditions.

In 2001, the Andhra Pradesh government had drawn up more plans. By 2005, it would buy 1,309 jeeps and motorcycles for 1,309 of the 1,585 police stations which did not have *a single* vehicle. By

July 2007, only 583 stations had jeeps. A few others were used in patrolling Naxalite-ridden areas, but that left a huge hole in the day-to-day policing, giving criminals a free run. Predictably, the bulk of the remaining jeeps was being used to escort VIPs.

If the Naxalites attacked those VIPs or other targets, police investigators at the crime scene collected splinters, bullet shells, torn clothes and dried blood as evidence – a routine exercise that probably seemed farcical to many people on the field. That is because when militant attacks occur in India, forensics is the last thing on people's minds. In Kamareddy town in Andhra Pradesh, at the regional forensic sciences laboratory, equipment worth Rs 1 crore, which is meant to help the police force, is lying idle. And in Hyderabad, late in 2007, the officials had not even got around to opening the boxes of sophisticated equipment bought in 2005 to establish a mobile toxicology unit at the Gandhi Medical College to assist the police. The buildings where the equipment was to be placed had somehow been neglected to be constructed. And if something went wrong with the machines once they were used, there would be nothing to do because the warranty offered by the manufacturers would have expired.

In the state's forensic science headquarters, a projective velocity machine bought for Rs 11 lakh in May 2004 was used only four times in 2004, four times in 2005 and not a single time during the next two years. Other equipment was also rarely used, often for silly reasons, such as a machine being bought without the software to run it. But taxpayers cannot blame government officials for not being able to buy and run complicated machines that could help tackle insurgency and crime more effectively. The truth is that the government could not even buy horses. Twenty-five mounted horses were to be bought for the police commissionerate of Hyderabad, for which Rs 20 lakh was released to the government in January 2006. Six horses were bought within three months, but there are no signs of any more purchases on the agenda. The money is still in its stable – the office of the police commissioner of Hyderabad.

Back in Chhattisgarh, the forces have more basic concerns to attend to.

Few know the story, for example, of how policemen in a remote police station in Jagarguda get their food in a land where there are zero logistics. The police station is 40 kilometres from Dantewada as the crow flies. 'But there is no road,' says Amaresh Mishra, superintendent of police. 'I walk fifty-nine kilometres over two days to reach there from the nearest road head.'

Once in three months rations are ferried to the distant police station. At dawn, a 1,000-member caravan hits the road. It involves hundreds of policemen, labourers, cooks, a tractor filled with sand, another with crushed stones, bomb disposal experts and sniffer dogs. Ambushes are common. Landmines are frequently found – mostly more than 100 kilograms in weight, which no landmine-protected vehicle can survive.

'That's how we deliver food to our men in Jagarguda,' says Mishra.

'Where is the honour?' The senior government official leaned over, put his hand into the plastic packet in front of him, rummaged around and came up with a trophy – his favourite salted snack. We were in the middle of a story. The pause was too long; he had stopped at a gritty point.

The story had taken us back to December 2002, when Naxalite platoon members had returned to their commanders with reports that the headman of Bitkilsoi village in Jharkhand's West Singhbhum district was, as they alleged, a police informer.

The sixteenth of December 2002 had brought two deaths. A forest officer was killed early that day when rebels surrounded him and asked him to hand over his gun. He refused, and was shot and killed instantly. Not too far away, a rebel platoon of lean young men and women, all dressed in green, most carrying guns, walked into Bitkilsoi and, using a megaphone, asked all the villagers to gather in a clearing in the middle of the village. A young boy was ordered to summon the *munda*. He stumbled off, terrified. A summary trial followed. Women watched from a distance, hugging their infants close to their chests. The men cowered.

Within minutes, the *munda*'s head lay severed on the ground.

'Get me some kerosene!' the leader of the platoon bellowed.

Another boy came forward in a daze, carrying a small canister of kerosene oil. It was poured over the dead *munda*'s body, already soaked in blood. Kerosene, blood and mud pooled together in the clearing, but the Maoists had still not had their fill of death. A matchstick was lit and thrown on to the body, now reeking of kerosene. Within seconds, it was engulfed in flames.

The flames spread. Word spread faster.

Two police teams from two different sides headed to the rugged rural area to investigate, driving over rocky terrain where roads barely existed, unaware that what had happened was only half of the bloody story. The police teams had little to protect themselves with despite a sweeping police modernization programme that had been put in place. There was no landmine-sweeping equipment, nor were there sophisticated guns and mine-protected vehicles.

The two police teams met at the small town of Digha, near Bitkilsoi. The decapitated body of the headman, charred beyond recognition, and that of a forest guard were handed over to them. It became dark as the police party began its long drive back to the government hospital mortuary to hand over the bodies for post-mortems.

The mortuary was where the Naxalites wanted to send the rest of them too, they realized shortly afterwards. As the police drove along the forest route from Bitkilsoi towards Tirilposi, dozens of guerrillas watched from their hidden posts in the forest. At least seventy Naxalites were keeping track of every movement of the sixty-man police convoy. The bodies were merely a decoy. The real attack was about to begin.

All that the survivors remember of the next moment is the series of explosions that ripped through the forest, hurling the jeeps into the air, sending bodies flying out. One after the other, five landmines went off. As the surviving policemen rushed out of the jeeps, guns began firing from behind the trees. The gun battle continued for two hours, from 7.00 p.m. to 9.00 p.m. Despite the prior call for reinforcements, none reached; there were no helicopters, no ambulances, no night-vision devices, no quick-reaction teams, and the police fought a virtually defenceless battle in the dark. The Naxalites had far superior weapons than the police – AK-47s and self-loading rifles against redundant World-War-II-era guns. Eighteen people died that day; the count included fourteen policemen. Then, an elderly woman emerged from the forest, leading more rebels. They surrounded the jeeps, burned at least seven, and fled with the weapons.

A helicopter was sent the next day to recover the bodies. The bodies of the policemen, their khaki uniforms stained with clotted blood, were dumped on the floor of the chopper heaped one upon the other like sacks of vegetables, hands twisted, legs knotted. A small, reeking pile of men who had given up their lives fighting a war created by someone else, with little by way of weapons, vehicles or even salaries, though the government was still tom-tomming the ambitious Rs 3,000-crore police modernization programme it had begun in 2000. There were no coffins and no *salaami*, or military salute.

As the bodies were being brought in, a sharp voice broke the deathly silence. 'Stop!' It was the pilot, a flight lieutenant formerly with the Indian Air Force. He asked for coffins. 'I won't have martyrs on the floor,' he said.

Similar traps would be set up year after year across states where the Maoists' writ ruled. In many instances, the police would just walk into the trap set by the rebels.

Early in the morning on 1 February 2009, Maharashtra Police Sub-Inspector Upendra Guladekar led fourteen of his men from their outpost in Gadchiroli's Gyarapatti post to Markegaon, a small village 9 kilometres away. Two days ago, on 30 January, the Naxalites had burnt down two tractor trolleys involved in a roadwork project. Guladekar was an experienced policeman. He knew that the Naxalites would commit small acts of arson to lure the police into traps. So, when the news of the burning tractor trolleys reached him, he did not react to it at all. He waited for two days, and on the morning of 1 February set out for Markegaon.

At about 10.00 a.m., an old man sat in his hut in Markegaon, thinking of beginning work in his fields. In five minutes, he thought to himself, as he chewed on some tobacco. Seconds later, he heard gunshots. The old man had lived in Gadchiroli all his life and knew what the gunshots meant. He fell flat on the floor and lay there for hours, at times even holding his breath.

Sub-Inspector Guladekar had waited for two days. Unfortunately, so had the Naxalites. Some two hundred of them had stayed back in the jungle behind the old man's fields. Armed with automatic rifles and grenades, the attack of the Naxalites was fierce. Taking position behind a tree, Guladekar sent a wireless message to his post, calling for reinforcements. The reinforcements left Gyarapatti immediately, but another group of Naxalites waylaid them, and cornered them in an encounter. Guladekar and his men fought for two hours. The old man's hut was hit by many bullets, as were Guladekar and his men.

Three months and fifteen days later, not very far from Markegaon, Inspector Ashok Iyer got a call on his mobile phone. A year ago, Iyer had requested that he be transferred to Gadchiroli, a request that had earned him the sobriquet of 'Daredevil' from his colleagues. Iyer saw the number flashing, and immediately pressed the tiny green button. A man whispered on the line. He was an informer. The two spoke for a few minutes. When he put the phone down, Iyer had an important piece of information. A top woman Naxal leader involved in February's attack in Markegaon was reportedly in a Naxal hideout in a village on the Maharashtra–Chhattisgarh highway. There was no time to lose. Iyer rushed to his police station and formed a team of fifteen officers, which included a sub-inspector and five women constables. The police party left in two jeeps.

Near a place called Tabitola, the police party spotted trees lying on the road. Iyer got down and asked some of his men to remove the trees. It is not clear how an experienced police officer like Iyer fell into this trap. A hundred Naxal rebels lay in hiding at the spot, and they opened fire from all directions. The police jeeps were the first to be blown up. Iyer had apparently not informed any senior officer about the operation he had hoped to conduct successfully. He tried sending SOS messages to his headquarters, but there had been heavy rainfall in the area and his messages could not be transmitted over the wireless. By the time additional troops rushed to the spot, it was too late. The ten policemen and five policewomen were dead.

The most startling aspect of these two encounters came to light after investigations by the top police brass. It was revealed that police informers had been used to give wrong information to both Inspector Iyer and Sub-Inspector Guladekar. The Naxalites had clearly managed to penetrate the police force, effectively using their own communication network against them.

Meanwhile, in Jharkhand, Mohapatra is no longer the police chief. On the outskirts of Ranchi, at the headquarters of the Jharkhand Police, we meet his successor, V.D. Ram, as he sits with two colleagues who are in charge of operations and modernization. (Ram has now been replaced by Neyaz Ahmad.) In all of India, this is perhaps the only place where anyone can park his vehicle right next to the police commissioner's car without being stopped by any security personnel. Barring a lone ceremonial guard outside his office, the police chief is bereft of any security.

So, how are the police doing in the fight against the Naxalites?

'We have the upper hand – we are proceeding in the right direction,' he says. 'We have been able to curb their activities to a great extent.'

His colleague, S.N. Pradhan, the inspector general in charge of modernization, is more pragmatic. 'I don't want to say that things are hunky-dory. Two to three years ago, things on the ground were totally hopeless. Now there is substantial change. Every constable on the frontline has weapons that are among the best possible.'

After we've finished our milky tea and Monaco biscuits, D.K. Pandey, the man responsible for all police operations in Jharkhand, leads us to a corner of his big office, where he opens up a version of Google Earth on his laptop, which shows up on a large projection screen on the wall.

'It's a battle of nerves,' says Pandey, as he zooms in on the Parasnath hills on the map. 'It requires convergence, and convergence requires time.'

'See this,' he takes his cursor to a particular spot. 'We have neutralized the Naxalite bases here, but they are still holding the ground over the adjacent Lagu Pahar hills.'

The Jharkhand Police have come a long way since the state was carved out of Bihar in 2000. Traditionally, Jharkhand is not a crime-prone area. But over the years, as Naxalism spread its wings, a policeman who was trained to handle the theft of a bicycle or a cow, found himself having to tackle a completely new adversary for which he had neither the training nor the orientation – armed militancy. With practically no resources at hand, as in other remote insurgency-affected areas, no buildings to house police stations and no weapons to face the Naxal onslaught, the forces were at a distinct disadvantage.

'We started with zilch. We had no buildings. Soon, we will have seventy-five police stations. Seventeen thousand boys have been recruited over two years, and one year down the line, you will see actual changes,' Pandey said in the mid-2008 interview.

Fifty-five companies of the district police have been converted into a paramilitary force to fight the Naxalites – a force named Sengail, which means fire. A contract with Sulabh International to run toilets in three hundred and thirty-nine police stations is in the final stages of completion. Things have certainly started to improve, but it is still a stark contrast from the warlike preparedness of the highly motivated Naxalite cadres.

The police–population ratio in 2004 was seventy-four per hundred thousand people. Since 2006, this ratio has improved, to a hundred and sixty-four policemen for every hundred thousand people. The state government has also lowered the age limit for sub-inspectors by eleven years, from thirty-five to twenty-four, so more recruitments are on the cards. The conventional .303 rifles had proved to be no match for the superior firepower of the Naxalites, who attacked police stations with machine guns. But now, the police say, 80 per cent of the police stations have AK-47s or INSAS rifles.

With all these changes, fewer policemen are now losing their lives in the state, but as the then union home minister, Shivraj Patil, admitted in November 2007, incidents related to left-wing extremism in Jharkhand had already gone up by 50 per cent, as compared to 2006. Jharkhand and Chhattisgarh accounted for 68 per cent of Naxalite attacks and more than 75 per cent of all casualties in 2007.

The state's record in terms of modernization has been quite poor in the past. According to the home ministry, Jharkhand received Rs 182.7 crore for modernization from 2000 to 2006. But its utilization of these funds remained abysmal. In 2004–05, for instance, it used only 7.33 per cent of the Rs 21 crore that was released for the purpose.

With a Martin Yale paper shredder displayed behind him, Pradhan, however, sounded quite upbeat about the modernization drive. 'Even if my boy is scared as hell, at least he has an INSAS, and the Naxalite will think thrice before attacking him,' he said.

He narrated a recent incident, which, he said, spoke volumes about the 'newly built confidence' of the police personnel fighting Naxalites on the ground.

At 3.00 a.m. on 29 March 2008, a two-hundred-and-fifty-strong Naxalite force attacked a police picket in Netrahat in Jharkhand's Gumla district. The operation, codenamed Daman Chakra by the rebels, was meant to be a repeat of what they had done in Nayagarh in Orissa. The picket was surrounded from three sides, but because of heavy firing from the police, the Naxalites couldn't make any headway. After two hours of fierce gun battle, they beat a retreat.

A little more than two months after Pradhan said this, the two policemen wounded in Hazaribagh died because the force's helicopter was not available to airlift them to a hospital.

~

'*Main shikaar pe ja raha hoon* (I am going on a hunt),' says Inspector Manoj Kumar Gupta in a matter-of-fact tone, pausing for a minute in the middle of a paddy field as he sets out on a patrol through the Jharkhand countryside.

Holding an AK-47 assault rifle in his right hand and surrounded by his two best men, Gupta is off to the forest in the Dumaria region for a 'kill'. A green hulk is on standby near him – a recently acquired medium mine-protected vehicle, a truck that is not likely to be blown up by even a landmine. Towards the other end of the village, soldiers of the CRPF are preparing for a long-range patrol alongside the Jharkhand Police to launch an offensive against the Naxalites.

Later, in Latehar district, another Naxal stronghold, we meet Inspector Awadh Kumar Yadav, who is on a routine patrol. Travelling in an armoured vehicle, he is kilometres away from the Latehar police station, but manages to stay in touch over the wireless, which he would have been unable to do earlier. 'Earlier we used to lose contact after four to five kilometres, but that is no longer the case now,' Yadav says.

Three years ago, it was in Latehar that the Naxalites had seized a train to protest the death of one of their commanders, and it is here that we get to see how the people who are left with no choice bow down silently before Maoist dominance.

In the town's small marketplace, a local resident meets us at a teashop. He smiles, but we can see that he is tense. We look like outsiders and we are carrying notebooks and cameras. The man, our guide now, looks around and whispers, 'Anybody can be a Naxalite here, you never know.'

We have to proceed a bit further, towards Matlaung village, which, our guide says, is a 'liberated zone'.

The road leading to Matlaung is kuchcha, not tarred. 'The Naxalites won't allow a pukka road to be built because that makes it difficult for them to lay mines,' says another man, whom we have given a ride. 'Most people here prefer to travel by foot rather than in vehicles – that reduces the chances of getting killed.'

The guide asks the driver to continuously blow the horn. 'This works as a signal here that we are Naxal sympathizers and not their enemies,' he clarifies.

Money is no problem for the Naxalites in a state like Jharkhand. They collect 'levies' from the local contractors as a matter of unquestioned routine. For every payment made, proper receipts are issued. According to police sources, the Naxalites generate an income of Rs 60 crore annually in the form of taxes.

We reach Matlaung, in the heart of Naxal-held territory, in the middle of a searing afternoon. In the Mile village cluster, we spot a few people working on the banks of what was probably a rivulet at one point of time. None of them have received any payment for work under the NREGS, we are told.

'*Dasta dikhta hai kabhi?* (Do you see the Naxalite squads?),' we ask them.

'Yes, we do. They keep on coming in and out from there,' an old man points towards the forest area behind the village.

We have heard that the Naxalites intervene in their areas of operation if there is any injustice. Surely, non-payment for hard work and toil under the NREGS counts as injustice, we say.

'Why would they intervene?' asks the man. 'They [the Naxalites] get their share – 5 per cent. Why would they care?'

As we speak to another labourer, our guide receives a call on his mobile phone. We don't pay it much importance, but after a while he comes to us pale-faced, urging us to leave. 'They just called on my mobile phone. The Naxal leader said, "*Yahan tak aaye ho, isse aage mat jaana* (You have come this far, don't go any further)."' So they know we are here. It is pointless to stay any longer.

This is just a snapshot of the extent of the rebels' control. More than twelve hundred of Jharkhand's four thousand and five hundred panchayats, or village councils, are reportedly under the control of the Maoists. The Maoists are in a position to dictate the electoral outcome in more than 30 per cent of the state's assembly constituencies, according to the Institute of Conflict Management, a prominent think-tank in New Delhi. In as many as fifteen districts, large areas have been converted into 'liberated zones', like the area we visited in Latehar district, where the rebels run a parallel administration.

If the police is upping its strength, the Naxalites are walking apace. According to intelligence inputs, Jharkhand has seen a threefold increase in Maoist cadres. The Naxalites are also acquiring sophisticated weapons and have been quite successful in creating a wider base of active sympathizers.

'The final Haldighati with the Naxalites will be fought in the Saranda forest of Jharkhand,' Inspector General Pandey says, referring to the historic sixteenth-century battle between the Rajputs and the Mughals.

Back from the 'liberated zone' of Latehar, we make another brief stopover at the market.

'I have hardly seen any electricity in the past two months,' our guide tells us. He runs his thumb over the Coca-Cola bottle he is holding. 'This drink reaches everywhere, but the government's schemes don't.'

In the town's fifty-bed hospital, he says, a generator acquired only a few months ago is not working. 'Surgeries are conducted in the light of lanterns,' he says. Another hundred-bed hospital was built recently, but there are no doctors.

'From east to west, Latehar is a hundred kilometres and yet we have only one affiliated college,' he informs us.

Latehar and other areas like it, which form the other, invisible India that has been bypassed by national growth, is the recruiting ground for insurgents. Yet, certain instances clearly indicate how the situation may best be turned around.

The 23-kilometre road from Chhattisgarh's Bijapur town to the rural hub of Gangalur winds through an expanse straddling the iron-ore-rich Bailadila hills, where rivers zigzag through forests laden with natural wealth. The road is the lifeline of tens of thousands of people across thirty villages, who earlier had to walk up to

25 kilometres through the heart of Naxalite territory to get to Bijapur. Now, they board public buses.

The road is soaked in blood. It was built at the cost of twenty-seven lives lost in one hundred and sixty-six attacks over thirty months. Public Works Department (PWD) officials, whose job it is to build the road, refused to undertake its construction, citing threats to their life.

'This is like a black hole for government money. Bridges have never been built, roads have never been built,' a senior police officer said. 'In the name of Naxalites, no work gets done and no one comes to check. No other department works here. Even fixing potholes seems to be our responsibility. The other departments are sleeping tight with sheets pulled over their heads.'

So in October 2007 the police decided to build the Gangalur road themselves and tackle the governance challenge head-on.

'It had become a question of prestige. The road had to be built by any means. We put four hundred policemen on guard,' said Ashok Singh, a police officer who was involved with providing security to the two-and-a-half-year operation in an area where there were no police stations over an 80-kilometre stretch. 'They used to plant bombs at night. They killed workers. There were face-to-face ambushes every few days.'

Two years on, Maoist influence has vastly decreased in the area. Following from this, a new experiment has been attempted in the neighbouring Dantewada district. Road building is to now be supervised by the police, with the PWD reporting to the superintendent of police.

'This fight cannot be won by the police alone,' says Ashok Pathak of the Jharkhand Police Union. 'Without development, we cannot win this war.'

5

It was not a grandmotherly action in the least. Draped in a simple white sari, the old woman tore across the narrow village path in the dark, panting heavily, the loose skin on her frail arms shaking as she proudly hugged her terrifying booty – a bunch of guns with bayonets.

She raced past a row of trees into a clearing outside her village, and then into the fields, where she fell down, exhausted, her body gashed and wounded. The guns – INSAS rifles and .303s – crashed around her with a clatter.

Back in the village of Lango in Jharkhand, from where the old woman had come, more blood was being spilled in a large open square. A group of shrieking, desperate young men had been surrounded and the gathered crowd was preparing for a massacre.

Hours later, on the morning of 8 August 2003, a row of blood-drenched bodies of Naxalite rebels lay on the ground in a clearing in the hilly village, watched by silent villagers. The old woman was inside a hut somewhere, being nursed by others. Outside, children huddled behind their parents. Goats sauntered around the village, past tribal homes neatly painted in cream and crimson. Police jeeps rushed in over the winding, bumpy village roads. Grumbling journalists were getting woken up in their homes by untimely calls. In the nearby town of Dumaria, on the Jharkhand–Orissa border, a press conference had been called. Something unimaginable had happened here. With help from the police, a group of villagers had killed several Naxalites.

How could this have happened here, in this land of peaceful Santhal and Ho tribals, who are patient with everything, even the landlords who have oppressed them for years, the politicians who have stabbed them in the back and the governments who have failed them for generations?

The answer takes us back to the summer of 1992, when Naxalite units first began showing up here. Units of nine men each descended on this region in what was then Bihar, armed with a tool with which they sought to change the order of things.

The world was certainly in the throes of change that year. Just some months previously, in January, thousands of kilometres across the globe, users had started toying with a new tool that would change the world, the World Wide Web. It was also the year of an apt landmark across the oceans: *The Silence of the Lambs* had won an Oscar.

The villagers would remain lambs, the Maoists told them, until they did something about it. 'Unless you pick up weapons, nothing will change,' the commander had said. The only weapons the commander's men had back then were axes, bows and arrows, and a few outdated guns. The rebel army had a long way to go.

Over the centuries, the Santhals and the other tribal people of the area had learnt how to coexist in peace. They were content with their farming, and picking and selling tendu leaves that would be rolled into beedis, but many villagers saw the truth in what the commander was saying, and the Maoists began to make the region their home. Their cadres used to frequent the place. No one informed the police. The villagers gave them water, food and even place to sleep in their homes.

Years passed. By 1999, the Maoists began to bring in real weapons, even if they were only .303s, often with bayonets. Slowly, their influence spread as more and more villagers began to support them.

The region slipped out of the government's hands, or rather, the government let it slip out of its hands. Officials had long stopped coming to the forests. Slowly, the other faces of the state – the village revenue official, the block development officer, the medical officer, the government school teacher – faded away. The government refused to accept that the Naxalites existed, or that they had a level of influence beyond what officials dismissively described at press conferences.

But at some level, there was something escaping the control of the local Maoists, too. The new recruits did not adhere as well to discipline; they took the power contained in the barrel of their guns too seriously. The normally tough regulations of the Naxalite cadres began to break down, as often happens when armies suddenly expand amid an unexpected sweep of influence. The rebels, villagers say, began to force them to provide food. They wanted the locally brewed liquor called mahua. They asked the men to guard the village, while they themselves entered the homes and slept with the women.

As part of their campaign against oppression by traders, the Naxalites issued orders to the tendu-leaf traders to pay higher prices to the farmers and commissions, or levies, to the cadre. Many traders shut down business and left the region. The livelihood of the Santhals depended on the tendu-leaf traders. Government officials say there was widespread resentment against the Naxalites there, a claim dismissed by pro-Naxalite voices.

The police decided to try and step up pressure in the area. One afternoon, the local superintendent of police, Arun Oram, a tribal himself, went on an operation in the Gudabanda region, a hotbed of Naxalism. Seemingly, Oram's aim was to show that the writ of the police still ruled in the area. He had two attendants with him, one of them a nightwatchman called Ultan Patar. The Naxalites swooped down on Patar's village hours after Oram went home. A platoon dragged Patar and the other attendant, who belonged to the same village, out of their homes and beat them to death before dozens of stunned and scared villagers. The two deaths hastened a secret plan that had been in the making for weeks in the area. For the first time, the police decided to embark on an adventurous – and lethal – experiment in the vast area now under Naxal influence. They planned to enable the villagers to fight their own battles. To that end they decided to arm ordinary people, hoping they would take on the Naxalites, and the Nagarik Suraksha Samiti (NSS), or People's Protection Committee, was formed.

Similar experiments had been tried out earlier in some other parts of the country, such as Jammu and Kashmir and the northeastern states. This model was different from the Village Defence Committees in Kashmir, where small groups of youth and ex-servicemen were given weapons and training, with the authority to use the weapons *only* when under attack. In Jharkhand – in a system that would be emulated at a much larger level in a few years in the neighbouring state of Chhattisgarh – a militia of villagers was created, an extra-judicial army that would virtually run under a parallel command and control. It was an audacious, double-edged sword.

By the end of 2002, the group began functioning, but remained underground. Spies were deployed in villages, moles infiltrated Naxal contingents. The police found a man to lead a ragtag group that would get weapons and money from the police and offer the Naxalites what they had never seen in the region – a challenge from the ordinary people.

The man in question was Dhanai Kisku, short, with an impassive face that rarely betrayed emotion except for a rare smile. He spoke little and was something of a community leader in parts of the district. Kisku had a red mark on his biodata because of his involvement in a bank robbery, but he was a rare man in that he was willing to take on the Naxalites openly, writing himself a death warrant from day one. Kisku began to campaign in the region. In a vast expanse where employment was a novelty, he found volunteers easily, especially since the work was mostly covert.

On 31 March 2003, the existence of the NSS was formally announced. The development was seen by government officials as a major achievement – a dent, they said, that they had created in their efforts to ram into the Naxal monolith.

Within months, the first battleground became clear: a village called Lango.

It began over a few plots of land. The Naxalites had taken over the fields of three farmers, whom they claimed were traitors. They accused the three men of not supporting their cause and of being police informers. Punishment was swift. Their sheep and goats were taken away and they were brutally beaten up and ordered out of the village. One of them, Jitendra Mardi, suffered serious injuries from being beaten with rifle butts and bamboo truncheons. He succumbed to his wounds before he could be taken to the hospital. Sido Mardi was luckier. He was badly injured, but reached the hospital on time. The third man escaped. The aggressive Naxal overtures on the village, the rebels' alleged assaults on women and the new wave of attacks on the farmers who were labelled traitors transformed Lango into a cauldron of fear.

About 13 kilometres away, a new police officer had recently been transferred to the Dumaria police station. The man, a Bengali, was short and stocky, passionate about his work, spoke animatedly, and was keen to prove that he could make a difference. He realized that the administration in the region had all but collapsed and the police rarely visited the villages there. So he began to frequent the villages. One of his first acts was to put Kisku behind bars for beating up a child. But, later, he and Kisku would work together to free the villagers from the Naxalite menace.

He began venturing deeper into territory that the police avoided, prompting many to call him foolhardy for travelling through a Naxal stronghold without patrol jeeps. Carrying just his service revolver, the officer – barely an officer in the larger scheme of things, just the police-station chief – began to visit Lango. Every other day, he would surprise the villagers by landing up on his motorcycle, not seeking any information, not forcing them to tell him when the Naxalites came, just being there to make them feel reassured. The villagers understood his language, Bangla. They soon developed a bond with the officer. They began calling him 'Dada', elder brother. Slowly, they opened up, talking to him as they had never talked before. They spoke of their impossible existence, narrated harrowing tales of how the security forces hounded them if they didn't reveal information about the rebels' movements and how the Naxalites persecuted them if the villagers didn't play good hosts.

One day, an old woman spoke up. 'Shall we poison them?' she asked, speaking softly, but in an assured, confident voice. She was a widow, she said, and had little to lose other than her impoverished life. The officer hushed her, telling her not to risk her life like that, but he found the idea feasible. On a subsequent visit, he asked the villagers: 'If you were to oppose the Naxalites, what would you do?' A brainstorming session ensued and yielded ideas for assaulting the Naxalites. The villagers were pushing the envelope, but they had reached the limit of their endurance.

The conversations continued. Summer came, and then the monsoon. The rains soaked the parched expanse, washed the trees to brilliant hues and brought alive the fragrance of wet soil. The officer asked the villagers to make a plan. The elders were brought on board. The reaction time was discussed. When the Naxalites attacked the village, how long could they be made to stay? And how long would it take for the villagers to inform Dada at the Dumaria police station of their presence? There were no mobile phones in the village because anyone who had one was usually declared a police informant by the Naxalites. There was no landline telephone anywhere between Lango village and the police station, or at least none that would be available for use at night when such an operation would presumably take place.

The officer made a simple promise: 'When they attack you next, inform me in any way you can. I promise you I shall come – even if I have to give up my life.'

The officer, like Kisku, had realized that Lango was their best chance to prove a point. They asked the villagers to make a gesture of defiance they had never shown before by starting to cultivate the three fields that the Naxalites had taken away from the three 'traitor' farmers.

'Grow paddy. That will show us where you stand,' Kisku dared the villagers.

One morning, a thousand people – men, women and children – assembled in the village and planted tiny saplings in the three fields in an act of mass defiance. Kisku's men, unarmed, mingled with the crowd and kept watch.

Word spread fast. By 2.30 p.m., a platoon of Naxalites descended from the densely forested Rani Jharna hills facing the village. It was an unusual move on the part of the cadre, which normally ventured out only in the late evenings, but events had taken an extraordinary turn and some reaction was in order. 'This is not good. You will have to pay for it,' the commander said. He meant every word – and the villagers knew that better than the rebels.

For the residents of Lango, it was time for battle. They had not been able to inform either Kisku or the officer. For now, it was a battle they would have to fight on their own. Men huddled in corners, planning their moves, but the women had already decided to take the lead. By the time evening fell, young men of the village had returned from the forest after collecting heaps of an exotic leaf, which the women then proceeded to crush in earthen pots. The plan was now in motion.

Darkness came and the villagers had their eyes fixed in the distance – towards the deep forest, where the first signs of attack would be seen. And, soon enough, there it was. One light, then more. Slowly, it became clearer – thirteen torch beams. In typical Naxal fashion, the torches were directing light at the feet of the walking platoon so that they did not illuminate a large area. The bright oval flashes dangled and moved with the troops, who were marching silently down the hill. In Lango, the villagers hurried home, sent their children indoors and prepared for what they anticipated would be the worst night of their lives.

As the others watched mesmerized, an old man walked briskly in the dark and stopped at the door of a hut. He summoned a young boy, barely sixteen, and snapped a quick, clear order: 'Rush to Dumaria! Tell Dada the time has come!'

'But I don't have a bicycle ... it is thirteen kilometres,' the nervous boy stammered.

'Then run!' the elder said. 'If we survive today, it shall be because of you!'

The boy stepped out of the house and ran – for his life, and for everyone else's.

The squad reached the village and walked right in. There were twenty rebels in all, including a few teenage boys. One of the men carried a 5-litre plastic can in which a transparent liquid sloshed as the man moved. The villagers knew well what it contained – kerosene – and what it was for. Naxalites were known to burn dissenters alive.

The platoon commander addressed the village. He was a wiry man of about thirty years, in a hostile mood today. There was a woman too, the only one in the group who was around his age. 'The man who ploughed first will be burned alive,' the commander announced. No one offered any information.

Outside the village, the boy was racing down the hill, wearing just one rubber slipper, wincing as his bare foot hit a sharp stone, panting, but trying to muffle his loud breathing. He could barely see where was going, but he knew that the lives of the people in his village depended on him. He was approaching another village now. He stormed into the home of a family he knew, mumbled something, took their bicycle and rushed out. No other words were exchanged – the family seemed to have guessed what the crisis was. The path down the hill was slightly better now, so he got on the bicycle and zoomed down as fast as he could.

Back in Lango, the platoon commander decided he knew what to do. Most of the villagers belonged to the Santhal or Munda ethnic groups, but there was one family of Gops, parallel to the intermediary Yadav caste in the Hindu caste order. One of the Naxalites viciously kicked the door to the hut of the Gop family – it crashed open. A nervous shriek was heard from inside the hut. The commander dragged a young and very scared man out into the open.

An old woman now stepped in. 'Wait! You are like my children. Don't do this ... we will do whatever you say. We are about to have dinner, why don't you join us? Then you can do whatever you want,' she told the commander. The other villagers joined in with their attempts to stall for time. The Naxalites let the Gop go. They placed their guns on the ground and sat down in a circle.

'Please wash your hands,' the old woman said. 'You can keep your belongings here on the side, no one is going to touch them.'

She went into her house. There, in a cauldron, a beverage was being brewed by a group of women working silently. It was mahua, the local liquor made from mahua flowers. But in this particular brew, there was an additional ingredient – a deadly poison made from the leaves collected earlier by the young men of the village in a process followed for centuries. It was believed that human beings died within seven days of ingesting the poison.

More than 10 kilometres away, Dada sat in his lungi, relaxing in the barracks after another tiring day, preparing to sleep. Other off-duty policemen were also getting ready to retire for the day. A sentry was posted with a light machine gun on the roof of the building, scanning the area for any movement. In the heart of Naxal land, where fear stalked every road, the first assumption about anyone who approached the station was that the person had to be an enemy.

Back in Lango, mahua liquor was being served to the group of Naxalites. As they gradually relaxed and their reflexes began to slow down, the quick-thinking old woman went back into her hut. Another round of the liquor was ready to be served, and the food was being readied. They had to hold the Naxalites in the village until Dada arrived. That was still hours away.

At the Dumaria police station, the sentry on the rooftop suddenly shouted: 'Sir, someone is approaching! It is a boy on a bicycle!' The sentry shouted at the boy to stop. The boy took the name of the village elder who had sent him and then shouted, 'Dada! Dada!' The policemen rushed to take their positions. The officer leaped up from his jute-rope cot, threw aside the newspaper he had been reading, and ran outside. He knew what the shouts meant.

'Wait! Don't shoot!' he ordered the sentry.

The boy, completely exhausted now, was offered water and a chair. The officer heard the story, then rushed for his mobile phone and dialled a number. It was the number of the one man who could reach the village the quickest, Dhanai Kisku.

Within ten minutes, two jeeps roared out into the silent night from the police station. The boy, still breathing heavily, had dumped his bicycle in one of them and now sat in the front seat, guiding the driver. The officer was right behind him, with policemen filling up the remaining seats. They drove down desolate roads, past streams and villages, past paddy fields and mahua plantations. They neared the hill on which Lango was perched, where the villagers were trying every possible trick they knew to keep the Naxalites distracted. As they approached the hill, the boy gave a simple instruction. The headlights had to be switched off. As the policemen listened in panic, the boy told them that Naxalites on the facing hill would see the headlights from a distance and, at this time of the night, they would have no doubt that the lights could only mean an assault from the police. So they switched off the lights and began the drive uphill – in the dark, with only faint moonlight guiding them, and the boy guessing his way over the narrow winding road, where one wrong swerve of the wheel would guarantee a painful death.

Meanwhile, Dhanai Kisku's men had reached Lango. As soon as the old woman saw the lone headlight from Kisku's jeep, she walked a few steps stealthily, bent low and, in a single swoop, gathered in her arms the Naxalites' guns, which were lying in a small heap. Then she ran out of the village. Before the rebels could react, she had passed rows of houses and made for the fringes of the village. Several rifles slipped out of her frail hands. Some hit her on her legs. As she slowed down and walked briskly, she began to feel sudden pain – the bayonets had jabbed her in several places. She walked on until she could not walk any more. Then she fell down in a paddy field, the rifles scattered around her.

A few kilometres away, two jeeps clattered forward in the dark on the narrow road. The policemen looked around nervously, wondering whether their invisible, powerful enemy was watching.

'Faster! Faster! How far is it now?' The officer was getting impatient and beginning to panic.

Back in Lango, with the guns out of the way, the villagers withdrew into their homes, but only for a few minutes. When they emerged, they held bows and arrows, bamboo truncheons, axes – anything sharp and strong and dangerous on which they could lay their hands. The rebels, their eyes drooping unable to move, realized they had been ambushed by the villagers. Soon, they were all tied up.

When the two police jeeps came to a halt outside the village, all that the Bengali officer heard was silence. Were they too late? But he soon spotted Kisku's jeep and was briefed on all that had transpired.

The three jeeps were placed in a loose circle and their headlights were turned on, lighting up a large clearing in the village.

The villagers, who had waited all day, wondering whether they would survive the night, victoriously dragged the rebels out in a long line. One of them even had a camera. The eyes of the rebels were half closed from the potent liquor and they were terrified, dazed at the turn of events that had placed them on the receiving end.

Watched by the police and the members of Kisku's NSS, the long, torturous process of eliminating the Naxalites began. The youngest boys in the group and the women were asked to stand aside. The others attacked the Naxalites with rocks, truncheons and sticks. They were gored with arrows. The assault carried on until daybreak.

When morning came, ten bodies were laid out in the village, soaked in blood. Word spread swiftly. It was the first incident of villagers defying and attacking Naxalites. It would make the headlines. Three other bodies were found in the nearby forest. It was announced that they were Naxalites who had challenged the police to a gunfight and been killed. They were, we were told later, members from the same platoon, who had been taken to the forest and shot. 'We had to show that an encounter took place,' one of the witnesses told us later.

The Lango killings created ripples across Jharkhand and outrage among human rights groups. Human rights activists flocked to the village, demanding to know why the Naxalites were killed in the manner that they were. In reply, the villagers simply asked, 'What about our human rights?'

For some, it was a far deeper trauma. The body of one of the young Naxalites killed in Lango, Boro Melgandi, was never claimed by his parents, Gelo Melgandi and Sompari, who lived in a nearby village. They chose not to see the body of their dead son or to perform his last rites because admitting he was their son might propel them into an unending cycle of police interrogations and lawsuits.

Whichever side of the fence one stood on, Lango had set a dangerous precedent. With governments becoming increasingly comfortable with giving civilians weapons to fight their own battles against rebels in different parts of India, it provided an example of how far citizens could go and how they could be no less brutal than the police or the Maoists themselves. Allowing, and at times enabling, common people to go out and kill militants was the worst sign of abdication of their roles by the police and the state because it opened up the doors to terrible retribution, even more bloody counter-attacks and, consequently, an unending cycle of violence.

The offensive did not end there, nor did governments stop arming villagers. Kisku's men infiltrated Naxal squads and formed a crack force of eight hundred men roaming incognito across districts.

Two years later, in 2005, in the neighbouring state of Chhattisgarh, the government created the worst monster of its kind in India. It relocated fifty thousand villagers from their homes to camps far away from their farms and villages, and armed hundreds of youth, transforming them into special units to fight the Naxalites. Christened 'Salwa Judum', meaning purification, the programme – which mysteriously brought together both the ruling BJP and the opposing Congress Party – illegally prevented the villagers from going back to their villages to work, and by mounting assaults on the Naxals through civilian forces put ordinary people at far greater risk of retaliation than ever before.

The supporters of this controversial experiment believed it to be the only solution. 'If we are attacked, we will retaliate. Our weapons are for our security,' Kisku said, sitting in a stuffy, dimly lit room in Ghatsila town, barely audible over the din of the evening traffic outside. He laid his .303 rifle on the table in front of us. Bodyguards sat on his left and right, looking repeatedly at their watches right through the interview. It was dark now, and Kisku, one of the main targets of the Naxalites in the region, did not travel at night because of safety concerns.

As bottles of soft drinks were brought in and Kisku took a sip of his, we told him frankly what we thought. We had seen it happen in Nepal's remote villages when we were there to investigate the Maoist insurgency. A young man in a village has the option to join the Maoists or the citizens' armed force and get a gun. If he joins the government-backed force, it will make him feel macho, women will like him, and he will have a relatively stable, though dangerous, job in a place where he cannot hope to get one in several light years. But unless the force he joins is disciplined, unless he obeys orders, knows the rules of engagement and is part of a command and control chain, he will end up being just a vigilante, a hired, unscrupulous killer.

Kisku spoke after a long pause. 'I do not support giving weapons to an unorganized force. Either the government should have guns, or they should be given to a B-team of the government. Otherwise, after a point, there will be no difference between the Naxalites and our men. You will have to do something to reform both. We are mindful that we do not want to go that way. But we want to show that the police cannot finish the Naxalites – only the villagers can fight them.'

Amidst national outrage and even after a reprimand from the Supreme Court, the Salwa Judum programme has continued unabated in Chhattisgarh.

The Naxalites got an opportunity to hit back at the NSS, the vigilante army created by the government, on a March afternoon in 2007.

In Baghuria, a small village in Jharkhand, around forty-eight kilometres from the city of Jamshedpur, where India's first modern iron and steel plant was built by the Tatas, a crowd of four thousand people had gathered to watch a football match on 4 March 2007. It was Holi, the festival of colours. In this part of India, more than the excitement of playing with colours, it was the prospect of playing football and watching young talented boys and girls rough it out on the field that attracted people. The village had its own football club and the day's events were particularly significant because the chief guest was the area's member of Parliament, Sunil Mahato. It is very rare that people in remote regions like these get to see their leaders. Mahato had actively supported the NSS, Kisku's army, which had tried to turn the tables on the Naxalites with the support of the police. Flanked by his bodyguards, wearing garlands offered by the crowd, he sat on a dais. The fun wouldn't stop with the match; a cockfight had been organized to begin right after.

A series of pictures taken in succession by a local photographer that day show a group of people, including a few women, inching towards the dais. Numbering around forty, the men and their female accomplices belonged neither to the village nor to any of the surrounding villages. No one had seen them before.

In one corner of the football field, fifty-six-year-old Sudheshwaran, former head of the village, was taking stock of the preparations. Some women admirers from among the strangers inched through the crowd, walking up to Mahato, apparently to greet him. That is when Sudheshwaran heard the sound. One of the women had shot at Mahato with a revolver fitted with a silencer.

'We felt as if electric wires had touched each other,' Sudheshwaran recalled later. He froze when he heard shouts of 'MCC! MCC!' It was a Naxalite attack. Though the MCC had merged with the PWG three years ago, the Naxalites active in this area were still known by their old name.

Mahato, wounded and bloodied, tried to drag himself to safety. At the same time, others from the rebel platoon pounced upon his bodyguards and snatched their automatic rifles. Two of the guards were shot - one died on the spot and the other's body was found later in a nearby field - and two of them managed to flee. Mahato fell on the football ground and bled to death within minutes.

For fifteen minutes, the villagers recall, there was absolute chaos. In the ensuing stampede, they left behind everything - slippers, cycles, motorcycles - and ran for safety. Then the entire village shut itself indoors.

When the superintendent of police arrived with his men half an hour later, he did not find a single window open. Mahato's body lay in the open field in front of the dais, a few metres from where he would have handed over a trophy to the winning team. He was rushed to the hospital where he was declared 'brought dead'.

The operation was meticulous. Not a single villager was injured. The Naxalite squad, after hitting its target effectively, retreated to the nearby jungle. Mahato was targeted because he had been openly issuing statements against the Naxalites. 'We do not kill everyone just because he/she is an MP or a minister ... it is mainly a small coterie of political leaders that plays a crucial role in finalizing the policies under the dictates of the imperialist–feudal combine. It is such political leaders that we single out for attack,' Naxalite supreme commander Ganapathi said in an email response to journalists' questions. 'In the case of Sunil Mahato, we had to eliminate him only because he had been actively involved in unleashing brutal repression on the revolutionary movement in Jharkhand. He is not just a leader of the Jharkhand Mukti Morcha [his political party], but is associated actively in the vigilante gang called the Nagarik Suraksha Samiti, which has taken part in the cold-blooded murder of our party cadres.'

The Naxalites had carried out the killing as a larger message against the arming of civilians to fight them. 'We have already had bitter experiences in Chhattisgarh where the so-called peace campaign in the name of Salwa Judum is playing havoc with the lives of thousands of adivasis,' Ganapathi wrote in his replies.

'Such punishments will be carried out where necessary on a case to case basis in a selective manner and this must not be treated as our general policy. We wish to make one thing clear: We are not for indiscriminate killing of leaders or ordinary members of political parties.'

Meanwhile, more bloodshed was being planned.

On Valentine's Day, 14 February 2008, Kisku's informers in the rebel squads called him at 4.00 p.m. and tipped him off about the presence of Naxalites in Bhitar Amda village on another flank of the Rani Jharna hills. At Kisku's instigation, the attacks began late in the evening. By nightfall, the villagers had cut down seven Naxalites.

When we reached Bhitar Amda, there was a lull, broken occasionally by the rumble of the armoured vehicles of the paramilitary forces on long-range patrols inside the jungles of Rani Jharna. A few children standing nearby, who were having fun getting themselves photographed, described the day in a matter-of-fact way. 'There was fighting in the village. The Naxalbaadi [Naxalites] had come, and everyone found out,' one of them said as he picked at his shirt, from which two buttons were missing. 'I heard firing, then the villagers started running away. Later, I saw one Naxalbaadi dead. He was shot. They brought him to the school from there. We were all taken in a tractor to another village.'

Paramilitary troops were rushed to the area on the morning following the massacre to protect the villagers, but there was no place for them to stay. So the local school, the Bhitar Amda Madhya Vidyalaya, was shut down. Sandbagged bunkers came up where children had played football till a day earlier. Soldiers took over the school where the bodies had been brought the previous day – the school where the Naxalites had once held court. The villagers could either protect their own lives or send their children to school. After taking up arms against the Naxalites, they had to choose self-preservation.

Villagers in Bhitar Amda and countless other villages are now paying a price that they will go on paying as long as Naxal influence remains. Mine-protected vehicles are a common sight now in their villages. Soldiers in fatigues are no more a novelty for the people.

Going to work on his ramshackle bicycle, Kaas Kisku stops near the school and looks at a soldier rinsing out his underwear at a hand pump. His youngest daughter, seven-year-old Guruwari Kisku who studied in the second standard, has been grounded at home since there is no school any more. There are many other children like her in the population of seven hundred, who now spend their time playing hopscotch or chasing ducks and goats.

'I am really worried about my daughter's education,' Kaas Kisku says, wiping sweat from his brow. 'She says every day that she wants to go to school.'

There is no electricity in the village. There are a few hand pumps and the nearest high school is 11 kilometres away. A nurse comes to the sub-health centre once or twice a week. A doctor is rare to come by, just like the other government officials responsible for implementing development schemes.

'We want irrigation facilities. We want the government to build a small dam here. We need a road. Our children have to go ten kilometres away to Bhalupara to study, and they cannot do that if there is no proper road. In the monsoon, it is terrible,' says Kaas Kisku.

Pukka roads would be one of the biggest weapons against the Naxalites. The rebels fiercely oppose the building of roads in any remote region, knowing that they will bring accessibility and police vehicles. Besides, it is much easier to set off landmines and remote-controlled bombs on mud roads. But the villagers have made up their minds. 'The Naxalites might oppose the building of roads, but we are here – if the government sanctions a road, we will oppose even the Naxalites for it,' Kaas Kisku says.

Kaas Kisku's neighbour, Bhaiyya Ram Soren, speaks of the incident of 14 February: 'The villagers had nothing to do with it; the other group was there.' The other group is the government-empowered citizen's committee, the NSS.

Kaas Kisku, a man of average height and lean build, stands on the roadside wearing a white shirt and a cream pyjama, which have been worn a few times too many. He was born in this village in 1973. The Naxalites began visiting his village in the mid-1980s, when he was still a teenager. 'Earlier when they came, they came without weapons and in civil dress. That was until 1985. Then, for several years, they went away to some other area. By 1992, they were back again, and this time they had weapons,' he says. By that time he was eighteen. The Naxalites, he remembers, would buy rice, salt and oil from the weekly market and return to their bases. Years passed and the Naxalites became familiar faces in Bhitar Amda. 'There were two groups. Our stance was to let them do what they were doing. We didn't even report them to the police. They weren't harming us,' Kisku says.

That is, until the day they dragged people out of their homes on suspicion of being police informers and beat them up mercilessly. Kaas Kisku's brother, Mohan Kisku, and his friend, Basudev Tudu, were among them.

'Everyone punished like that was brought here, to this school. The Naxalites said my brother and his friend were police informers. That wasn't true. So we all assembled right here. We argued with them. We said, "If you live here, you cannot oppress us."'

The long, tentative association of many years had come to a sudden end with the incident of 14 February, and whichever side of the fence they might be on, the residents of the village feared – or rather knew – that the Naxalites would hit back with fury.

Not a single child had gone to study since the day the school was converted into a near-permanent security base. Paramilitary soldiers, fighting someone else's battle, slept in its classrooms, with peeling plaster and moss-covered the walls. There were broken chalk sticks on the floor. Troopers walked past an empty blackboard that announced the 'Word of the Day'. A war kitchen had been set up where children had streamed out to play at lunchtime.

'We want to educate our children. Our elders never studied. Earlier, only the upper-caste people could study. My father and grandfather were so passionate about us getting an education. They were so keen that my elder brother study English,' Kaas Kisku says.

'We are safe as long as these people are here,' he continues, gesturing with his eyes towards the school and the paramilitary camp. 'After they are gone, we cannot say what will happen to us.'

Safety or a better future – the residents of Bhitar Amda village have been forced to choose between the two. It is a heart-wrenching choice because this is a village that treasures the safety of its residents and knows the value of education. Even so far away from the nearest high school and college, the village has thirty-five people who have completed their matriculation (tenth standard) and twelve college graduates. 'My brother Ghasiram Kisku is the only MA in English in the entire village!' Kaas Kisku says with pride. 'I too wanted to study, but I could not go to school after Class 10 due to family problems. I guess only one of us could carry on with schooling and my brother got the opportunity.'

'I want my children to do what I could not,' he says, looking blankly at the security camp as a mine-protected vehicle leaves on patrol, kicking up a storm of dust, with a man in dark glasses holding a light machine gun standing atop. 'But now, if we have to feel safe, our children cannot study.'

On the morning of 5 January 2010, Dhanai Kisku stepped out of his house in the former copper-mining town of Mosaboni in Ghatsila to go to a nearby tea stall. His bodyguards were not with him. As he lifted a glass of tea to his mouth, two motorcycles stopped in front of the stall. Two of the three men on the bikes walked towards him and one of them took out a pistol. A bullet was fired. Immediately after, the other took out an AK-47 rifle and fired a few more shots. Kisku took five bullets in all. He died at a local hospital less than an hour later.

The Naxalites had killed the head of the force created by the government to kill them, and another blood-drenched saga had come full circle.

6

In today's India, it is easy to make people militants. The police do it all the time. The guerrillas do it all the time.

Take the twenty-year-old who set out to walk 28 kilometres across sixty-three hills to meet his sister, with just one ulterior motive: He would get to play in the football tournament the next day under the easy excuse of meeting her. The winners of the tournament were to be treated to *khassi*, goat meat.

It was a December day in 2005 when Shiv Charan Soi set out for his sister's marital home in Hatnaburu village in Jharkhand. He wasn't alone – twenty others were headed to the same village, some with him, others separately.

Soi was one among many young men whom India had left behind in its journey for development. He had finished school, but there was little now to look forward to in his life. College was an unattainable dream. He had never been to Ranchi, the state capital and the big city nearest to his village, and it was unlikely that he ever would. He occasionally found work on someone else's field or at a brick kiln to earn a few rupees a month. Down the mud path from his house, homes were emptying out as young men headed to the metropolises of Mumbai, Kolkata and New Delhi to chase their sweatshop dreams. Some, of course, had vanished in the opposite direction. Naxalite platoons had been coming to the village for weeks, asking for 'one child from every home for the cause'. Many villagers responded positively. A monthly stipend of up to Rs 3,000 was on offer, and the promise of a life full of respect, not crushed under the local landowner's whims.

Today, all that Shiv Charan Soi wanted was to play a game of football and eat some *khassi*. The youth reached the village. A fiery game of football followed, and Soi's team won. The *khassi* was delicious. As it turned out, the game had been organized by the Naxalites. The commander of the platoon was known to Soi and the others from his village. Members of both teams were asked, peacefully, to accompany them. For good measure, they took along Soi's sister, Meera, to join the Naari Mukti Sangh (Women's Liberation Union). The brother and sister pair had become militants.

For months, Soi and his sister begged to be let go. Finally, a local commander agreed to free them on the condition that they join one of their overground units that serve as a powerful intelligence-gathering and propaganda wing for the movement. The Krantikari Kisan Committee (Revolutionary Farmers' Committee) was being formed around that time, and Soi and his sister were enlisted in it.

For the next year, Soi remained with the overground group, until he and his sister were detained by the police and accused of being terrorists. For two months before that, the police had been looking for explosives believed to have been hidden by Naxalites in the area. Soi insisted that he was not a militant and he could help the police find the explosives, but no one paid him much attention. One day, he found a sympathetic police officer who did.

'The bomb is in a bucket under a mahua tree on the way to the military camp,' Soi said. Sure enough, the bomb was found there. But worse was to follow. Despite the protests of the officer to whom Soi had revealed the information, possibly helping to avert several deaths in a future attack, Soi and Meera were branded terrorists and are now being prosecuted.

'I knew they were being wrongly kept in prison, I knew that all the poor young man wanted to do was to visit his sister and play a football match, but others in the force were hungry to show results, whether we had the wrong man or not,' said the officer, declining to be named. 'This is how we often make militants in this country.'

When incidents like this happen and people are wronged, many come rushing to the tiny town of Ghatsila in Jharkhand, where a doughty woman sits in a shed behind a row of unevenly placed desks.

Ghatsila is a small town leaning against the highway, on the banks of the Subarnarekha river. The town is best known for being the place where Bibhutibhushan Bandopadhyaya wrote his celebrated novel *Pather Panchali*, which was later made into an internationally acclaimed film by Satyajit Ray. But now, Ghatsila is gathering fame because Deepti Singh lives here. Forty-year-old Deepti Singh has proven that dozens of people arrested on charges of being terrorists were actually innocent. The growing list of people acquitted with the lawyer's help after being accused of being terrorists has made her a sort of messiah in the tiny town and its surrounding villages.

'People are being blackmailed. If someone has any wealth, however little, the police threaten them – to give money or they will be taken away and charged with terrorism,' says Singh, sitting in the sun on a rope cot near the local courthouse. 'There are women who are not Naxalites – it's their husbands who are in the cadre – but they are also labelled Naxalites. The police say, "Get him to surrender or else..."'

Singh knows about adversity. In a land of lost opportunities and deep discrimination, in a village where it was easier for her to become a Naxalite, she was the first woman to study and become a lawyer.

Singh was born in the hilly Choira village, some 19 kilometres from Ghatsila. Unlike her peers, she grew up with a deep yearning to be educated. But the girls in her village did not, or were not allowed to, study. She somehow managed to complete her primary studies at the local school, which had only one teacher. The nearest high school was several kilometres away. She would walk to school with the boys, participate in table tennis and badminton matches, even compete with teams of other girls from West Bengal. That was the last straw. There was a backlash based on centuries of conservative, oppressive customs, which the Naxalites were trying to capitalize on in other parts of the country.

'People thought that if a girl went out of her village, she became characterless. They wanted me and my father to drink and offer them alcohol as well, but we did not,' says Singh. 'The *pradhan* used to molest girls. I opposed it. The girls used to come to me for shelter and I tried to protect them. It continues even now. They do whatever they want to do with the girls. Then they threaten them, "If you report this, we will evict you from the village."'

Back then, the village *pradhan* and the village council tried to crush her into submission. Singh and her family were banned from walking on the village paths and they were not invited to weddings and other social occasions. Both father and daughter received death threats. There were two occasions when Singh was surrounded by assailants at her college but was saved by her teachers. Undeterred, she completed her post-graduation, obtained her legal degree and became a lawyer with the support of several well-wishers in Ghatsila.

'If I had not received help in my life, I might have become a Naxalite myself. I would certainly have been a zonal commander by now,' Singh says.

It was the year 2000. The Naxalites had entrenched themselves in the area and the campaign was spiralling across the region. Not too far away, in Jiam village in the Gudabanda area, a land squabble was underway and taking a sinister turn in the absence of any police presence or intervention. 'The people of the Munda tribe had worked really hard for a long time on a large piece of barren land to make it fertile. Now the Santhals wanted it. There was a big tussle over the land,' Singh recounts. 'The Santhals began beating up and oppressing the Mundas, who, in turn, began to lean towards the Naxalites. They could not go to the police, which did not exist for them, so they went to the Naxalites for justice.'

The police on their part, unable to get to their invisible adversaries, the Naxalites, cracked down instead on the villagers. Arrests were made on the slightest suspicion and, often, as later court judgements have shown, without reason. After the land tussle in Jiam, the police arrested a twenty-three-year-old man called Lele Singh and imprisoned him without a trial for one and a half years.

'The villagers came to me. The trial went on for two years,' said Deepti Singh. She proved he was innocent and won him his freedom.

Numerous such cases followed. A thirty-five-year-old woman, identified only as Baishali, was arrested because her husband was a Naxalite. She was accused of illegally carrying weapons and of damaging and burning the house of a member of the NSS. 'The police told her that she would be released only if she could get her husband to surrender, but she did not know where her husband was. She was in prison for a year and eight months till I got her acquitted,' says Singh.

By the end of 2008, Singh had won acquittals for forty-two people wrongfully accused of being terrorists. The charge of being a terrorist could come from the most innocuous of acts: If a Naxalite platoon was walking through a village and its commander asked a villager to give them some water or cook them some food, that act – mostly carried out at gunpoint and not due to ideological or political sympathies – could invite a terrorism charge.

And for those who don't have to face injustice or oppression, there is unemployment to deal with. 'Very few people become

Naxalites out of their own free will. Earlier, whoever went into the jungles, went because of torture. Now it has become a fashion or pastime for many, to earn money,' she says. 'An educated person has nothing to do here, you see.'

~

In these murky lands where few outsiders ever venture, the shadow-boxing between the state and its opponents has little accountability, and a gap between perception and reality ends up shaping government policy and public opinion, and influences courts of law.

'I am so glad that journalists from Delhi are finally coming to Bastar,' said Suresh Mahapatra, editor of the Dantewada-based newspaper *Bastar Impact*. 'For a quarter of a century, after the start of the Naxalite movement here, it has been totally ignored. Now the issues here, and the truth, will be portrayed in a correct way.' He knows that seeking the little-known truths in insurgency-affected lands is as tough as battling the insurgency itself.

Take the NGOs, for instance.

In the winter of 2009, a damning human rights report, hit the headlines. Titled 'Burnt in Oil', the report cited numerous cases of alleged human rights abuses of civilians by paramilitary soldiers in forest raids against Naxalite rebels. The title came from a grisly and damning case study reported by Himanshu Kumar of the Vanvasi Chetna Ashram and others, including members of the independent Public Union for Democratic Rights (PUDR).

Torture: Burnt in oil

> Muchaki Deva (60 yrs) of Onderpara was grazing cattle on the morning of 17 September. He was caught, beaten and dragged into the village by security forces. He was hung on a branch of a tree and pushed into a pot of hot oil which was kept ready under the tree.

> He was then pulled out and poured over with water. As a result, the upper part of his body is severely burnt and he has developed maggots in his wounds. He is gravely ill and has no access to medical aid. He has been taken to Bhadrachalam by members of the fact-finding team.

The report was showcased in different parts of the country and presented as clinching evidence of widespread human rights violations in Chhattisgarh.

Then the truth emerged. No man had been burnt in oil. The report was part of the other great battle of insurgency lands, of truth versus fiction.

The so-called fact-finding committee hadn't met the 'victim' in question but had managed to invent the colourful details of his being hung upside down from a tree and pushed into hot oil. Nor had he been taken to a hospital across the border to the town of Bhadrachalam in Andhra Pradesh. When an investigation was conducted by one of the authors for the *Hindustan Times*, Himanshu Kumar sent out bulk text messages insinuating that the reporter had been influenced by corporate interests that advertise in the paper.

Kumar's assertion, however, was in keeping with the trends that emerged from the biggest ever investigation by the National Human Rights Commission in 2008 into alleged human rights violations in Chhattisgarh. The investigation, which came after a petition submitted in the Supreme Court by activist Nandini Sundar, involved officials trudging to twenty-six villages in Bastar's remote areas, where they faced three Naxalite ambushes and held interviews away from the police. Their findings from a hundred and sixty-eight investigations into alleged human-rights violations by paramilitary forces and the police were as follows:

a) Many of the allegations are based on hearsay;
b) Many villagers listed as having been killed by state forces were actually killed by Naxalites – or were Naxalites killed by security forces;

c) A few villagers listed as killed died of natural causes;
d) Some other villagers who are listed by complainants among the dead were found to be alive.

The commission found human rights excesses by the police and paramilitary as well, and listed some cases of relevance. The portions of the report criticizing the state forces were quoted by human rights NGOs to slam the government, but they questioned the other damning contents of the report.

Kumar alleged that security forces were routinely killing people. 'Villages have been attacked twenty times in some cases. The security forces are killing the same people they are claiming to protect,' he said.

Some of his peers do not agree. A senior executive of an international NGO working in the state said: 'I don't subscribe to that view. It's not that people are being mauled or killed every other day in the fight between both sides ... We do hear of stray incidents of people being caught in incidents of violence ... [but] we have not come across that extreme.'

Across the border, in Bhadrachalam, where the burnt man was purported to have been taken, doctors say no such case has been reported. At the town's government hospital, the only place where such a case can be treated, Medical Superintendent Dr Jayaram Reddy says: 'Nothing – no patient with that name has been brought to us. No patient with even 10 per cent oil burns in six months. All the other doctors in the town, seven of them, say they haven't heard of the case either.'

At the Vanvasi Chetna Ashram, Himanshu Kumar tells villagers not to complain to the police, and asks them to only give their thumb impressions on identical printed letters in which details are filled out as required. About fifteen villagers from Munder are sitting in front of him, waiting for the journalist whom Kumar has called, saying, 'The victims are here.' He says that the police have told the villagers that they will burn and destroy their village in the next two days.

When questioned in front of Kumar, the villagers say no such thing happened. 'Police did not make that threat,' says Moti Ram Kadti, twenty-five, sitting a few metres away from Kumar's desk. 'A man called Badru read something in the paper and got that impression.'

Days later, word has spread about the wrong facts in the fact-finding report. Himanshu Kumar calls the reporter and shouts into the phone, 'I am bringing the burnt man to Delhi!'

The man does not materialize. Instead, the PUDR points to a documentary by journalist Gopal Menon who says he met the same man and he was not burnt, but had been tortured. The allegation cannot be substantiated because Kumar's team refused to give access to the elusive oil-dipped man. And tucked away in a letter from the PUDR to the editor of the *Hindustan Times* are the following words: 'While we were at wrong in alleging that Muchaki Deva was burnt in hot oil ...'

7

On the flickering television screen, the chief minister of West Bengal gazed at the man who wanted him dead. A towel wrapped around his head and an AK-56 rifle hanging upside down from his shoulder, the man stood with his back to the cameras.

Thirteen years younger than Chief Minister Buddhadeb Bhattacharya, the Maoists' second-in-command, frail-looking, short, soft-spoken Kishenji spoke to journalists in an unwavering voice. 'Let the security forces enter Lalgarh,' he said, 'we will turn it into their grave.'

As a Marxist, the chief minister did not believe in god, but it was nothing less than divine intervention that had saved his life on 2 November 2008. To blow up the chief minister's vehicle, the Maoists had laid cables that ran a kilometre through the fields, but as they waited for their target, the rebels realized that rats had chewed at the cable in various places, weakening the impact. The landmine went off, but Bhattacharya, who was travelling that day with the then union steel and mines minister, Ram Vilas Paswan, had a miraculous escape. Now, eight months later, Kishenji was on television and the man he wanted dead was watching him, only too aware that the three-decade-old edifice of his party, the Communist Party of India (Marxist), the CPM, was crumbling in West Bengal.

Kishenji was only nine when Bhattacharya had taken a vow to fight for the cause of the downtrodden by joining the CPM. As Bhattacharya was raising his clenched fist in anti-United States rallies, Kishenji was fulfilling similar vows of fighting the rich and the powerful for the sake of the poor in Andhra Pradesh. At fourteen, Kishenji had joined the Naxalite ranks, and seven years later, in 1978, he had gone underground.

In the early 1980s, when Bhattacharya was learning the ropes of politics, Kishenji was receiving arms training from a faction of the Liberation Tigers of Tamil Eelam (LTTE) that had come from Sri Lanka. The CPM had come to power in West Bengal in 1977 and, since then, it had continued to be in power, winning election after election with the help of its thirty-four thousand worker units spread across the state. Over the years, however, Marx had been replaced by money. The CPM leaders, big and small, used their influence to further their own interests. And whenever the CPM faced any challenge from its political adversaries, they were ruthlessly quelled.

In 2000, the CPM had taken the help of the Maoists to contain the growing influence of its biggest political opponent in the state, the Trinamool Congress. By Kishenji's own admission, he had collected five thousand cartridges from a local CPM office and distributed them among his cadre to be used against Trinamool workers. Yet, once it had strengthened its position, the CPM turned its back on the Maoists, targeting the rebels wherever possible.

In 2007, leaving behind all that Marxism stood for, Buddhadeb Bhattacharya sent a four-thousand-strong police force to the Nandigram area to suppress a people's movement against the acquisition of land by an Indonesian business group to start a chemical hub. The police were helped by the armed cadre of the CPM and, in the ensuing brutality, at least fourteen people lost their lives. Many women, whose family members were Trinamool supporters, were raped by CPM goons.

Defending his actions in Nandigram, Bhattacharya went a step further by commenting that 'they [the people of Nandigram] had been paid back in the same coin'. This statement was – in letter and spirit – not very different from the utterances of Gujarat's chief minister Narendra Modi, under whose rule hundreds of Muslims had died in communal riots.

The CPM would have to pay for their mistakes, and the payment would be extracted by its former ally the CPI (Maoist). It would happen in West Midnapore itself, with the help of the Trinamool Congress, in a place called Lalgarh, which ironically means 'red bastion'.

The CRPF soldier collapsed on the way to the Lalgarh police station and began to cry softly.

He had been walking for hours on a serpentine road. On both sides of the road was a dense jungle of sal trees. The temperature hovered at 45 degrees Celsius and the relative humidity was 90 per cent. The jawan walked in the sweltering heat, carrying about 20 kilograms of explosives and two rifles, wearing a heavy bulletproof jacket. He had no water to drink. The jawan knew that a day earlier another CRPF soldier, Nabakanta Roy, had died of dehydration under similar circumstances. That was not all. The Jhitka jungle through which he was walking was still infested with Maoists and their supporters. They could come out at any moment and slit his throat – nobody would notice.

'Please give me a lift to the police station,' he pleaded in Hindi, signalling to us to stop. We couldn't say no, even though we knew that this could compromise our own safety. Police personnel are known to travel mostly in civilian vehicles, and if the Maoists spotted the soldier's uniform, we ran the risk of being attacked. But the soldier would have died if we had left him to cover the remaining distance on foot. We rolled up the windows of the car, which were thankfully covered with a dark film, and offered the soldier some water with glucose in it. This was on the day the security forces reclaimed the Lalgarh police station, which had been taken over by Maoists eight months ago.

Less than 2 kilometres away from the police station, we met Ranjit Mahato, sitting on a rope cot, leaning against a huge branch of a tree. The police had not reached where he sat, and he spat frequently, running his hand over a bandaged leg. The tree that lay behind him had been felled by the Maoists and he prayed that the police would not be able to cross it.

'Every fire begins in the belly,' he told us.

Until the explosion that almost ended Chief Minister Bhattacharya's life, Lalgarh had been an unknown entity, like thousands of other regions in the Indian hinterland. Now, Lalgarh was big news. Pushing aside the staple glamour and gore of television news, Lalgarh had begun to ride the primetime satellite waves as the second 'liberated zone' of the Maoists, after Dandakaranya.

The police had swung into action immediately after the blast. Since the Maoists would not have waited for their arrival, the police began to shoot in the dark. The first target of their ire was the poor tribals living in the Lalgarh area because their dwellings were closest to the blast site. Three teenagers were picked up while they were returning from a village festival at night. Without an iota of evidence, serious charges were pressed against them, including waging war against the state. Two days later, on 4 November, the police arrested a man while he was buying medicines for his pregnant wife. His wife, too, was beaten up and had to be hospitalized. Ten people were arrested, including a retired school teacher. On the night of 6 November, a police contingent entered Lalgarh town. They unleashed terror in dozens of villages across Lalgarh. Women were beaten up mercilessly. One woman, Panamani Hansda, was kicked in her chest and suffered multiple fractures. Eight other women received serious injuries.

But, unknown to the police's intelligence apparatus, the tribals were not as helpless as they had been a few years ago. They had the support now of certain armed people who had been galvanizing them against the state machinery. Before the police could make further use of their batons, rifle butts and boots, the fire erupted. Thousands of tribals, armed with traditional weapons such as machetes and bows and arrows took the police by surprise. They surrounded the Lalgarh police station in the heart of the town, cries of revenge on their lips. The few policemen working inside were trapped. The electric supply to the police station was cut off and the frightened policemen cowered in various corners of the building. With the aid of the Maoists, the tribals dug up roads and felled trees, leading to a complete cut-off. Lalgarh was no longer a part of West Bengal. The siege of Lalgarh had begun.

With the Lok Sabha elections scheduled to take place a few months later, the state government tried negotiating with the people. The people's committee, which had been formed to act against police repression, said it would call off the siege only if the government acceded to its thirteen-point list of demands. Some of the demands on the list were: The superintendent of police should hold his ears and apologize to them. The police officers who had assaulted the women in the village of Chhotopeliya should crawl on the road, rub their noses on it and ask for forgiveness. Each of the injured women should be paid a compensation of Rs 2 lakh. The villagers also demanded that the police release all the people arrested in connection with the attack on the chief minister's convoy. And that they remove all the police camps set up in schools, hospitals and panchayat offices.

The government was now dealing with fire – a conflagration that had been simmering for some time. Simmering, as Ranjit Mahato had said, in the people's bellies.

For more than three decades, Lalgarh had been a bastion of the ruling CPM. In the neat and tidy tribal houses, CPM flags bearing the hammer and sickle shared space with tribal deities. 'We were all CPM,' Mahato said.

Over the years, life had become tougher. Electricity was yet to reach most of the villages. The local CPM leaders distributed ration cards meant for people living below the poverty line among their own friends and relatives. In the ration shop, though the Rs 2 per kilo rice was available all the time, Mahato and many others like him had no access to it. 'We were forced to buy the same rice for Rs 7,' Mahato said. Job cards under the NREGS were given out, but there was no work. Many people went hungry.

At around this time, Lalgarh received unknown guests. A few strangers had begun to hang around the villages, occasionally asking people if they needed anything. They would ferry sick villagers to the town, and after a few days follow up on their status, offering free medicine and even monetary help. They demanded nothing in return, except occasional requests to cook a bag of rice, which they would bring with them.

In the coming years, the dissatisfaction with the CPM increased further. Meanwhile, the unknown men would pay visits to the weekly *haat* in the villages, now with rifles slung on their shoulders. One of them would speak about how the tribals were being exploited and how the politicians were becoming richer. 'The people would listen to them,' said Mahato.

The local CPM cadre began sensing the discontentment among the people and grew increasingly insecure. Before the last panchayat elections, the CPM leaders began clamping down on villages in Lalgarh. They forced the villagers to nominate CPM leaders. 'One night, CPM workers came with the police. They said, "CPM supporters stand towards the left and others towards the right." Those on the right were all taken away,' said Mahato. Seventy people were arrested in the Lalgarh block alone.

By this time, anger against the CPM had reached an all-time high. It erupted when the police began committing excesses. CPM insignias and flags outside houses were covered with mud or black paint. Instead, flags of the Trinamool Congress began to be seen flying all over. Of course, that was just on the surface. Inside, it was the Maoists who now held sway in Lalgarh. The police had deserted their positions, and the Maoists had taken over.

'They encouraged us to fight with whatever was in our possession,' said a villager. In various villages, the Maoists would arrive at night, asking the people to join them. 'They knocked at my door and said they wanted my help in transporting weapons and other supplies,' said another.

Gradually, the Maoists went on to destroy the CPM's might in the area. The tribals, aided by the Maoists, demolished the local party office of the CPM. Then, amidst the beating of drums and tribal dances, they tore down the CPM's party secretary Anuj Pandey's two-storey house, ironically, with hammers and sickles – the CPM's emblems.

For years, Pandey had been a terror in this area. His house stood out in a sea of poverty. As people around him struggled for one meal in a day, he moved around surrounded by guards carrying AK-47 rifles. Pandey's own story is a reflection of how the CPM, the self-acknowledged saviours of the marginalized, had gone against the principles of Karl Marx, and had, over the years, worked only towards their own prosperity instead of working for the people whom they represented. Pandey's grandfather had migrated to Lalgarh years ago from Uttar Pradesh to work as a priest. The family had lived in a small hut, like everyone else around them. Pandey's father had also chosen to become a priest. But Anuj Pandey had a different aim in life. Mesmerized by the kind of power even small-time politicians enjoyed, he joined the student's wing of the CPM. Because of his hard work and his staunch devotion to the party, he quickly climbed the ranks. By the late 1990s, he had become the undisputed king of Lalgarh, amassing wealth, while the condition of the poor tribals around him deteriorated.

When the Maoists began to call the shots in Lalgarh, Pandey was naturally one of their first targets. No one really sympathized when the horde guided by a senior Maoist leader tore down his house.

Pandey himself managed to escape to Midnapore town, where he was put under police protection.

Later, as Lalgarh came under siege, hundreds of CPM workers fled to escape imminent death. Not all of them succeeded.

On a muggy morning in June, three men sat outside a tea stall on ancient wooden benches, reading Bengali newspapers and sipping tea from small cups without handles. One of them was twenty-seven-year-old Tinku Mahato, recently employed as a teacher for his services to the CPM. With him were twenty-three-year-old Abhijit Mahato, a CPM supporter, and forty-eight-year-old Anil Mahato, the branch committee secretary of the CPM.

Tinku also ran a syndicate for providing security cover to vehicles passing through a forest stretch on National Highway 6, which was vulnerable to robbery. Armed robbers would routinely strike with impunity, relieving travellers of their cash, jewellery and other valuables. It was the police's job to secure the safety of those who passed on this road, but they had outsourced the work to Tinku, who had employed two hundred men to help him. His men would guard the road every day from 6.00 p.m. to 6.00 a.m. In return, the police allowed Tinku's men to collect a 'safety tax' from each vehicle, ranging from Rs 50 to Rs 500.

That morning, as the men sipped their tea, Maoist rebels appeared on motorcycles. They shouted slogans and fired at the three. Tinku and Abhijit were killed on the spot, while Anil Mahato ran away. He was chased by the Maoists for about a kilometre and then gunned down. 'He had been receiving threats from the Maoists to close down his syndicate,' said Tinku's tearful father. 'I had told the police about it, but they did nothing. And now my son is dead – they have killed him so brutally.'

Elsewhere in Lalgarh, a corpse lay covered in a blood-stained sheet on a cot outside the CPM's destroyed office, unattended, not for hours, but for almost a week. The corpse was that of another CPM member, Shaflu Soren, who had been shot dead by the Maoists. Many people, including Soren's own brother, passed by, but nobody dared touch the body out of fear of the Naxalites.

Though he couldn't smell it on his television screen, the helpless chief minister of West Bengal felt sick as he watched the visuals of flies crawling over Soren's body. Then he saw Kishenji.

Someone else was watching the same visuals on television. P. Chidambaram, who had replaced the old Congress hand Shivraj Patil as union home minister, was of the view that most of the Maoist were 'simply bandits'. The time had come to act tough.

On 18 June 2009, five hundred soldiers of the CRPF, which included two hundred commandoes from the elite Cobra force, entered Lalgarh. They secured the Lalgarh police station within two days. The security forces inched forward through Lalgarh, and the Maoists retreated deeper into the forest, leaving the villagers to their fate. The police had not been issued any specific guidelines except to 'flush out' the rebels. Since the Maoists rarely indulged in direct encounters, the police treated every villager as a suspect. They swooped down upon village after village, beating up and torturing people, accusing them of being Maoist supporters.

In Kuldiha village the security forces didn't spare anyone, not even an eighty-year-old woman, who was dragged around by her hair by a policeman. Two motorcycles were destroyed and thrown into the village pond. A jackfruit tree was destroyed. 'One of them ordered me to raise my hands and the other started beating me,' said forty-five-year-old Vijay Mahato. Before leaving, the policemen took away his radio and torch. Shortly afterwards, the villagers fled from their homes and took shelter in a nearby school. Vijay and his family stayed behind because they had to tend to their cows. Many young men were picked up. Dozens of villages began emptying out.

In Kamarpara village, an old man was the only one left behind. He fell to the ground, cringing, the moment he saw us entering the village. 'I have done nothing,' he pleaded. He was too scared after all that he had witnessed. Though he did not reveal anything, other villagers who had taken refuge in the school building in Kamarpara spoke of the police brutality. Janardhan Mahato from a neighbouring village had watched helplessly as policemen beat up his son and kicked his daughter-in-law when she fell at their feet begging for her husband's life to be spared. A policewoman continued to slap her even after she had lost consciousness, he said.

Tarun from a village near Pirakata had begun walking at dawn. The night before, CPM workers had come to his village and beaten up many of the residents. Tarun and his family had escaped at dawn with a few others, fearing yet another beating at the hands of the police. Shops had been closed for many days and food was hard to come by.

'God only knows how we have survived all these days,' Tarun said. He was on his way to Midnapore with his wife and three children, he informed us. They were carrying a few utensils and a change of clothes, and their most prized possession, a packet of Britannia Tiger biscuits. Midnapore town is about 40 kilometres from their village. They would have to walk for hours in the heat to reach there.

Before the Lalgarh police station was taken over by the police, journalists waited with their notebooks and mikes for the security forces to make their move. The heat was so extreme it could kill a person in a matter of a few hours, draining all the water from the body. A hen fluttered around cautiously, stopping every now and then on one leg. There was nothing to do except wait. The journalists passed around bottles of water and handfuls of puffed rice. The security men had nothing except their weapons and dirty water bottles that they carried on their belts.

Then came the news that the few stretches that had been secured earlier by the police had been retaken by the angry villagers. A few armed Maoists had also been spotted nearby. Some journalists and a police party rushed towards the area. There was a confrontation. From a village nearby, the tribals let out their traditional battle cries to scare the policemen. 'Doesn't it look like they are fighting the British?' a photographer remarked.

That evening, five minutes after the media left in their cars for Midnapore town, where they were staying at two hotels that had doubled their rates, there was a landmine blast. Two policemen were injured. Deep in the forest, the Cobra forces had begun their hunt for the Maoists, but the senior members of the cadre had already been shifted to a secure area.

From his hideout, Kishenji said he was readying the Maoist bulletin. He was on the phone continuously, giving interviews to television channels. The day the police stormed into Lalgarh town, Kishenji had been interviewed by at least two dozen media organizations. That morning, most newspapers had quoted the founder of the Naxalbari uprising, Kanu Sanyal, as saying that the upheaval at Lalgarh was not a communist movement. Kishenji thundered back, his mellow voice turning hard for a while: 'Kanu Sanyal is a *pheriwala*, a hawker, for the CPM. If you have further questions, please call me in the morning. I have two more interviews lined up.' It was already way past midnight.

Amidst the police offensive, a government jeep approached the Lalgarh police station. Several senior government officials had come on a visit. Two of them passed by the police station and saw a long queue of people – men, women and children – pressed against each other in the sweltering heat.

'What are they here for?' one of them asked a constable.

'To collect ration, sir,' came the reply.

'But isn't there a block office for ...' the official stopped midway. He had understood the crux of the matter. All those who had queued up outside the police station had never been given cards by the ration dealers, who made a profit by selling the subsidized ration in the open market.

Afterwards, some of the officials went to the local health centre. They found vaccines and other medicines lying open in a termite-ridden cupboard.

'You don't have a refrigerator to store these?' one of them asked the medical assistant.

'Refrigerator!' the assistant repeated in amazement. 'We don't even have a proper almirah to store these.'

At Pirakata, the officials were shown two local embankments that had collapsed about a year ago and were still to be repaired. A panchayat member told the visiting officials that hundreds of square kilometres of land had been lying unused due to lack of water. They were also shown a 12 kilometre stretch of road that had last been repaired in the 1970s.

Meanwhile, the heat had intensified. On the serpentine road surrounded by jungles, the police and the paramilitary jawans took their positions against an enemy they couldn't see. They had no clarity about the operation. 'We do nothing except wait in this dense jungle, and that is killing us,' said a soldier.

And it is not the wait alone that kills them. In the absence of the most basic facilities like water, many die of heat stroke. Some fifty soldiers had to be admitted in hospital because they were severely dehydrated. Six of them had to be airlifted for urgent medical intervention. In the hospital, the visiting officials saw that the ward in which the jawans suffering from heatstroke had been kept had air-conditioners but no doors.

A jawan camping at a government high school spoke about fifty soldiers having been housed in a single room. 'I am on duty for eight hours in the sun, and when I come back the fan doesn't work. When it does, it moves like it is suffering from constipation,' he said.

Sitting with his back against a tree, another jawan was waiting for food to arrive. A fellow soldier had gone in search of water. 'There is no action and this heat is killing me,' he said. 'And look at this uniform – I haven't been able to change it in four days.' There was a pause, and in the silence of the Jhitka jungle, his stomach rumbled. He looked away. 'I cannot fight when I am hungry,' he mumbled.

Ranjit Mahato had said that every fire began in the belly. He was only partially correct. Some fires, it seemed, died in the belly as well.

Postscript

Months have passed, but Operation Lalgarh is far from over. The Maoists are still holding ground and apart from some arrests the police haven't been able to make major headway in the area. The Maoists are still carrying out attacks at will, including a deadly attack on a camp of the Eastern Frontier Rifles, which resulted in the death of twenty-four policemen. Even after pushing in thousands of soldiers the area has not been completely 'sanitized', as a senior home ministry official put it. Senior Maoist leaders, including Kishenji, are still camping in the area, speaking unhindered to journalists over mobile phones.

Lalgarh has now been dubbed 'Naxalbari 2'.

There are clear indications that the government is looking at a long-term offensive against the Maoists. Troops, numbering over a lakh mainly from paramilitary forces like the CRPF, have been deployed across Maoist-affected areas. Some believe, the main thrust of the operation will begin after the monsoons are over. So far, the Centre has said that the army will not be deployed, but now, there are indications that the army will play at least some role even if it is not directly involved. The central government expects the security forces to 'cleanse' the area of Maoists and be prepared for an extended deployment. 'At least for two years,' a senior home ministry official said.

The CPI (Maoist) is also gearing up for the central government's proposed offensive. In a party circular titled 'Post-Election Situation – Our Tasks', the Naxal leadership talks about the ruling United

Progressive Alliance government getting an absolute majority in the 2009 Lok Sabha elections. 'The results have given scope for the UPA government to enact more draconian legislations and implement more fascist measures and suppression of the people's struggles,' the circular says. It also says that there are lessons to be learnt from the recent debacle of the LTTE in Sri Lanka. 'The mistake of the LTTE lay in its lack of study of the changes in the enemy tactics, capabilities, international support and open assistance by imperialist powers, i.e., an underestimation of the enemy along with an overestimation of its own forces and capabilities.'

The circular asks the party members to 'prepare the people, the party and the PLGA [the Naxalite army] to confront the brutal enemy onslaught.' It advises them to 'take the initiative to unite with other struggling organizations and forces to forge strong united fronts ... enthuse them with the daring counter-offensives carried out by our forces in various parts of the country and prepare them to undertake similar operations.'

The top Naxalite leadership believes that it will be difficult for the central government to deploy a huge force against them, but they are well aware of the government's plan to increase the deployment of central forces and create special forces. Through the circular, the leaders are telling the Naxalite cadre to 'further aggravate the situation and create more difficulties for the enemy forces by expanding our guerrilla war to new areas on the one hand and intensifying the mass resistance in the existing areas so as to disperse the enemy forces over a sufficiently wider area.'

Referring to the security forces' operations in Abujhmaad, the circular speaks of mobilizing adivasi organizations. 'The bigger conspiracy of the reactionary rulers to extend mining from Raoghat to the innumerable hills in Maad [Abujhmaad] and to loot the natural mineral wealth of the region should be exposed and a broad-based movement should be built against displacement,' says the circular.

The central government might be serious about replicating the Lalgarh model across all Naxalite-infested areas, but it has conveniently ignored the lessons that this small area in West Bengal has offered. When the ill-equipped CRPF and other forces try to enter the Naxal strongholds, the Maoists will play a cat-and-mouse game with them, as they did in Lalgarh. That is already clear from the attack on CRPF jawans in Dantewada in Chhattisgarh on 6 April 2010, in which seventy-five jawans died in an ambush. This is probably the highest casualty the military has faced in a single act of insurgency. There have been many other such assaults that have caused heavy casualties among the CRPF ranks. Since 1991, the central government and the Naxalite-affected states have spent crores of rupees in tackling the Naxalites. Yet, on the morning of 12 July 2008, the Naxalites managed to shoot two policemen in Chhattisgarh because they had to go into the jungle to answer nature's call. Their police station had no toilets. In all Naxalite-affected areas – and this is true of almost all of India – the average policeman is highly demoralized and poorly equipped, and lives in his barracks in abysmal conditions.

Soldiers who have been packed in their dozens into a single room under 'a constipated fan', as the CRPF soldier in Lalgarh put it, seldom succeed. And when clueless forces are pressed into action, they end up further alienating the people, as has been witnessed in Lalgarh.

The fight against militancy in India will have to be imaginative and wise, keeping in view the concerns of millions of poor people who, spontaneously or under duress, end up supporting the militants. It is a battle that cannot be won by putting together a few thousand police or paramilitary personnel and naming them Cobra or anything else.

After a major Naxal attack in Orissa in 2009, Home Minister P. Chidambaram said that the belief that police action and development can go hand in hand in Naxalite areas was a 'naïve theory'. Clearly, the government has taken off one set of blinkers and put on a new one.

Part Two

The Valley of Denial

'THE AMOUNT OF MONEY NEW DELHI HAS SPENT HERE ... THEY COULD HAVE BUILT A NEW KASHMIR'

1

From a distant pore in the unending stretch of the Himalayas, an unexpected blade of sunlight peeped out on to the frozen Dal Lake. A hush had blanketed its white icy expanse during the night. Now, that silence was gradually being broken by the twitter of hidden birds, the muffled clatter of utensils in lakeside kitchens and the rustle of the flaming red leaves of the chinar trees. Like streamers at a birthday party, red streaks broke through the golden waves splashing across the sky. Another morning was dawning in Kashmir.

Clouds drifted lazily across the sky, past mountains draped in sheets of snow and valleys decked with scarves of dazzling flowers. After many years, the Dal Lake was again covered in ice. Children lay snuggled in their beds in cosy timber houses around the lake, but they would wake up soon and scamper on the ice, defying warnings from their angry mothers. On a small part of the lake which had yet to freeze over, a few early-bird adventurers rowed their small boats, weaving through clusters of lotuses in the water, teasing tiny fish into scurrying below the surface, and trying to ignore the morning chill that numbed their faces.

From a small window on the bank, a man watched the shrunken lake. It was 5.00 a.m. and seventy-year-old Abdul Aziz was awake, defying the December chill as he had all his life. Along the manicured grass banks of the picturesque lake floated a row of ten houseboats made of the best teak and walnut wood, with chandeliers hanging above their carpeted floors and ornate cutlery laid out on dining tables next to cosy fireplaces. These were the most popular addresses in Kashmir for honeymooners, politicians, heads of state, movie stars and, lately, journalists hungry for updates on the latest incidents of bombings, killings and terrorist swoops.

Warmly cocooned in his winter gear, Abdul Aziz walked out on to the green stretch of lawn, kneeled, raised his shrivelled hands and began offering his daily prayers to Allah. There was much to thank the Almighty for on regular days. Aziz was well aware that behind the picturesque image held out by Kashmir lurked a crisis that went far beyond guns and blood. At a time like this, at his age, he was lucky to have a job at all. Thousands of young men and women were jobless in the state of Jammu and Kashmir. Insurgency had severely dented the tourism industry. There was barely any supply of electricity, so children could not study and factories could not be run efficiently. Partially constructed Roads, power projects, schools and health centres lay in a state of suspended animation, often unfinished for years in the name of insurgency.

A closer look at the placid waters of the 314-square kilometre stretch of the Dal Lake, one of the most photographed water bodies in the world, would reveal that the panoramic lake was rotting and shrinking, despite the Rs 240 crore – US$53 million – spent on cleaning it. We could have used a cliché and said that the money had vanished into the waters of the Dal, but that would be practically unfeasible. The lake had been abused to the extent that it was now only an average three metres deep. Fish were disappearing every day. Thousands of weeds were gobbling up the take, but not as quickly as the famous Kashmiri houseboats and the settlers who had encroached on its shores and silt islands, built concrete houses and kept pumping sewage into the water. The silt clogging the lake had suddenly gone up from 7,200 tonnes per year in August 2003 to 2,300 tonnes per year in August 2005, when it was last measured.

In Kashmir, failure of governance had for years been concealed behind the façade of a twenty-year-old insurgency. No militant had ever bombed a civic official or seized a dredger meant for cleaning the Dal Lake. It was Kashmir's government that was choking the state's most prized asset. Nevertheless, officials like to blame militants for the disappearance of the sprawling expanse of water, as they do for everything else, from poor roads to missing doctors at health centres to the crippling lack of education and jobs. Just as Inspector General of Police S.M. Sahai did, when a young carpenter was killed by a policeman and buried after being branded as a Pakistani terrorist: 'When you have a situation like this, systems break down,' he said.

'So much money is coming in from the Government of India, but our capacity to spend – and spend well – is still not very good,' Khursheed Ahmad Ganai, principal secretary, General Administration Department, tells us candidly.

The capacity to destroy the state's resources seems to have developed well, though. In a state celebrated for its greenery and beautiful forests, jungles have been polished off by the timber mafia at a rate that is unmatched anywhere else in the world, even though all the forests in the valley are marked and watched by security forces because they could hide militants. Jammu and Kashmir is officially estimated to have only 20,000 square kilometres of forest now, about 20 per cent of the state's area, against the legally prescribed norm of 66 per cent. However, in a recent investigation the CAG found that state government officials had lied about this – the forest cover was in reality 17,000 square kilometres, and that too was a misleading figure because half of this area was clear, with tree density of only about 40 per cent. It was discovered that even after spending more than Rs 18 crore on planting trees, the bald patches on the mountains had *increased* from 7,000 square kilometres to 10,000 square kilometres between 2002 and 2007.

How exactly did hundreds of square kilometres of lush coniferous forest vanish from a region that was perhaps under the sharpest scrutiny in India? Common sense and local reports suggest that this state of affairs could not have come about without the connivance of government and security officials. Kashmir's finest wood, illegally smuggled, can be found in living and dining rooms from Chandigarh to Chennai. Since the insurgency flared two decades ago, around Rs 50,000 crore, US$12 billion, have been pumped into Kashmir by the central government for development aid alone. Kashmiris, and taxpayers across the country, could be forgiven for wondering where it has all vanished. It is also unfortunate that, just like the government officials, most of Kashmir's residents have also let go of some simple duties in the name of insurgency, like paying income tax or electricity bills.

There are other unpaid dues. Funerals to attend. Friends to mourn. Memories to nurse.

This morning, Abdul Aziz said a special prayer in his mind. Aziz prayed for a twenty-eight-year-old man who had been killed along with thirteen others in a huge explosion and shootout in the border district of Uri. Word had reached him barely minutes ago when the ancient black telephone in the office lobby had shattered the silence of the tranquil morning. It was his old friend Manzoor Ahmad Wani on the line giving him news he would rather not have heard. The town in Uri was more than four hours away by road and there was no way Aziz could attend the funeral to take place at noon that day. He closed his eyes and prayed. Aziz's mind wandered to his friend's choked description of his son's final few minutes. There had been no novelty in the account; it was how thousands had died before and would die in the future, Aziz told himself. Like most Kashmiris, he was deeply emotional. He had no hope for the future of his stunningly beautiful, paradisiacal homeland. His dreams were long dead, like those of most Kashmiris.

Death had stalked Kashmir daily for twenty endless years now, claiming at least a life a day, sometimes ten and, on a few bloody days a hundred. On that Friday afternoon, shortly before the muezzin in the local mosque was to summon the devout on the booming public address systems, death had chosen to strike in Uri.

The bomb went off ten minutes after noon, ten minutes after the school bell rang to announce the end of another day of classes. Some thirty children in white shirts and blue ties, the boys in grey trousers and the girls in long skirts, strolled out of the large metal school gates. It seemed unusually warm for a December afternoon. Unknown to the school children, the day would soon begin to sizzle in their small town on the frontier of India and Pakistan.

Most of the children stopped to buy candy and fried peanuts from the nearby shops. Five teachers – three young men and two women – walked a few steps behind, clutching notebooks from the day's classes, all covered in glossy brown paper. A long, shrill whistle rung out on Uri's main road, a thoroughfare flanked by a wooded hill on one side and the town's main business district on the other. A long convoy of army jeeps, trucks and water tankers was winding along the narrow roads, with a stern-looking, machine-gun-toting soldier in the jeep leading the convoy blowing the whistle, ordering Kashmiris to clear the way. The soldiers clutched their weapons tightly. They knew the drill of watching out carefully for their enemy in crowded areas, though their enemy was invisible and he changed his face each day. As the convoy wove its way through the busy area, three men, all wearing long gray Kashmiri coats, or *pherans*, slipped through the crowd. Under the woollen coats, two men nervously held machine guns. The third held a grenade in his hand. He had slipped his finger inside the pin, ready to release it at any second. Their faces impassive, they walked from a cluster of grocery and meat shops towards the main road. Most people in the small town knew or recognized each other, but these were new faces. Beneath their *pherans* and their long shirts, they had distinct marks on their shoulders and their ankles, indicating that they had walked a long distance, through treacherous mountain passes, carrying heavy loads on their backs. Their *pherans* bore the same label - of the tailor who had stitched their clothes, Karamat and Sons, Karachi. One of them had in his pocket the receipt of a guest house in Pakistan, where they had stayed for three weeks before moving to India-controlled Kashmir. Allah Baksh Musafirkhana, the shabby receipt said, indicating that a payment of Rs 2,000 had been settled. Two of the men had photographs of their icons in their battered wallets. One was of their supreme commander, Maulana Masood Azhar, the strong-bodied, bearded Islamic cleric who had founded the Jaish-e-Mohammed (JeM) militant group after he was released in a swap for civilian hostages at the dramatic hijacking of an Indian Airlines jetliner in 1999. Soon after it was founded, the JeM had attracted hundreds of new recruits with its quickfire ways and dramatic strikes, its cult of suicide attacks and its close links with the al-Qaeda. The other was a picture of Osama bin Laden, apparently torn off the glossy page of an Urdu magazine. The pictures, and the tailor's labels, would later become a little difficult to read in the blood-and-sweat-smeared clothes of the three mujahideen recently returned from Pakistan.

These men were among the thousands of Kashmiris who had, since 1989, sneaked across the border in small groups, always headed by a nimble and expert guide, to safe houses in Pakistan where they were trained to carry out a jihad when they returned to Kashmir. Several arrested rebels would later describe how they were taught to shoot, bomb and initiate guerrilla warfare in dozens of weapon-stacked training camps run by Pakistan's establishment, before they were ready to return along the same mountain routes to wage war within India. World leaders from Washington to Moscow to London would soon be clamouring for these training camps to be shut down, for the infiltration to be controlled. But that day was some time away from this December afternoon in Uri.

At the curve of the road, another young man sat in a parked three-wheeler auto-rickshaw, ostensibly waiting for commuters, his left leg dangling outside the vehicle, his right leg resting at the edge of the seat. He gazed blankly at the market.

The convoy was close now.

The man with the grenade – the youngest of the three – suddenly lunged forward and lobbed his weapon at a clear area on the slope of the hill. It exploded about a hundred feet from the first jeep and the soldier with the whistle ducked in a split-second drill he had learned over and over at the base but had prayed he would never need to perform. He was too late. He tumbled out of the jeep, a fatal bullet wound in his neck. Another soldier behind him spotted the young man and began firing at him, bringing him down quickly, along with two civilians. The man with the grenade died instantly, with bullets in his head and abdomen. The civilians would struggle for a few days in a hospital in the state capital of Srinagar before they, too, succumbed to their wounds.

The two other *pheran*-clad men raised their guns, fired a burst of bullets each, and rushed to the area in front of the convoy. They tried to bring down as many soldiers as they could with a hail of automatic-weapon fire, but fell, instead, to the barrage of gunfire from the soldiers. The army convoy ground to a halt. Officers leaped out of their jeeps shouting emergency instructions. The soldiers scampered and surrounded the convoy, their whistles going berserk. They crouched on the road, taking cover behind the bulky vehicles, and took aim.

'Clear the area!' an officer screamed in Hindi from behind a truck.

Less than a hundred feet away, the market had by now broken into chaos. Traders froze in their chairs, customers tore out of shops, bystanders ran in every direction because they knew what each soldier knew at that moment: The invisible enemy was right here somewhere in the crowd and there was no knowing what he would do next.

At the curve of the road, the man waiting in the auto-rickshaw stumbled out of the vehicle and ran, the keys still dangling in the ignition. A few seconds passed. Nothing happened. A few hundred feet above them, near the top of the low hill running along the road, another man, who had been squatting there for an hour now, clenched his jaws, clasped his hands together and pressed a button. The explosion that resulted was the loudest many had heard in years in the region. On the road, a minute before he died an agonizing death, the army captain at the rear of the convoy had a flash of realization. The grenade, which had done little more than set a barren tree on fire, had been a diversion from the main weapon in that afternoon's attack, the auto-rickshaw. Several kilograms of RDX, one of the most lethal explosives used in Kashmir, packed neatly in a plastic sack behind the rough black leather seats, blew up in a deafening, remote-controlled explosion, like a furious volcano suddenly blasting out of the belly of a silent mountain.

The harmless vehicle was flung more than six metres into the air. The impact of the explosion travelled swiftly along the road, clawing away at the sides of the trucks and the jeeps, past the crouching soldiers, taking three shrieking children with it. The lifeless bodies of the children dropped down on the ground a few feet from where they had stood. Screams echoed in the thin mountain air, as fleeing men and women kicked up clouds of dust and dried mule dung.

As the echo of the explosion died, the soldiers regrouped. Apart from the soldier with the whistle, a captain and four others of their battalion lay on the road, their bodies blown apart, their limbs in bloodied shreds. The soldiers trained their guns at the hilltop and started firing in a frenzied, frantic response. They were not firing at anyone in particular, just churning out all the bullets that they wanted to pump into their enemy as if he were there before them. They screamed abuses and invoked the name of God as they fired into the air. The women in the crowd screamed. The men hunkered down. They knew what was coming. Several soldiers clenched their jaws and started spraying bullets into the crowd. They wanted their revenge. They had fired several rounds before an officer rushed forward and asked them to stop. Three children, five teachers and six soldiers lay on the road, some whole, others dismembered. The small white shirts were mostly red. So were the grey trousers and the soldiers' well-ironed greens. Thirty-six people were wounded. Most had died in the first impact of the explosion, but some of the dead, and many of the injured, bore bullet wounds. Teacher Shaukat Wani was among those dead. A government spokesman later claimed he, like the others, had been caught in the crossfire.

On the grass lawn beside the Dal Lake, Aziz opened his eyes and took a deep breath. He had finished saying his prayers.

Images of the past day, which, for him, were no different from the images of the past decade, flickered through his angry mind. Kashmir, his beautiful homeland, where a million dreams had bloomed for centuries, had long stopped being a paradise. It was now a war zone, dealing with the debris of a prolonged battle in which automatic-weapon fire had ricocheted through apple orchards, bomb explosions had ripped apart narrow roads in lush pastures and fear had stalked the flower-laden Mughal-era gardens.

Sometimes Aziz was not sure whom to blame. Could he blame Pakistan for giving the Kashmiris dreams of independence, training two generations of youth in its camps, pumping money and weapons into the Kashmir valley and setting loose a Frankenstein that had gone out of control? Could he blame India for responding to this campaign of terror with terror of its own, a ruthless state response backed by half a million people, which had been unable to crush the militancy or Pakistan's support for it but had instead routed the lives of thousands of innocent people? Or were the Kashmiris themselves to blame for letting Islamic fundamentalism and jihad seep into their centuries-old secular traditions, for allowing their aspiration for a free nation to get hijacked by an unending cycle of violence, for not standing up to resist when the tens of thousands of Hindus, with whom they had lived for generations, had been terrorized and forced to flee their homes? Nothing was black and white in Kashmir; there was just the haze of death.

The feeling of being helpless and trapped had swept over Aziz a million times in his life. More than a decade ago, liberation had been sought from this entrapment by the launch of a successful rebellion by an entire generation of youth, which believed that its future was safer in a free homeland, or as part of Pakistan. Weapons had been plentiful, there had been an unending supply of resources. All that was needed was passion and blood.

The journey of dissent had begun years ago on a sunny afternoon in the late 1980s in Kashmir, as four angry men talked over cups of steaming, cardamom-redolent *kahwa* and plates of meatballs. One of them had just lost a heart valve. His name was Yasin Malik. The tall, frail young man nurtured a deep anger rooted in a seemingly insignificant event that had unfolded one July afternoon even further back in the past.

It had been unusually hot that afternoon in 1980 in Srinagar. *Bhishtis* sprinkled water on the roads from their leather bags. The Palladium cinema in Lal Chowk, the market square in the heart of the state capital, bore a deserted look. The clock tower at the chowk showed the wrong time, as usual. There were no ice cream carts or stalls selling sheep-trotter soup. Boatmen plying their shikaras on the Dal Lake had taken a break for their siesta under the shade of the chinar trees on Boulevard Road. It was the month of Ramzan, the time for fasting and prayers for Muslims all over the world.

Hundreds of kilometres away from Srinagar, Soviet troops were facing stiff resistance from the mujahideen in Afghanistan. The Olympic flame had arrived in Moscow, and India had launched its first orbiting satellite. There were no twenty-four-hour news channels then, but the Kashmiris had their own way of deciphering the script of the gods. At sunset, old men would point towards the crimson sky and tell their grandchildren, 'There has been *khoonrizi* (bloodshed) somewhere.'

Late on that afternoon in July 1980, children, most of them wearing Bata's Naughty Boy shoes and laden with schoolbags, were sauntering back home. Many government employees, especially women, left their offices early, stopping at Lal Chowk to buy slabs of dates for that day's Iftar, the ritual breaking of their fast after sunset. Young men smoked secretly behind half-closed shop shutters, fearing rebuke from their elders. On Badshah Bridge, named after the most tolerant king to have ruled Kashmir, life was moving at its usual pace.

A Shaktiman truck of the Indian Army had left the Badami Bagh cantonment and was on its way to another camp on the outskirts of Srinagar. Usually, drivers would slow down their vehicles near Badshah Bridge, to change gear and begin the slow climb up the gradient. But the army truck, with its solo driver, was being driven impatiently, and when it reached the top of the bridge it swerved uncontrollably towards the left and climbed on to the pavement. Eyewitnesses say that a child was injured. The army had always been seen as the most distinct symbol of India's 'hegemony' in Kashmir. As the injured child was rescued by passersby, tempers ran high. Seeing that the driver was alone in the truck, the crowd pulled him out. He was reportedly found drunk.

In a fit of rage, someone from the crowd slapped him. A young man hurled a stone at the truck. 'Kill the kafir,' another shouted. The driver managed to save himself with much difficulty and sped away, leaving behind a trail of smoke. After he was gone, the people shouted a few slogans and went back to their work.

Some shops closed down as sunset approached. As the sky turned crimson, the muezzin in a nearby mosque consulted a calendar from Mecca. In a few minutes, he would have to announce the Iftar, asking the believers to break their fast.

Those who were in Lal Chowk that evening swear they heard a rumble that felt like the earth was churning. As they wondered what was happening, some three hundred army vehicles, moving in a convoy, halted in the middle of the market square. Hundreds of soldiers, wearing round-necked T-shirts and shorts, descended from the rear of the vehicles and fanned across the square. Then they went on a rampage. People were beaten up, shops vandalized, some of them even set on fire.

A few minutes before the army soldiers took their revenge, fourteen-year-old Yasin Malik had reached Lal Chowk. He lived in the neighbouring locality of Maisuma. 'I saw a soldier looking directly in my eyes and I was so scared, I ran away and hid in a ticket booth of the state roadways,' Malik would recall twenty-seven years after that fateful evening. The boy watched from his hiding place as the soldiers set a poultry shop on fire. As he peeped out from behind the ticket window, he could see dozens of chickens being roasted alive. The police tried to control the agitated soldiers, but they too were subjected to the soldiers' wrath. A senior police officer from the Kothibagh police station was slapped by a junior commissioned officer of the army.

Almost ten years later, when he jumped from the fifth floor of a building to escape arrest, the images of that evening would come back to haunt Yasin Malik.

2

The roots of anger run thick and deep in Kashmir. British colonialists had sold the princely state of Jammu and Kashmir – its mountains, meadows, rivers and two and a half million people – to a Hindu king for Rs 75 lakh, one horse, twelve goats and three cashmere shawls. By that measure, the Kashmiris told themselves, each of them had been bought for Rs 3. It is a slur that has refused to leave the Kashmiri mind over generations.

The Treaty of Amritsar was just one of the things the Kashmiris have kept in their hearts for decades as an angry memory. The day on which the treaty was signed – 16 March 1846 – was the first of many significant and bitter days in Kashmir's history, when the fate of the land and its people was decided by foreigners, resulting in transfers of power over which Kashmir's people had little control.

It was not as if the people in the rest of colonial India had any such control. Bombay (now Mumbai), which has now become India's financial powerhouse, was given away by the Portuguese to the British as part of Catherine of Braganza's dowry when she married Charles II of England. But for the emotional and proud Kashmiris these pinpricks would become part of folklore, politicians' fiery speeches and angry arguments for independence around crackling bonfires. These passions were evoked partly because of the religious equations in the state. For, during the last century before the British rulers left India, Jammu and Kashmir, a Himalayan state predominantly populated by Muslims, was governed by Hindu rulers of the Dogra dynasty.

With the 1846 treaty, the British, unable to rule over the sprawling princely state of Kashmir because of geographical and logistical problems, handed it over to the fifty-four-year-old King Gulab Singh. Gulab Singh used to be the prime minister of the Sikh rulers in Lahore, the arch rivals of the British. Historians say he betrayed his king during the razor-edge Battle of Sobraon, delaying his soldiers' advances and positioning them in such a way that the Sikhs were crushed by the colonial troops. Gulab Singh took control of a territory that included the flatlands of Jammu, the stunning Himalayan landscape of Kashmir and the picture-perfect cold desert plateau of Ladakh. But neither he nor his successors did much to nurture the land.

Contemporary writers and historians put the Hindu Dogra kings in the same league as many of the oppressive Muslim rulers of medieval India, including some of the Mughal emperors. Gulab Singh, seemingly in a hurry to reclaim the fortune he had spent buying his kingdom, began an aggressive and ruthless taxation campaign. He is also known to have blatantly favoured Hindus over Kashmiri Muslims in government, education and all areas of governance. Sir Walter Lawrence, a contemporary visitor and an officer of the Indian Civil Service, wrote of how little remained to be taxed in the Dogra kingdom. There were taxes on 'fruit trees, birch bark, violets, hides, silk, saffron, hemp, tobacco, water nuts and paper ... the right to legalize marriage was farmed out, the office of [the] gravedigger was taxed. Prostitutes were taxed, and everything save air and water was brought under taxation.' All these taxes were appropriated by violent means. The oppression, which was continued by the king's successors, intensified the hatred of the subjects for their monarchs and eventually made their aspiration of independence even fiercer.

The three Dogra kings who followed Gulab Singh were more orthodox than him in their religious leanings and means of governance, and keen to remain in the good books of the British.

Gulab Singh's son, Ranjit Singh, has been described as doing little more than building Hindu temples across the kingdom. Ranjit Singh's successor, Pratap Singh, was painted by the British as being an imbecile and an agent of the Tsar of Russia – the first apparently an exaggeration and the second a false allegation backed by forged letters leaked to the press. Pratap Singh was deposed in 1889 by the British viceroy. In protest, he went without food for two days, languished without his throne for sixteen years and got it back only in 1905, although only as a matter of ceremony.

But the most colourful Dogra ruler was yet to take over, and he sprang into the public eye in a rather bizarre manner. Hari Singh, Pratap Singh's nephew, took over the reins of Kashmir in September 1925 and was gobbled up by the British tabloids soon after, when he was reportedly set upon by a criminal gang in London. Published accounts say that the king was caught in bed in a state of undress with a woman planted by the gang, which later demanded, and received, a huge sum of money as payoff for blackmail. According to British writer Leonard Mosley, 'The Maharaja of Kashmir was so rich that he bought hundreds of concubines and dancing girls at £20,000–£50,000 apiece and once paid £1,50,000 for one hour with a female crook in a London hotel bedroom.' After that lustful beginning to his reign, Hari Singh returned to Kashmir and picked up the mantle of repression worn by his predecessors. But as Kashmir entered the second quarter of the twentieth century, the first sparks began to show in the lush land strewn with the maple-shaped leaves of the flaming red chinar trees.

A burden of bitter memories weighed upon generations, and it was these collective memories that formed the foundation for popular unrest and provoked uncomfortable questions, such as why a Muslim-majority state was ruled by an oppressive Hindu-dominated government. One of the most powerful voices that raised these issues was that of a young man who wanted to be a doctor but became, instead, a champion of Kashmiri nationhood. Sheikh

Mohammad Abdullah, who would become the father-figure leader of Kashmiri Muslims, was born into a family that was, until two generations before his, Hindu. His ancestors were Kashmiri Pandits belonging to the highest caste of Brahmins and the family lived in a picture-postcard village on the banks of the Anchar Sar Lake in Kashmir. The family converted to Islam in the eighteenth century and Abdullah was born into a Muslim shawl-weaver's family in 1905.

Abdullah was the man whom India's federal government would hail as a patriotic hero for decades, and then imprison as a traitor. Riding, and guiding, the turbulent wave of his political destiny, Abdullah became the most influential, and a hugely popular, opponent of the century-old Dogra dynasty. He came to symbolize what had ignited the passions of a million Kashmiri dreams for decades – a Kashmir for Kashmiris. Using his powerful skills of oratory born of his masterful recitation of Koranic verses, Abdullah could move thousands of people to tears, or rebellion.

The first sparks flew on a spring afternoon in 1931. A group of young Kashmiri Muslims returned to Jammu and Kashmir from a rhetoric-laced conference of Muslims in Lahore, a bustling trading town that would later become part of Pakistan. Fired by Islamic zeal, the men led protests in Jammu, trying to stoke a pan-Muslim movement, along the lines of what hardline Islamic leaders were provoking in other parts of undivided India. The movement met with police repression. What happened during the next few days and weeks is not certain, but has been loosely reconstructed from contemporary accounts and those described by Abdullah himself.

As the protesters screamed slogans in Jammu, Head Constable Labho Ram briskly walked forward, taunted the protesters, took a copy of the Koran from one of the men and allegedly tore it up. Many protesters were arrested. In a separate incident, the police are said to have forced a Muslim cleric to stop offering his prayers. Abdullah started a campaign demanding punishment for the officers who had desecrated the Koran. Alongside him, a former cook called Abdul Qadir delivered a blistering address to thousands of people, in which, according to some accounts, Qadir urged a general massacre of Hindus, and according to others asked the people to rise against oppression. The electric speech landed Qadir in prison. On 13 July 1931, the day his trial began, more than five thousand people assembled outside the prison, screaming angry slogans against the maharaja and his forces. Emotions soared and they rushed to force open the gates of the prison to free Qadir. The police surrounded the prison and asked the people to stop. The protesters responded by pelting stones. The police opened fire, and at least twenty-one people were killed.

Within hours, the miasma of silent rage spread through the city. The bodies of the dead were laid out on bamboo cots, draped in white shrouds, and a funeral procession began to make its way through the streets. The protests soon turned violent, and Hindus became the targets of the screaming, frenzied mob as it pelted stones and set shops on fire. It was the most serious occurrence ever of Hindu–Muslim violence in Jammu and Kashmir. At the end of the rioting, three Hindus lay dead, many more were wounded, and hundreds of shops had been burnt, looted or razed to the ground. Most of all, the clash had created a wide chasm between Hindus and Muslims in the state, something that had never been witnessed so prominently before in the region.

Unknown to most people trying to storm the prison that day, on 13 July 1789, a hundred and forty-two years before, the people of Paris had broken into the prison of St Lazare to seize arms. The French Revolution had begun the following morning with the storming of the Bastille and the beheading of the governor. Kashmir's revolution, too, had now begun.

More than fifteen years passed. The angst of the Kashmiris simmered and often boiled over in protests and demonstrations against the king's rule. The British were getting tired of their lengthy war with Nazi Germany. On the Indian mainland, the campaign for independence was reaching a climax; the Quit India movement of 1942 shook the British. It was clear that colonial rule would have to end soon, and to increase the pressure the United States, Britain's close ally, was insisting on independence and self-rule for the British colonies.

Abdullah and his political party, the National Conference, began a Quit Kashmir movement against Hari Singh, along the lines of the campaign against the British in the rest of India. Hari Singh's forces tried to crush the movement with severe force and brutality. According to historical accounts, twenty people were killed in the state's ruthless response to the campaign. Hundreds were wounded in truncheon charges and firing and hundreds of others were arrested. Political activists were detained, arrested and tried for sedition. The public anger spread to the security forces, the state's police force reportedly refusing to beat back civilian demonstrators. Hari Singh had to recall his soldiers, including detachments that had been sent to West Asia to aid the British. The royal soldiers – mostly the feared Dogras – stalked the streets of Srinagar, the kingdom's summer capital, sending waves of terror among the common people. Abdullah was arrested. Describing the situation in Kashmir at the time, Jawaharlal Nehru said, 'Srinagar is almost a city of the dead.'

On the threshold of India's independence, Kashmir, too, stood at the crossroads of history. It had to decide – like the five hundred and sixty-four other princely states in India – whether it wanted to remain in India, merge with Pakistan or preserve its independence.

There were two men in Kashmir who could most likely decide the province's destiny. The shapers of destiny – Mahatma Gandhi, Jawaharlal Nehru, Viceroy Louis Mountbatten and Home Minister Vallabhbhai Patel – keenly awaited a decision from both Hari Singh and the other history-charting man of the moment, Abdullah, the icon of millions of Kashmiri Muslims.

Cables were exchanged, telephone calls were made, and emissaries from both sides exchanged bluff and bluster, but Hari Singh continued to wait and watch as all the other states signed the Instrument of Accession. At his end, Abdullah pleaded an upset stomach and avoided a meeting with Mountbatten when the viceroy travelled to Kashmir in 1947 to hear his decision. Nehru followed the viceroy, and was detained. Gandhi returned empty-handed.

On 8 July 1947, with a little more than a month to go before India declared its independence, a British judge named Cyril Radcliffe arrived in the country to partition the destinies of 400 million people. Radcliffe ran his pen across a map of undivided India to carve out the borders of a new Islamic nation called Pakistan, 'the pure land'. Meanwhile, Abdullah finally opted for his Muslim-majority state merging with Hindu-dominated India. His foresight had made him a fierce and often bitter rival of the proponent of the Islamic nation, Mohammad Ali Jinnah. Abdullah wanted Hindus and Muslims to live together in the new Kashmir. Jinnah wanted, and got, Pakistan.

Pakistan was created on 14 August 1947. India gained its freedom the next day. The crown of Kashmir was still perched on the northern frontier. Hari Singh remained undecided, and the kingdom was now seething with anger against him.

Two months later, Hari Singh's complacence was shattered. On 22 October 1947 hundreds of trucks, buses and trailers rolled towards India along the road that was considered the lifeline of Jammu and Kashmir, the Muzaffarabad–Srinagar highway, which brought the Kashmir valley its salt, rations, rice, fuel and key supplies from what later became Pakistan. Riding the more than three hundred trucks and lorries were some five thousand tribal warriors – Mahsuds, Afridis, Wazirs, Swatis, Daurs, Bhittanis and Khattaks – and sections of Hari Singh's royal army, who had switched sides at the last moment believing that Kashmir was going to become part of Pakistan. Hours earlier, the raiders had taken over Muzaffarabad, and the king's soldiers posted there had revolted and killed their commanding officer and several fellow soldiers before joining the raiders.

According to historian H.V. Hodson and other contemporary foreign accounts, the attackers also included 'soldiers of the Pakistan army on leave', who 'were being directed by Pakistani army officers and armed by Pakistani authorities'. Pakistan's government said it had nothing to do with the invasion. Days earlier, the Pakistani authorities had cut off food supplies to Kashmir, transporters were reluctant to carry supplies into Kashmir.

The invaders crossed the Jhelum river, their aim being to conquer Kashmir's capital, Srinagar, and celebrate Eid in the city's grand Jama Masjid on 26 October. Led by Major General Akbar Khan of the Pakistan Army, who used the alias of General Tariq, their plan was that the father of their nation, Mohammad Ali Jinnah, would drive triumphantly into the summer capital of Jammu and Kashmir, which the forces would have conquered and made a part of Pakistan.

Town upon town was crushed under the fury of the invasion. But the tribesmen veered off their schedule, falling prey to carnal pleasures in the towns they had raided. There were reports of widespread rape, loot and arson. Militarily, the raiders won a prize victory. As they pushed forward, the commander of the Kashmir state army, Brigadier Rajendra Singh, who had ordered that several bridges be blown up in an attempt to delay the attack, then personally leaped into battle, and was killed near Uri.

On 24 October, the lights went off in Srinagar. It was not a pre-war blackout; the Pathan raiders had seized the nearest power station at Mahura, only 50 kilometres from Srinagar, and cut off the city's electricity supply. Srinagar seemed set to fall soon – in a matter of hours, it seemed. Almost immediately, the deputy prime minister of Jammu and Kashmir flew out of Srinagar for Delhi, carrying the crucial document that both India and Pakistan had been eyeing for months: Hari Singh's letter of accession. The king had realized that if he prevaricated any further, he would lose what little he had left.

Hours later, hundreds of kilometres to the south in New Delhi, a noisy party was underway at 1 Teen Murti Road, the residence of the then Indian prime minister, Jawaharlal Nehru. It was a cool afternoon on 24 October 1947; the winter chill was just beginning to sweep across Delhi. Waiters in plumed hats and long white tunics walked around the opulent lawns of the mansion, bowing gently as they served the men and women who were going to be independent India's destiny makers. Nehru and Mountbatten were present, along with senior members of India's new cabinet, at a dinner reception for the foreign minister of Siam (now Thailand).

As the guests raised toasts and conversed politely, Nehru walked up to Mountbatten and sombrely pulled him to the side. He had received a piece of intelligence a short while ago. Kashmir was under attack. After months of dithering, Hari Singh had dispatched a letter merging his princely state with India. It was time for New Delhi to step in. However, caught in bureaucratic wrangles, Delhi was not able to take action and send military aid to the embattled king for another three days. Meanwhile, in Kashmir, the raids continued.

Little is known of the rampage in the other towns, including Domel, Pattan and Garhi, but the fall of Baramulla, a key town located 53 kilometres from Srinagar on the Muzaffarabad–Srinagar highway, remains one of the best documented events of what would turn into the first war between the newly independent nations.

It was 26 October, the day that the tribesmen had planned to celebrate Eid in Srinagar. In a story that appeared in *The New York Times* on 10 November 1947, its correspondent, Robert Trumbull, wrote from Baramulla: 'The city had been stripped of its wealth and young women ... Surviving residents estimate that three thousand of their fellow townsmen, including four Europeans and a retired British Army officer, known only as Colonel Dykes, and his pregnant wife, were slain.' When the raiders rushed into the town on 26 October, witnesses said, 'One party of Mahsud tribesmen immediately scaled the walls of the St Joseph Franciscan Convent and stormed the convent hospital and the little church ... the raiders' greed triumphed over their blood lust.'

One woman would live to tell the story of how five thousand Pakistani tribesmen went on a rampage in the small town, raping women, killing and looting residents and draping the roads with dead bodies. Sister Emilia Monlowani, a timid Italian Catholic nun, took refuge in the chapel and survived the massacre. But the images of the attack would haunt her for the rest of her life. Fifty-four years later, at the age of ninety-seven, she would tell the authors how she still spent nights struggling with nightmares about the attackers and of how their faces had become etched on her terrified mind.

'When I am sleeping, he suddenly appears at the window and stares hard. He says: "You have spoilt my name. I won't spare you",' the nun said softly as we sat before her at the convent that had been raided by the armed tribesmen. 'Then I see a big light and I am so scared. He wants to kill me. So I run to the church. They are coming to do their business.' The stocky nun in the grey habit covers her face with her wrinkled hands. Born in Verona, Italy, in 1905, Sister Emilia had taken a ship from France in 1930. The ship, which was crowded with other missionaries, sailed past the Suez Canal and arrived in southern India. Three years later, she went to Kashmir, where she would remain for the rest of her life, learning Urdu, the local language, and Kashmiri culture. For years she had travelled to remote Kashmiri villages on horseback with her mobile clinic, nursing sick children and pregnant women.

Gunshots, war cries and cries of terror rang across the mountain town of Baramulla for three days. Thousands of raiders ran amok, hunting down women, raping them, snatching away their gold ornaments and money, and then killing them. Those trying to escape the attackers leapt into wells to commit suicide. Hundreds of houses along the Jhelum river were set on fire. The town was engulfed in smoke. 'If one woman died, they took another one,' Sister Emilia told us.

Terror-stricken people tore through the streets, chased by the raiders. Most of those killed were Hindus. Many were burned alive. Flames raged for kilometres, razing down hundreds of villages. There were gun battles between Hari Singh's soldiers and the Pakistanis, but the royal army was completely outnumbered and routed.

'They were killing everybody. They were shooting recklessly. They didn't care. They just went thichun-thichun-thichun,' Sister Emilia remembered even five decades later, grimacing and pretending to hold a gun as she mimicked the gunshots. 'They robbed young girls as much as they could. The Pakistanis sent the tribesmen. They paid them to do the job. They started killing only the Hindus. They didn't want the Hindus.' Muslims in the town were asked by the tribesmen to wear a distinguishing green mark on their arms. They were spared.

Then, they went for the most vulnerable targets, the nuns. A group of the Mahsud tribesmen climbed the walls of Sister Emilia's convent and broke into the main building of its hospital. The frenzied men ransacked the hospital. Medicines, equipment and furniture were thrown around. Whatever valuables they found were carried away in sacks. Then the shooting began. The first one to be shot down was a nun who was running towards the hospital gate to help an injured civilian. Three other nuns and a British military doctor identified as Colonel Dykes were the next to fall in the hail of bullets. Dykes had brought his pregnant wife to the convent from faraway Calcutta for her delivery. She was also killed. 'They threw the body of the wife of Colonel Dykes into a well. After a few days, when there was less danger, I went with a servant and he pulled it out,' Sister Emilia recalled. Sister Thereselina was shot in the stomach though she hid behind a pillar. She was dragged to the nearby babies' ward of the hospital, where she bled for eleven hours before she died. A black marble slab with a cross would be placed later in the ward at the spot where she died. Another nun was accosted by an armed tribal who demanded money and gold. He tore away her veil. 'I have no money,' the nun told the tribal. He slapped her brutally across her face. Several of her teeth broke and her mouth was covered in blood.

The tribesmen arranged chairs in a circle in the hospital compound and sat around a fire. A cow was brought and slaughtered, roasted for a short while, and then eaten. The nuns and other missionaries were then lined up outside the building. Sister Lucla Este was among those standing in the line, waiting to be shot. Sister Emilia remembers how, in an unlikely gesture, the other nun smiled. 'I was just thinking how nice it would be to reach Heaven and God … and only for that, I smiled thinking of that,' the nun would write later in a published account. 'Then he saw my gold tooth and pulled me from the line and he tried [to pull it out] … of course, I said I cannot give [it to] you because it is my own tooth,' she wrote. 'Then he pulled his big knife and tried.'

At that point help came from an unlikely quarter. A Pakistan Army officer, who was sympathetic to the nuns because he had studied in a Catholic convent, stepped in. 'These devils are completely out of our hands,' an eyewitness, Father Shanks, an American priest, would quote the officer, Major Sohrab Hayat, as stating later in a written account. The major persuaded the tribesmen to spare the nuns and took them to the babies' ward, where they were guarded by six of his men, who shielded them from the tribesmen keen to plunder the ward, Father Shanks wrote. Almost a hundred other people, including terrified nuns and patients, huddled in the ward, a single candle burning through the night next to the dying nun. They would stay there for twenty days, until they felt safe again. The tribesmen stared from outside, their faces pressed to the window, a sight Sister Emilia would never forget.

Bodies were strewn outside. At night, journalists, including reporters from *The New York Times, The Times* (of London) and *The Observer*, stole into the compound, wrapped in blankets, seeking shelter. The missionaries escaped during the night to the city of Rawalpindi in Pakistan, under protection provided by George Cunningham, the British governor of the frontier province. They remained there for a few months.

The Baramulla massacre would remain one of the worst memories in the Indian subconscious, one of a series of events that would colour the subcontinent's collective memory for five decades even as political leaders tried, and failed, to pursue peace. The carnage and the desecration of the convent would also bring the tribal attack to international prominence at a time when the issue of Kashmir's destiny was at a crucial stage.

Militarily, the three-day delay at Baramulla proved to be a blessing for the Indian forces and a strategic loss for Pakistan. It gave the Indian Army and the Indian Air Force crucial time to take over the air strip at Srinagar and to consolidate their gains in what could otherwise have been a lost battle. If the raiders had not stopped for three days in Baramulla, they would have reached Srinagar in a couple of hours, and a possible capture of the Srinagar airport by the Pakistani raiders could have overturned history.

With the Pakistanis knocking at his door and then forcing themselves in, the vacillating maharaja, Hari Singh, had fled his summer capital of Srinagar and ensconced himself in his winter capital and traditional base, Jammu. He was now resting in the palace and his instructions to his chief aide-de-camp were quite clear – no one was to wake him up. If the government of India sent an emissary to him, it meant that Delhi had agreed to send emergency military help to beat back the invasion, which meant that his worries were over. Even if that did not happen, and the emissary did not come with help, Hari Singh had asked not to be woken up because then all would be over. The ADC was given orders to shoot the king in his sleep in that eventuality.

Luckily for Hari Singh, the emissary from New Delhi was on a plane to Jammu with a promise of help from India. V.P. Menon, a secretary in the Indian government who had been sent to convey the message to the king that day, described the chaotic scene at the palace of the Dogra dynasty, now crumbling after a century of unbridled rule in Jammu and Kashmir: 'On arrival at the palace, I found it in a state of utter turmoil with valuable articles strewn all over the place. The maharaja was asleep; he had left Srinagar the previous evening and had been driving all night. I woke him up and told him of what had taken place at the Defence Committee meeting [in Delhi].'

With the attackers barely eight kilometres from the airfield, on 27 October, Dakotas of the Indian Air Force swooped down on them, dropping bombs. Hari Singh, bowing before popular pressure, appointed an interim government headed by his former arch rival Sheikh Mohammad Abdullah, the man he had put in prison. Abdullah, Kashmir's most popular leader, would later head the province's first popular government as well. The bombing and fighting continued for months after this as the Indian troops tried to flush out the raiders. In May 1948, Pakistan's army formally went to war with India and the confrontation continued through the year. On 1 January 1949, a United Nations-administered truce came into effect in the state and a ceasefire line was established.

The war was over, but guns would boom again. The calm silence of Kashmir's picture-postcard valleys had been broken forever.

3

The soldier's eyes are red because he has been drinking too much rum. Above him, in the strategically located bunker, several giant searchlights have been placed with their backs to each other. Along the barbed-wire fence that surrounds the bunker, empty bottles of Old Monk rum have been placed in pairs; they are meant to alert the sentries by producing a jangling sound if someone tries to cross the wire. Soibug does not register in the widely circulated tourist maps of Kashmir, but at one point of time Soibug was a militant stronghold. In one of the villages in this district was born a man who is wanted in India as badly as Osama bin Laden is wanted in the United States.

It is 2007, a fortnight before India's sixty-first Independence Day, Yasin Malik is in the village of Vatryihel adjoining Soibug. Vatryihel is the one-thousand-and-six-hundredth village that Malik is covering as a part of his campaign, Safar-e-Azadi, his campaign for a free Kashmir. The gun-wielding Malik of yesteryears, who is still the chairman of the Jammu and Kashmir Liberation Front (JKLF), is trying hard to inculcate the image of a non-violent leader, a militant-turned-Gandhian.

Standing atop an open truck, Malik waves at the crowd that has gathered to see him. On one side of the truck is a board bearing the portrait of a man with a moustache and back-brushed hair. Young girls climb in from the rear of the truck with the help of Malik's aides and garland him. Scattered groups of women sing traditional Kashmiri wedding songs. In one corner, two women lament Malik's lean frame. 'This is because of years of torture by Hindustan,' one says to the other.

'In 1988, we realized that there is no space for argument in a non-violent movement. Gandhi was successful because of the genuine political space offered to him by the British,' Malik speaks feebly in his camp, smoking a Gold Flake cigarette.

Budgam district, where Vatryihel is located, is the smallest district in Jammu and Kashmir, home to 6 per cent of its people. Off the road leading to Srinagar's airport, palatial houses fade away, as if they were being manually wiped off to give way to a predominantly rural landscape, with thatched mud houses, vast fields of rice and mustard, slushy, pot-holed roads, and shops selling cheap fabric, plastic shoes and local Kashmiri bread.

In 1987, Budgam was abuzz with news. A local preacher who delivered Koranic sermons had fought the assembly elections against the candidate put up by the ruling party, the National Conference (NC). Mohammed Yusuf Shah was certain of his victory, to the extent that he had been seen visiting one of the most popular sweet shops in Kashmir, Shakti Sweets, to buy sweets for his supporters upon announcement of his victory. Yasin Malik and three of his friends were Shah's polling agents. But, in the elections, alleged to be rigged heavily in favour of the ruling NC, men like Shah stood no chance of winning. His rival was declared the winner from the Amira Kadal constituency. Amira Kadal is one of the seven bridges built over the Jhelum river in Kashmir. Shah and his close supporters, Yasin Malik among them, were arrested, beaten up and imprisoned.

A year later, Malik and his three friends were the first four, after Maqbool Butt, another icon of resistance, to travel across the border for arms training. Yasin Malik was in Class 11 when Maqbool Butt was hanged on 11 February 1984. Four years after Butt's death, guided by Butt's brother, Ghulam Nabi Butt, Malik and his three friends took a taxi to the border district of Kupwara. After a halt of three days, they crossed the border from a place called Rationpora.

We meet Malik in Vatryihel on 31 July 2007. It was, in fact, on the very same day nineteen years ago, that Malik and three of his friends had lobbed two bombs in Srinagar – one at the Central Telegraph Office and the other at the golf course. That day is often seen as the starting point of the now twenty-year-old insurgency in the state.

In 2007, however, Malik has turned into a political leader. In every village, he delivers a small speech, urging people to remain 'awake'. He reads out a list of 'martyrs' from each village: 'Shoolipora village: Bashir Ahmed Dar, Muzammil Ahmed, Inayatullah ...' He invokes the famous Urdu poet, Iqbal, reciting one of his couplets, which talks about a flame struggling against strong winds.

'We requested everyone to lead us, but no one came forward. Then we took the plunge ourselves,' says Javed Mir, who was among the four. The four men came to be known as the HAJY group, an acronym derived from their collective initials. Two of them, Hamid Sheikh and Ashfaq Majid, were killed during the early days of the insurgency. Majid died on 31 March 1990 when a grenade exploded in his hands, killing him instantly. Malik jumped from the fifth floor, trying to evade arrest when the security forces surrounded his hideout. He was seriously injured and the security personnel took him to hospital. There, a few doctors who were sympathetic to the cause of freedom recognized Malik, who had, by then, slipped into a coma.

'Even the BBC said that evening that I was no more,' Malik lets slip a smile recalling the incident. But he survived, with broken limbs. Once he had recovered, he was arrested on 6 August 1990. Two days later, he was shifted to Tihar Jail, where his idol, Maqbool Butt, whose portrait now adorned the side of Malik's truck, had been hanged. Meanwhile, their mentor, Mohammed Yusuf Shah, had crossed over to Pakistan. He emerged as a new man with a new name – Syed Salahuddin, the supreme commander of the Hizb-ul Mujahideen, Kashmir's largest militant group.

Around the same time that Malik is busy running his campaign, a police operation is underway in Soibug. It is a Sunday afternoon when our vehicle halts at Soibug's main bus stop. On a wooden platform outside a small shop, three old men are sharing a hookah, their eyes staring at nothing in particular. Young children, most of them barefoot, stare greedily at cheap toffees in a jar. A man selling bananas on a cart is trying to ward off flies. Soibug is stuck in a time warp. It would seem that nothing has changed here for decades. Someone who visited Soibug thirty years ago might have seen the three old men sitting idly in the same pose, taking deep puffs from a common hookah. But then we remember the red-eyed soldier, the barbed wire and empty bottles dangling from it and the searchlights that we encountered when we entered the town, and we are quickly reminded that we have entered one of the world's most densely militarized zones.

Those who know Soibug also know that at least one inhabitant of this village has changed, too, and changed, in turn, the contours of the insurgency in the Kashmir valley. That man is Mohammed Yusuf Shah now better known by his nom-de-guerre Salahuddin.

'You can't go out – the police has cordoned off the entire area.' A young boy comes rushing into the room where we are sitting with our host, Manzoor, a little later. Police commandoes from the Special Operation Group are looking for a militant who has reportedly returned after receiving arms training in one of the camps across the border. Manzoor lets out a sigh and looks meaningfully at us. 'There are many young men in this village who are missing,' he says.

'I tried looking for Soibug in historical documents and found a twelve-hundred-year-old mention of the place,' Manzoor resumes after a pause, urging us to try the local sesame bread. Manzoor is a research scholar, studying for an MPhil degree at the University of Kashmir. 'We only have a primary health centre here. The nearest hospital is eight kilometres away. We had no tap water till a year ago. It is only last year that a storage tank was built here,' he says.

'This is Salahuddin's village, so the government has never brought about any development here,' says a villager, who has come inside out of curiosity.

Manzoor's father, his forehead bearing the mark of offering prayers five times every day, sits nearby. 'Manzoor always liked to read. He was a good student also, probably the only one in the village who will be awarded a doctoral degree,' the smalltime businessman says of his son with a gleam in his eyes.

'Tell them about Salahuddin's family,' Manzoor interrupts his father.

A day before we fixed a meeting with Manzoor in his village, we had a conversation with a professor of law on the picturesque campus of the University of Kashmir. The professor shared an interesting anecdote with us. A Kashmiri Hindu, forced to leave the valley because of the militancy, met a Kashmiri Muslim in Canada. Both of them recognized each other by their distinctive features and mannerisms and ended up having a friendly chat. Learning that the other man was from Soibug, the Hindu let out a sigh. 'I have so many fond memories of Soibug, where I taught for a while in a government school. I was particularly close to a man called Mohammed Yusuf Shah. In my life, I have not known a more decent person than him. If, once in a while, my wife failed to pack my lunch, he would forcibly take me to his home and feed me,' he said. Heaving another deep sigh, he let out a curse: 'May lightning strike that man called Salahuddin – all that is lost now.'

The Muslim heard this and chuckled. 'I have to tell you something, brother,' he told the Hindu. 'Do you know – and I realize that you don't – that Mohammed Yusuf Shah and Salahuddin are the same person?'

We share this anecdote with Manzoor's father. He looks out of the window. 'Yes, all that is lost now,' he mutters. 'I have known Mohammed Yusuf Shah since he was a boy,' he almost whispers.

Once the search operation in Manzoor's neighbourhood is over, we make our way over a short distance to the house of the supreme commander of the Hizb-ul Mujahideen. Set in a small plot of land, Salahuddin's family's old house is still intact, but now used for storing grains and fodder for the cattle. Salahuddin's family, comprising his wife and five sons, has just come back to live in Soibug after many years. Some construction work is going on in the house. As we sit inside a room, two men come and greet us. One of them is Salahuddin's son. He introduces the other man as Bashir. 'You are lucky. Abba's closest friend is here,' he says, looking at the older man next to him. Both of them are wearing long Pathani shirts and pyjamas. As they sit on the carpet, a young boy appears with tea and biscuits. 'I am sorry we cannot offer you much here,' Salahuddin's son tells us apologetically. 'Actually, all of us are busy with the construction.' He tells us how the Ikhwanis, renegade militants, 'at the behest of the security forces', had attacked them in 1995, destroying their house. 'They forced the neighbours to break even the toilet bowl,' he says.

'Whenever I see this house, I become nostalgic. It is here that I dyed Yusuf sahib's beard for the first time in 1985,' Bashir says. He takes a sip from his cup. 'My family disliked him. My mother used to say sarcastically, "Yusuf is your father?" But I paid no heed because I was very close to Yusuf. I even drove his vehicle. When I came to this house for the first time, it was like any other ordinary village house. I still remember there was dry straw as flooring and the house didn't even have a radio.'

In 1984, a small sticker had caught the attention of intelligence agencies in Kashmir. A few hundred kilometres away from Kashmir,

Maqbool Butt had been hanged in Tihar Jail in West Delhi, and the place where the stickers had been printed was not far from the prison. The stickers showed all of Jammu and Kashmir as an independent nation. Acting on some leads, the police began searching for a teenage boy who had been modelling for a Japanese fashion accessories company in Srinagar.

Meanwhile, another young man already knew what the police merely suspected. Javed Mir had received eight stitches on his head for injuries he had received during a protest demonstration against Maqbool Butt's death sentence in Srinagar's downtown area. Like his father, Mir had acquired a job in the state Public Health Engineering Department. But instead of tending to the sanitation of the city, Javed Nulka, as Mir was nicknamed ('nulka' is tap in Kashmiri), would organize protest marches against the Israeli occupation of the Al-Aqsa mosque in Jerusalem. Mir knew well that after the printed stickers had arrived in Kashmir, they had been hidden in the model's house in Maisuma till they were ready to be distributed all over the valley.

A day or two after the police began their search, the stickers were traced to the Maisuma house. And Yasin Malik, who had modelled for a Japanese company for six months, was arrested for the first time. In the next two decades, he would be arrested over two hundred times. That first time, however, Malik was kept in custody in Sonawar, the Jammu and Kashmir Police's counter-intelligence wing's interrogation centre, codenamed Red16, and interrogated for three months and fifteen days.

By that time the man from Soibug, Mohammed Yusuf Shah, was already an advanced member of the Rukun rank of the Jamaat-e-Islami. The stage of Rukun, as the most loyal members of the Jamaat is called, could be achieved only by those who chose to dedicate their lives to the cause of the organization. A member had to pass the three stages of Mutasir, Hamdard and Umeedwaar to become a Rukun.

Shah possessed a strong, intelligent mind and was, in fact, one of the few men from his village who had actually been to college. It is said that it was in college that he came in touch with Saaduddin Tarabali, the founder of the Jamaat in Kashmir. After completing his BA, Shah went on to study MA in political science from the University of Kashmir. He belonged to a prosperous family. His father, fondly known as Lassa Bab, owned more than 700 square kilometres of land. The family also ran a cloth shop. In his village, Shah was known for his humility and down-to-earth manner. He is also said to have initiated cordial settlements of many disputes among the villagers.

As a child, the elders of Soibug remember Shah climbing a tree and urging his friends to listen to him. Later, as a preacher of the Jamaat ideology, he held regular sermons in a mosque near the exhibition ground in Srinagar. It is said that his sermons were so popular that even top bureaucrats and politicians would come to listen to them.

In 1983, Shah became the poll agent for senior Jamaat leader Syed Ali Shah Geelani. Soon after the assembly elections were over, a number of Jamaat leaders were put behind bars by the reigning government, allegedly for their anti-national activities. His friend and long-time associate, Bashir, remembers being put in prison with Shah. While they were in prison in 1985, Kashmir faced a very harsh winter. The Dal Lake froze completely after many years. Young boys would come in hordes to play cricket on the firm ice. People would try to drive their vehicles on the frozen lake. But even the freezing cold did not deter Yusuf Shah from offering his midnight prayers in prison. 'I would tell Yusuf-sahib to have a bath, but he would refuse; he had a bath only on Fridays,' says Bashir. 'Perhaps Allah was preparing him for the days ahead,' he adds as an afterthought.

After an outrageous incident in Iqbal Park, which involved Kashmiri men sitting naked, waving their genitals at Indira Gandhi when she had come visiting, the central government, then under

Indira Gandhi's prime ministership, had put Kashmir under governor's rule. After Indira Gandhi's assassination, her son, the new prime minister, Rajiv Gandhi, tried to mend fences with Farooq Abdullah the chief minister of Jammu and Kashmir. Srinagar's Iqbal Park witnessed another high-voltage drama as Farooq Abdullah and Rajiv Gandhi joined hands for a new political innings, which saw Abdullah play lead batsman in the 1987 Jammu and Kashmir assembly elections. At this time, the Jamaat created a sort of third front against the NC–Congress combine. It became the leading party under the political umbrella called the Muslim United Front (MUF). The MUF decided to fight the elections and fielded its most charismatic candidates. Yusuf Shah was pitted against NC stalwart Ghulam Mohinuddin Shah. Yasin Malik chose to be Yusuf Shah's polling agent. The MUF was confident of winning a comfortable majority, but it is alleged that blatant rigging swung the poll in favour of the NC. By the evening, Ghulam Mohinuddin Shah's name was announced as the winner on Radio Kashmir. The NC won thirty-nine seats, while its partner, the Congress, bagged twenty-four. The MUF was allowed to win only four seats. But there was more to come. Yusuf Shah and other MUF leaders were picked up directly from the polling booth and imprisoned, although Shah was released right after.

On 18 May 1989, Shah was again picked up from his house under the Jammu and Kashmir Public Safety Act 1978 and released in January 1990. On 6 April 1990, the vice-chancellor of the University of Kashmir, Professor Mushir-ul-Haq, and the general manager of Hindustan Machine Tools, H.L. Khera, were kidnapped and both were later found dead. That morning, Shah left his home, he crossed over to Pakistan on the same day. He later returned to India as one of the key members of the dreaded militant group, Hizb-ul Mujahideen.

The last time Yusuf Shah, alias Syed Salahuddin, was seen in the valley was in 1994, when he attended a marriage. He now handles all the terror activities in Kashmir as the leader of the militant conglomerate United Jehad Council, from the headquarters of the Hizb-ul Mujahideen in Muzaffarabad in Pakistan-occupied-Kashmir.

Kabir Sheikh knows a bit about those times. His son was one of the four that had formed the first band of militant leaders in the valley, the HAJY.

For two decades, the stocky man with the skullcap and a face marked by deep lines of pain has been among the busiest men in Kashmir, for he is a gravedigger. By his own admission, Sheikh has dug graves for some twenty thousand bodies. 'And I am only counting those that came through the police control room.' The twenty thousand included the body of his own son, Hamid Sheikh.

Kabir Sheikh leads us along a narrow lane outside his house to his workplace, Kashmir's first graveyard. He knows the names of all the dead there. He knows how each one died. 'He was sleeping by the roadside, he was seven,' he says, pointing to a small grave and bringing his palms together under his chin in a gesture denoting sleep. 'The security forces started firing on protesters on the street. He died just like that, as he was sleeping.'

There were too many graves to be dug, and not enough space. So a fresh layer of mud was laid on top of the existing graves and another set of graves made over it. But death is not what riles Kabir Sheikh these days. He speaks only of the lack of governance and of his rage against Kashmir's separatist leaders.

'The amount of money New Delhi has spent here in Kashmir – they could have built a new Kashmir,' he says. 'Kashmir had the potential of becoming a prosperous castle, like Lanka of the *Ramayana*. But look at this,' he points at a choked drain outside his house. 'This is supposed to be part of a river.' The people of the neighbourhood gather around him. 'My house is just about a kilometre and a half from the Secretariat,' he says. 'Go to the locality on the airport road and just see the kind of mansions government officials have built. They have built them from the money meant for ordinary Kashmiris. We've got nothing.'

We are sitting in his house in Srinagar's Magarmal Bagh area. Across the road is Hari Singh High Street, where Justice Neelkanth Ganjoo, the Kashmiri Pandit judge who sentenced Maqbool Butt to death, was shot dead twenty years ago. Sheikh remembers each and every detail of those days in the late 1980s. The young men of Magarmal Bagh had realized that Hamid Sheikh had crossed over to Pakistan. They wanted to follow him.

'They would come in hordes, carrying dates and flowers. First they would beg and, when I told them I had no idea how my son had done it, they would grab me by the neck and threaten me,' reminisces Sheikh. His most vivid memory of those times is how Hamid and his men would leave the house after being told of an imminent police raid. 'They would tell me to pour a few buckets of water on the veranda so that the police dogs would not be able to pick up their trail.'

Even today the police raids continue. Although there has been a significant slowdown, militancy still continues to haunt the Kashmir valley. But, increasingly for ordinary Kashmiris, their political destiny has begun to take second place. Many people are beginning to talk about what has long been pushed under the carpet – the issues of governance and the future of ordinary Kashmiris.

Sheikh says there is a government-run middle school in his neighbourhood. 'For around forty-five students, can you imagine, there are twenty-one teachers.' Most of the teachers are the wives of government officials. 'They come in official cars at 11.00 a.m. and leave by 2.00 p.m.'

Yet, as they speak out against the government, many are speaking out against the separatists as well. Outside the house, anger resonates. 'There was a time when Sheikh Mohammad Abdullah would walk on the streets with a stick in his hand and Kashmiris would bow before him, requesting him to touch them with his stick [in benediction],' says a shopkeeper outside Sheikh Abdullah's residence. 'And now,' he says, 'we have leaders like Geelani who ask teachers to teach the children properly and call for a strike the very next day.'

4

'*Hum kya chahte? Azadi!* (What do we want? Freedom!)'

In 1990, this was the slogan that became an anthem for hundreds of thousands of Kashmiris. Two Kashmiris would meet in a ration shop and one would tell the other, 'Inshallah, God willing, our next ration will come from Islamabad.' The conductor of a bus running from Srinagar to the border town of Handwara would shout in Kashmiri, 'Sopore, Handwor, Upore! (Sopore, Handwara, Across [the border]!)' In December 1989, five militants were released in exchange for the daughter of the then union home minister, Mufti Mohammed Sayeed. A jubilant crowd dressed in shrouds appeared in Lal Chowk, shouting pro-freedom and pro-Pakistan slogans. The released militants received a hero's welcome. Alongside, a few farewells were being planned in the weeks ahead.

On the night of 19 January 1990, a small community sat huddled in their houses, fearing for their lives. They were Hindus, known as Kashmiri Pandits, a minority community that had become a symbol for India in Muslim-majority Kashmir. Every night, at around 10.00 p.m., threatening slogans would break the silence. Raised against them from mosques all over the valley, the most prominent slogan was: '*Asi gachhe panunuy Pakistan, batav rostuy batyanin saan.* (We want our Pakistan; without the Pandit men, but with their women.)' Sometimes the slogans would reverberate for weeks, even during the day. It was a traumatic psychological assault on a community that would soon be targeted with guns as well.

This was not the first time the Kashmiri Pandits were facing such violence. In 1986, in Anantnag in south Kashmir, riots triggered against the Pandits saw a number of their houses and temples razed to the ground. Riots would break out on any issue and the target would invariably be the Pandits. Even during the demonstrations against Salman Rushdie's controversial book, *Satanic Verses*, Kashmiri Pandits were the main targets, as they were when Operation Blue Star unfolded in Amritsar's Golden Temple in 1984. There were reports of rape as well.

The Pandits remember how they had been forced to switch off their lights on 15 August when all of India was celebrating Independence Day. They often found the window panes of their houses broken if India won a cricket match against Pakistan. And now, in 1990, in the euphoria of what was viewed as fast-approaching freedom, they were being hunted down again.

Pandit community groups that have listed the names of those who died say some five hundred of their community were killed between 1989 and 1992, some of them mercilessly by people whom they had known for decades. But more chilling than the numbers of the dead was the valley-wide reign of terror that was cascading every day. The so-called Kashmiriyat, the secular fibre of Kashmir, which Mahatma Gandhi had boasted of during the partition in 1947, had been torn apart. Corpses of Kashmiri Pandits would be found with cigarette burns on their body, their eyes and tongues gouged out, and a nail hammered in on the spot on their forehead where they put a tilak. A nurse from the community was gang-raped and then cut alive with a mechanical saw.

The exodus began soon afterwards. Fearing for their lives, some three hundred and fifty thousand Kashmiri Pandits left their homes, many with ovens still warm and food still cooking, and migrated to Jammu and other parts of India. Some were housed in refugee camps set up by the government. In the initial years, many Pandits died due to the harsh weather and the pathetic conditions in the refugee camps. Dozens died of snake bites. Skin diseases were rampant and hundreds fell victim to stress-induced diabetes and depression. Hypertension and heart disease became common. Young, newly married couples were forced to live in small rooms, a mere two and a half metres in length and breadth, with their families, and the simple act of having sex became a luxury. This led to reduced birth rates in the Kashmiri Pandit community.

Those who had unleashed the terror in the valley went unscathed. Until now, there has not been a single conviction for the killings of Kashmiri Pandits, the sole exception being the case involving the murder of the human rights activist, H.N. Wanchoo.

Even a man who admitted openly on television that he had killed scores of Kashmiri Pandits roams free today.

It was October 2006 when the phone rang late one night in a house in Srinagar's Guru Bazaar area. Within two rings, Fatima picked up the receiver. 'Your son is free,' said a police officer from the other end. The next morning, it was celebration time in the locality. By afternoon, Farooq Ahmad Dar, alias Bitta Karate, was home. He was garlanded, and kisses were planted on his forehead. He had been set free after spending sixteen years in prison.

Some 880 kilometres away, a distraught man watched these images beaming on his television set. Ramesh Tikku had waited for justice for years. Sixteen years ago, his brother, Satish, was waylaid and shot dead by Dar outside his home in Srinagar. Satish was Dar's first victim. In the next few months, he would kill many innocent people, most of them Kashmiri Pandits. Some of them were murdered gruesomely in front of their children and the women of their household. In a television interview soon after his arrest, Dar – a martial-arts expert, hence the name 'Bitta Karate' – had confessed to killing twenty people, though many believe the count was twice that. The state government, which for years had issued appeals to the Kashmiri Pandits to return home, had shown no interest in having Bitta Karate convicted, though the case would have been the single largest confidence-boosting exercise for the Pandit community, helping to convince them that they would indeed be safe in the state they called their home.

In 2006, while ordering Bitta Karate to be released on bail, a judge of an anti-terror court had remarked: 'The court is aware of the fact that the allegations levelled against the accused are of a serious nature and carry a punishment of death sentence or life imprisonment, but the fact is that the prosecution has shown total disinterest in arguing the case, which is in complete violation of Article 21 of the Constitution.'

On 6 July 2007 a Kashmiri activist filed an application with the ministry of home affairs under the Right to Information Act 2005, seeking information about Bitta Karate. Among other queries, the application sought answers to the following questions:

a) What is the total number of cases registered against Dar?
b) Is the bail granted to Dar for any specified timeframe or is it indefinite?
c) What action has been taken against the state police for what the designated judge N.D. Wani called 'total disinterest in arguing the case'?
d) Is it true that the designated officer/s (both public prosecutor and police officer) on behalf of the state was/were absent on the day of final hearing of arguments in the case? If so, please explain the reasons for the absence of the designated officer/s in the court on the day of final hearing of arguments in the case?

In a letter dated 20 July 2007, the Kashmir division of the ministry of home affairs wrote six lines in reply: 'The information you have asked for is not available in the Kashmir division of the ministry of home affairs.'

The knock came soon after the 2003 Cricket World Cup final turned one-sided in Australia's favour. It was about 10.30 p.m. when twelve Kashmiri Pandit families in Nadimarg village in south Kashmir's Pulwama district switched off their TV sets, knowing well that India now stood no chance of winning the World Cup. Mohan Bhat had just slipped into the warmth of his quilt when he heard a noise outside, followed by a knock on the door. Sensing danger, he leapt for the door, pressing his body hard against it. But he was overpowered. As the door came crashing down, Bhat jumped out of a window and hung on to a ledge outside. Within seconds, there was gunfire, and Bhat turned numb. His father, mother, sister and uncle did not get a chance to escape.

That night, twenty-four of the thirty Hindus in the village were killed, many of them women and children. 'The terrorists were accompanied by policemen, who guided them towards our houses,' Bhat says.

After waiting on the ledge for a few minutes, Bhat jumped down to the ground below and ran towards a nearby field, where he saw his dead father, his head resting against a chinar tree. Bhat's uncle's head lay in his father's lap. He knew his mother and sister were lying dead inside the house. From a corner of the village, where he was hiding, he saw the terrorists fleeing. 'They heard a child crying and one of them shouted to another in Kashmiri, ordering him to silence it,' Bhat says. There were more gunshots – the command had been obeyed.

Six years later, Mohan Bhat still wakes up in a cold sweat in the dead of the night. After the massacre, he moved to Jammu, where he now works as a laboratory assistant in a government school. Two years ago, he went back to Nadimarg with his wife. 'But I did not enter my house,' he says. Bhat had lost everything that fateful night. 'Still, life has to move on, and that is what I tried to do,' he says.

Yet, his nightmare is still to end. Police parties from Kashmir keep visiting him in Jammu, asking him to identify an arrested foreign militant, Zia Mustafa. 'They threaten me, saying I will have to do it at any cost,' he complains. The police, he says, have occupied his house in Nadimarg, but do not pay him rent despite repeated requests. He is most angry at the words of the then chief minister of Jammu and Kashmir, Mufti Mohammed Sayeed. 'He told me that he would like to see what my "Hindu brethren" would do for me in Jammu,' says Bhat.

A few hours after Bhat's entire family was wiped out, a man from his village was caught selling a piece of his mother's jewellery in the marketplace. 'That piece, which is all that remains of my mother, is still lying in the court's custody,' he says. 'At least, they could give it back to me.'

A time-tested mathematical formula has been proven correct over and over again in Jammu and Kashmir:

stupidity + arrogance = disaster

In a state where continuing militancy has long served the interests of everyone, from security forces to intelligence officials to separatist politicians to armed militants – everyone, that is, except the people of Kashmir – that particular equation would play out with stunning consequences in the summer of 2008. But first, as the same summer set in, Kashmir's mathematics was showing up in a completely different way. Journalists and officials were beginning to use that word most hated in the valley – normalcy.

True enough, things had been changing swiftly. Hordes of tourists – Malaysian, American, Israeli and from within India itself

– were flying in, Kashmir's hotels and houseboats were packed and no bookings were available for weeks. Taxi drivers who once ferried only journalists had no time for them now. The arrival of tourists had long been seen as a simple barometer of how things stood in Kashmir. But this time things were a little different because thousands were flying out as well. Suddenly, every national airline, and even a few regional ones, had started flights out of Srinagar. Srinagar's tiny, once-deserted airport was undergoing renovation on a massive scale because it was being upgraded to an international airport. It wasn't just that more flights were taking off. Ambitions and aspirations were soaring as well. Young men and women were flying out of the valley to seek education and work with a passion they had never shown before. Foreign travel was at an all-time high. Business was booming. And in this churn, questions that had not been asked for years, such as about governance, long been brushed aside with the excuse of militancy, were emerging again.

Hundreds of men marching down Residency Road in the heart of Srinagar, day after day, shouting angry slogans, their fists clenched, had been a clichéd sight in Kashmir. But this time it was not a group of idealistic youth demanding independence. These were teachers employed on a temporary basis, demanding that their jobs be made permanent.

It was a summer of discontent in Kashmir, like many earlier summers, but the colour of discontentment seemed to be changing. People were beginning to ask questions on where the estimated Rs 50,000 crore – US$12 billion – in central government aid sent to the state over two decades, had vanished. They wanted to know why officials had been sleeping on their jobs and using the imagined fear of militant attacks as an excuse to not perform their duties, despite the fall in the frequency of violent incidents.

The story of Kashmir's change could be told most eloquently, perhaps, at the one place that the protesting teachers passed during their march – Lal Chowk, which must surely be among the town centres that have seen the most violence in the world. Lal Chowk is where India's first prime minister, Jawaharlal Nehru, stood alongside the legendary Kashmiri leader Sheikh Mohammad Abdullah and promised the Kashmiris a plebiscite, a promise that thousands of them would remind India of through the 1990s through marches and bombings at the same venue. Over the years Lal Chowk had become the crucible of Kashmiri angst – the clock tower that had been silent for sixteen years, the long stretch of bullet-ridden walls, the splinter marks from grenade attacks on the blue signboard of a radio shop and, not too far from the radio shop, the spot where an unexpected bullet brought down an unsuspecting fisherwoman, who died without a gasp even as the catch she had come to sell spilt over on the concrete. It was also the site of the first military bunker in the valley constructed in the late 1980s.

Some years ago, people stopped getting killed at Lal Chowk. Now, Tamil tourists and British backpackers haggle here with Kashmiri memento-sellers. The soldier frisking the random civilian is less aggressive and less rude. The shopkeepers are doing good business, though their sons and daughters are jobless. The pigeons are back in their dozens at the square. The herbal medicine shop has been shut down, making way for a store selling expensive LCD TVs. The large, old-fashioned clock in the tower has been replaced with a new, digital one.

Ordinary Kashmiris like Ali Mohammed, a veteran taxi driver, look back in disbelief at the summer that the plebiscite was announced. 'There would be traffic jams on Boulevard Road and I would pinch myself looking at them and say, "Allah, is this a reality?"' he says.

There was, however, another reality that was about to play out in this pleasant lull – the hauteur of the Indian policymakers and the directionless stubbornness of the Kashmiri separatists.

There had been few hand-grenade attacks or ambushes in Kashmir in some time, and the then home minister, Shivraj Patil, and the national security advisor, Mayankote Kelath Narayanan, took the tentative peace that had descended over the state for granted.

In Srinagar, the Jammu and Kashmir government had decided to transfer almost half a square kilometre of forest land to the Sri Amarnathji Shrine Board, which helps organize the pilgrimage of thousands of Hindus every year to a Himalayan cave where Lord Shiva is believed to reside. The land was to be used to set up temporary shelters for the pilgrims.

It was a whimsical act. The land had been used for decades for the same purpose and the transfer of ownership was not necessary or done for any practical reason. But the Congress-led UPA government in New Delhi, its nominee who headed the Amarnath Trust, the governor of Jammu and Kashmir, Srinivas Kumar Sinha, and the Congress-led Ghulam Nabi Azad government in the state all assumed that there would be no repercussions. No Hindu organization had ever asked for the land to be transferred. For as long as any Kashmiri could remember, pilgrims from all over India would come to Kashmir and travel to the Amarnath caves unharmed. Even when militancy was at its peak, the Amarnath Yatra had never been stalled and Hindu pilgrims had continued to enjoy the hospitality of Kashmiri Muslims. The pilgrims, as a senior police officer who has supervised the security arrangements for the Amarnath Yatra for many years told us, had been using large stretches of land along the Yatra route, where both temporary and permanent structures existed. No one had ever raised an objection.

But the other half of the story was to come from Kashmir itself. After the decision to transfer the land was taken by the state cabinet, which included ministers from former chief minister Mufti Mohammed Sayeed's People's Democratic Party, the same party went to town screaming that the land transfer was a great attack on the special status of Kashmir as laid down under the Constitution of India and that it was an assault on Kashmir's rights.

With that, the time-tested mathematical formula came into play. Jammu and Kashmir burned for weeks, having suddenly become Jammu versus Kashmir. First, thousands of protestors in Kashmir held the region under their control, throwing stones, burning vehicles, waving Pakistani flags, forcing the security forces to watch silently, and finally pressuring the government to revoke the land transfer. Then, thousands of Hindu youth retaliated in Jammu with protests of their own, defying curfew and indulging in arson, rioting and stone-throwing. In all, fifty-six people ended up dead on both sides of the divide. The crisis was unnecessary, a combination of a series of mistakes and naivety by New Delhi and Srinagar.

In Srinagar, a man long revered by Kalashnikov-wielding fighters, was struck once again by chest pain.

As he woke up as usual before sunrise, Syed Ali Shah Geelani took his cup of tea to the front lawn of his residence, which stands on the road leading to the Srinagar airport. The doctors had advised the patriarch to get his pacemaker replaced and he should have travelled to Delhi for the procedure, but right now he had no time. Right now, he was busying contemplating recent events that had shaken Kashmir.

Five years ago, in 2003, Geelani's party had split. Two years later, the moderate faction of the Hurriyat Conference, led by the young Mirwaiz, had chosen to open negotiations with New Delhi. The talks had eroded Geelani's authority. Even the Jamaat-e-Islami, a party which he had led for many years, had not been according him much importance.

Around the time that the Amarnath land controversy broke, Geelani had been detained in order to prevent him from travelling to Amritsar, where he was invited by Sikh radicals to speak on the twenty-fourth anniversary of Operation Blue Star, the 1984 military operation ordered by the then prime minister, Indira Gandhi, to flush out militants holed up in the Golden Temple, the holiest of shrines of the Sikh community.

Geelani had had to skip his meeting with fellow radicals, but the arrest had truly been a godsend. For a pro-Pakistan icon, now increasingly out of fashion in Kashmir, it was an opportunity that had fallen into his lap like the proverbial apple. Within a fortnight, Geelani's influence rose so much that on 19 June 2008, the moderate faction of the Hurriyat announced that it had set up a committee for the unification of the party, which would come up with a joint action plan on the land transfer issue.

On 24 June, Feroze Ahmed, a thirty-five-year-old bus conductor, became the first victim of firing by the security forces, aimed at quelling the protests. Hundreds of men, women and children came out on the streets in defiance of the curfew. The situation was so tense that many Kashmiris believed it to be worse than in 1990, when pro-freedom sentiments had been at their zenith in the state. The fresh lease of protests by ordinary Kashmiris took even the separatist leaders by surprise. 'Till just a few weeks ago, these leaders had lost their hopes of reviving the so-called movement,' said a senior Kashmiri journalist. 'I remember that a senior leader stood at Lal Chowk to make a speech. People would look, wait for a moment, and then turn back to their work. No one listened to his speech.' Following the agitation on the transfer of land, however, large groups of Kashmiris hit the streets shouting pro-Pakistan slogans. 'The separatist leaders couldn't hide their glee,' said the journalist.

During one of the protest gatherings, Geelani climbed on to a stage and addressed the people. 'Do you accept me as your leader?' he roared into the microphone. Thousands of hands went up in acquiescence. The response of the people was so resounding that many leaders did not know what to do, how to lead, or where to steer the course of the agitation.

'I mean, calls for bandhs and hartals are fine, but what do you do when thousands of angry and restless youth accost you and ask you for guidance? What do you do?' said a senior police officer. 'At least a couple of separatist leaders requested us to put them under arrest since they didn't know how to channel the anger.'

Tempers ran high across the state. The smallest of incidents sparked extreme reactions. A man had parked his car outside Srinagar's Residency Hotel and gone across the road to meet a local businessman. Five minutes later, when he came out he discovered that the traffic police was preparing to tow away his car with a crane. He rushed back and requested the policemen to fine him on the spot, instead of taking his car away. 'I told them that towing it would damage the car and that they were free to challan me on the spot,' the man said later. But the policemen wouldn't budge. 'You can collect your car from SP sahib's office,' they told him. He put his foot down. Meanwhile, a crowd of shopkeepers and curious onlookers had gathered, and all hell broke loose. The crowd started shouting slogans against the police. 'Why do you harass Kashmiris? Do you have the guts to say something to a CRPF man who parks his vehicle in the middle of the road?' they asked the policemen. 'Let freedom come, we will take you to task,' someone else shouted. Sensing the belligerent mood, the policemen slipped away.

In the late 1980s, civil administration had virtually collapsed in Kashmir. The militants were openly defying the state and the state police had just not been equipped to handle militancy. In some cases, the police were even seen as being sympathetic to the militants' cause. This continued till the mid-1990s, when the police infrastructure was in absolute shambles. However, the situation changed over a period of time until, towards the beginning of 2002, the Jammu and Kashmir Police was at the forefront of counter-insurgency operations, so much so that within a couple of years Budgam, the hotspot of militancy and a Hizb-ul Mujahideen stronghold, had become the first militant-free district.

Now, the Amarnath controversy and the violence that erupted were threatening to bring an end to whatever had been achieved so far. 'Years of hard work has gone down the drain,' rued Aashiq Bukhari, the police officer credited with transforming Budgam.

With no directions from New Delhi, the Amarnath agitation took the security forces in Kashmir by surprise. They decided to clamp down heavily on any anti-India sentiment. Of course, in places where the crowds swelled up to almost half a million, they thought it best to watch silently as angry Kashmiris threw themselves on the bunkers occupied by the soldiers, tearing the structures apart in a rage. But when the soldiers got their way, innocent Kashmiris had to bear the brunt.

In Srinagar's Dalgate area, a small, shabby neighbourhood along the picturesque Dal Lake, hidden behind shops selling dry fruits and handicrafts, thirty-five-year-old Mohammed Yaqub Jan lies on a bed with a urine bag dangling on one side. His neck is covered with thick wads of bandage, a blood stain faintly visible on it. Nine days after Prime Minister Manmohan Singh expressed concern over what he euphemistically referred to as 'recent incidents in the state of Jammu and Kashmir' during his speech on Independence Day that year, Yaqub had stepped out of his home. Though curfew still prevailed all over the Kashmir valley, college students, medical representatives, shopkeepers and drivers would assemble in small and large groups on the roads and fight pitched battles with the security forces.

It was about 5.00 p.m. when Yaqub's mother told him there was no milk at home to make sheer chai, the pink salty tea that is a must in every Kashmiri home. Yaqub was not worried. CRPF soldiers from the nearby camp stood guard outside. Some of them frequented his provision store, and he had offered them tea several times. He stepped out on to the street, an aluminium vessel in his hand. As he had expected, two soldiers were standing at the corner of the street, a few metres away from the entrance to his home. He knew them. 'Milk,' he said, pointing to the vessel. 'Go, but come back fast,' one soldier said. Yaqub was on his way back in ten minutes, the vessel full of milk in his right hand. At the entrance to the road leading to his house, he noticed that the two soldiers on duty earlier were not at their posts. Three other soldiers had taken over. Yaqub didn't know them. Before he could say anything, the soldiers started beating him up.

Inside his house, Yaqub's father, Ghulam Qadir Hajjam, a barber by profession was waiting for his son when he heard anguished cries. 'Come, I think Yaqub is in trouble,' he told his other son. Together, they came out. Yaqub's brother tried to reason with the soldiers. 'Please spare him,' he begged. And then, as their neighbours watched from gaps in their heavily curtained windows, the soldiers fired four bullets. One of them hit Yaqub's father in the chest. He died on the spot. Two bullets hit Yaqub, one narrowly missing his wind pipe. While he was in hospital, his family didn't tell Yaqub that his father was dead.

'Have some tea,' one of Yaqub's uncles insists when we visit his home. In the background, Yaqub writhes in pain every now and then. 'Tell me, if Yaqub or his brother turn into a militant tomorrow, whose fault would it be?' asks his cousin angrily.

Such incidents have angered the Kashmiris even more and isolated them further. With every such incident, anti-India sentiment in the state has grown stronger.

In Nawhatta, where the first protester fell to CRPF bullets, the maze of lanes and by-lanes has come to be known as Kashmir's Gaza Strip. Here, young Kashmiris battle it out daily, throwing stones at a CRPF contingent and the state police. For decades, anyone who was a non-Kashmiri was dubbed as a Punjabi by the average Kashmiri, but the two-decade-old insurgency has changed that. Now, an outsider, more so if he was in uniform, was a Bihari. In a by-lane in

Nawhatta, a young boy throws a stone at an armoured vehicle of the CRPF and shouts, 'Bihari, Bhelpuri.' He also shouts what he would like to do to the sisters and mothers of the men inside the vehicle. The CRPF soldiers do not react, but their fingers are firmly placed on the triggers of their Kalashnikov rifles.

After moving to a safe zone, the soldiers come out of their vehicle. One of them is puffing nervously at a Wills Navy Cut cigarette that has turned limp with sweat. 'We don't know what to do,' the soldier says, 'the other day they threw shit over us from a house.' In many localities, a truckload of stones arrive, paid for with contributions from every household. Families then share out the stones in their courtyards and break up the large stones for use the next day.

In the two decades of violence in the state, about ten thousand people have gone missing. Drivers, labourers, shopkeepers – almost all of them ordinary people. Some of them were picked up by security forces and never seen again. Some others are believed to have crossed the border. They are possibly stuck in Pakistan-occupied-Kashmir, or lie in unmarked graves near border towns like Uri, shot dead by security forces while trying to cross over.

In a state which has more than half a million pairs of combat boots on the ground, words like 'crackdown' and 'crossfire' have become part of the daily lexicon. There has never been so much rush in psychiatry departments across the state's hospitals as there is now. A young boy committed suicide because his father refused to buy him a mobile phone. Ironically, there is no mobile network coverage in his village. A girl had a tiff with her boyfriend and, when he turned away, she jumped off the Badshah Bridge into the waters of the Jhelum river. Another girl from Srinagar's Women's College wrote a letter to the editor of a prominent local daily about the bridge the administration had built near the college. It will not serve any purpose other than enabling love-struck Romeos to commit suicide by jumping from there, she wrote.

At a cafeteria called Escape outside Srinagar's Press Lane, where journalists generally take refuge after covering incidents of stone-pelting and the consequent firing, a young photographer's mobile phone has stopped working. 'Have you seen Mirwaiz?' he says dreamily, referring to Mirwaiz Umar Farooq, Kashmir's topmost Islamic cleric. 'He has an iPhone.' This sparks off another round of discussions on the prevailing situation. His friend, an aspiring journalist who holds a wad of resumés in his hand, takes a long gulp of scalding tea and mutters: 'Why is it that only people from poor families die in police firing?'

5

When they brought him in through the huge iron gates of the graveyard, thirty-seven-year-old carpenter Abdul Rehman Padder had six fingers on one hand and no face on the right side. He wore two pairs of socks and two trousers, one over the other, to fight off the cold. But the layers of clothing would not be of any help now – he was stone-cold already. The carpenter had been killed by the police after being branded as a Pakistani terrorist. The graveyard in Sumbal town, not too far from Srinagar, is where foreign militants – Pakistanis and Afghans – are usually buried.

Kashmir's crippling unemployment had zigzagged through the lives of both Padder and the man who lowered him into the grave, thirty-year-old Mushtaq Ahmed Baba. Both wanted desperately to be police officers, but that required them to pay a bribe. Unemployment is rampant in Kashmir, and the seventy-nine-thousand-strong police force is probably the largest employer in the state. Baba did not have the money to pay off the police personnel who claimed they could help get people recruited in the force. 'I was qualified. They did not hire me. I went for the interviews so many times,' said Baba, who was studying science at Srinagar's government college when militancy raged in the state. 'The other applicants told me, "Why are you wasting your time if you don't have money to give?"' There are just no jobs here. That was one of the reasons why the militancy started,' Baba said, looking at the rows of graves. 'I could not do much for myself. So I started doing this – digging graves.'

Padder, on the other hand, was able to arrange for the money and, his family alleges, paid his tall, lanky policeman cousin Farrukh Ahmed Padder Rs 75,000 to be passed onward in the quest for a job with the police. Farrukh worked for the dreaded Special Operations Group, the police wing often accused of having made extrajudicial killings their USP. A year went by. The job did not materialize. Abdul Rehman kept asking his cousin to get him the job or return the money. Finally, one day, Farrukh – now under trial – allegedly summoned him. Rehman was last seen at the Batmaloo bus station in Srinagar.

A few days later the police found a bullet-ridden body and buried it, identifying it as that of Abu Hafiz, a Pakistani militant. They said they knew his name because a diary had been found on him. But, unknown to the police officers, a missing report filed by Padder's family led to his mobile SIM card, still in use, being traced – and thereon to his alleged killers. The body was exhumed forty-five days after it was buried and a DNA test revealed it to belong, not to a Pakistani terrorist, but to a young, jobless Kashmiri carpenter.

In November 2008, a year after Padder's death jolted the region, we return to Sumbal. It is a day after the state elections, in which the Kashmiris have stunned everyone, including themselves, by turning up to vote in overwhelmingly large numbers, despite the boycott call by separatists and just a few months after unprecedented anti-India protests had shut down the Kashmir valley for weeks.

We meet another gravedigger who helped Baba bury Padder, Manzoor Ahmed, who has not studied beyond twelfth grade. 'Many people who were boycotting the elections themselves went to vote,' Ahmed said angrily. 'I just don't know what to say. They must have been paid off by the candidates.'

A few metres away from the graveyard gate, forty-five-year-old kerosene oil dealer, Ali Mohammed, is also furious, but for a different reason. 'I am tired of these boycotts. I get nothing from the boycotts. These people go on strikes, what is the use? The same people demanding the boycott then got on top of buses and went around asking for votes,' he says. 'If a government is made, we will gain from it, won't we? We want peace.' Ali Mohammed's twenty-six-year-old son, Shakil Ahmed, however, was among those who had boycotted the elections.

And azadi, freedom? 'Azadi is a separate equation,' Ali Mohammed says, matter-of-factly.

Abdul Ghani Mir, a seventy-two-year-old gravedigger, knows the changing equations well. He wants freedom for Kashmir, but he left home early on voting day to line up at the polling booth a few hundred metres away at the local school. He said he voted for the National Conference because his father was a die-hard supporter of the late Sheikh Abdullah. 'My father had the fortune of meeting the Sheikh once and promised him that our family would always vote for his party,' Mir says animatedly, standing in his *pheran* on the same road that was choked a year ago with furious protesters when the case of the extrajudicial killing of the dead carpenter was unravelled.

Not too far from Sumbal village, in a neighbourhood called Wah, slush and black filth lines the roads. The women of Wah abandoned their husbands temporarily at 8.00 a.m. on election day and went in groups to vote, even though many of their husbands stayed indoors. The women knew what they wanted. It was a sign that the voices of ordinary Kashmiris were emerging after two decades, asking for the basic things that they had not been able to ask for earlier.

When we reached Wah, the neighbourhood had virtually not had electricity for ten days. Taps spewed water for only a few hours in a day. A strong stench rose from the overfull sewers and the mounds of sewage lining the cobbled road. Six white ducks ambled by, their wings blackened in places from grazing past the filth.

'Look here, look at this road,' sixty-year-old Asha Begum said in rapid-fire Kashmiri, through an interpreter, as she tapped one of us on the chest. 'We are part of the town, but we clean this road ourselves. We voted to change that.' Slowly, people stepped out of their homes. Many surrounded us. 'Can you write about the dogs please? They are catching dogs in Srinagar and releasing them here. I want the new MLA to look into this,' said twenty-six-year-old Jahangir Rashid, a long-distance sociology student, who had also voted the day before. The loudest woman of the neighbourhood stepped out with her daughter. 'My daughter is a graduate – she is unemployed. I thought if I vote, she might get a job some day,' said Rahat Begum, who estimated her own age to be around seventy. Standing beside her, her daughter, Afroza, blushed.

At the edge of the town, outside a roadside tea shop, sixty-year-old Mukhtyar Sheikh frowned. 'I did not send my two sons for the processions. You just have to throw stones,' said Sheikh, a woodcutter whose sons, twenty and twenty-five years old, help him at work. 'What use are these [separatist] strikes? If I am able to use my hands to cut wood, I will eat. If I don't, what will I eat?' he said, soaking in the sun as he sipped his tea.

The angry women and teenage girls of Nunner village, eyes flaring, cheeks flushed and fists clenched, are not seeking votes outside Ganderbal town on this nippy November morning. In the village, which is just 30 kilometres north of Srinagar, they have decided to take things into their own hands. They are looking for the men and women who have been coming to seek their votes.

With headscarves wrapped tightly around their heads like bandanas to protect them against the cold, some with infants in their arms and others with their daughters clinging to them, the women have choked traffic on the road that is optimistically called the National Highway, a key artery connecting the Kashmir valley to the cold desert of Ladakh. They have dragged out part of a massive tree trunk, bamboo poles, metal sheets and other junk and laid them across the tarred road as a barricade.

The road is lined with grocery shops, a butcher's shop and two photo studios promising posed portraits before a cloth backdrop of the Gulmarg valley and the best and cheapest postcard-size pictures for job applications. A traffic jam extends for kilometres on both sides. Hundreds of vehicles have been held up for hours. The women are doing what many Kashmiris are beginning to do for the first time – asking their government tough questions.

Hundreds of people – including the women's husbands – watch from the windows of their homes along the road. The women stand in their *pherans* behind the barricade they have created. In a shrill, uneven chorus, they scream a slogan that has echoed every other day in the Kashmir valley for twenty years: '*Hum kya chahte hai?* What do we want?' It's the catchline of Kashmir's rebellion. Even a three-year-old knows how to respond: '*Azadi!* Freedom!'

But the protesting women shout a different reply: 'Transformer!' The crowd looks on in amazement.

'*Hum kya chahte hai?* Transformer! *Hum kya chahte hai?* Transformer!' Others join in.

In a land with no patience for dissent, patience is being tested. A small posse of policemen with guns and tear-gas shells watches in silence. The long lines of waiting vehicles include several military vehicles with soldiers on the edge; they know the drill to make such pinpricks of protest evaporate in minutes. The tension is rising. What will it be? A swing of a baton? A shove into the side streets? A bullet?

The slogans continue. '*Hum kya chahte hai?* Transformer!'

This is truly the new face of Kashmir. It is a moment not often experienced in this troubled region. While the Kashmiris themselves frequently stage political protests demanding freedom, few have raised questions of governance in the past. In earlier times, groups of women – from Nunner village, or anywhere else – would never have dared to come out on the streets, defying their men and the police, to ask for something as basic and crucial to their lives as better electric supply.

'We need hot water in the winters. We need electricity so that our children can study. We want to watch TV,' says thirty-two-year-old Haseena Bano, wearing a *pheran*, a scarf wrapped around her head.

'Don't you need *azadi*?' a bystander – a man – says, teasing her.

'We don't need *azadi-vazadi*, we need a transformer,' she snaps.

'There is no power, so I can't see what I am writing and I do my homework all wrong. Then I make mistakes and my teacher beats me,' says eight-year-old Iqra Sultan, a frown creasing her face.

'I can't watch films. And I have to study with a candle,' says fourteen-year-old Razia Sultan.

'I can't watch TV serials,' says homemaker Fehmida Bano.

The policemen pace anxiously. This is unprecedented. The women will just not disperse. They have skipped breakfast. They have refused lunch. They have been raising slogans for more than three hours.

It didn't have to be like this. Kashmir, crisscrossed by raging rivers, is an ideal production centre for hydro-electricity. Its waters, experts say, could generate 25,000 megawatts of electricity. Of this, 20,000 megawatts can be generated on running water, as the Indus Water Treaty between India and Pakistan imposes limits on Kashmir's river water storage. It is believed that the state incurs a loss of Rs 6,000 crore annually because it cannot use its waters for irrigation or power generation.

'Hydro-electricity is the oil of the Kashmir valley,' says Mubeen Shah, president of the Kashmir Chamber of Commerce and Industries.

'Just imagine the kind of revenue we could have generated if we built dams on our rivers. But India signed the treaty with Pakistan without taking the Kashmiris into confidence,' says Shakeel Qalander, who heads the Federation of Industries in Kashmir.

Even with those restrictions, the water in Kashmir can generate around 6,000 megawatts of power in ten years. But that, experts say, requires an investment of Rs 50,000 crore. The state currently requires 2,000 megawatts of electricity, but gets only 600 megawatts during the peak period. As a result, it imports power worth Rs 1,600 crore each year. Everything is tied up in sloth. The National Hydroelectric Power Corporation Limited (NHPCL) took decades to build power projects in the state and is only able to generate 1,600 megawatts of electricity even now. One of the power projects, the Dul Hasti project, was scheduled to be finished in five years, but took twenty-three years. 'They used all our natural resources and yet, during peak time, we have to buy electricity from the Northern Grid at an exorbitant rate,' says Qalander.

The anger is spilling over now, and so are the questions. 'What all do we tell you? We get mud in our water. Our children drink it and get jaundice. The health centre is far away and the doctor comes one day and sits at home for four days,' says Sultana Bano. 'There is no power supply. The lineman is always busy flirting,' she says, as the other women in the group giggle.

A wireless set crackles. Reinforcements have been called in. 'Sir, why confront them? It will get worse,' a subordinate tells Superintendent of Police Shahid Khursheed, the officer handling the situation.

Khursheed walks up to the women. 'You are like my mothers and sisters. I am one of you,' Khursheed says. 'I have been watching patiently for hours, you must disperse now.'

The response is totally unexpected. His voice is drowned by the cackle of a dozen angry women, all pointing their fingers at him and talking at the same time.

'Please, we do not want to use any force. You must understand,' Khursheed says. Two policemen with boxes of menacing tear-gas shells walk up nonchalantly, as if offering a glimpse of what could come. After about ten minutes, an agreement has been reached. 'I swear on Allah the Almighty, you will have the transformer by 5.00 p.m. today,' the officer says.

The women begin to remove the blockade, but forty-year-old Fehmida Bano won't go home without laying down the terms. 'If we do not get our transformer, we will beat up the police next.'

In the small town of Hiranagar in the Jammu region, not too far from the Pakistan border, one of the faces of the disastrous consequences of callousness and neglect was about to emerge from a small home hidden in a narrow alley. Balwant Khajuria, a sixty-five-year-old, silver-haired Ayurvedic doctor, had decided to kill himself.

Outside his home, hundreds of people had been on a twenty-four-hour vigil for days, raising angry slogans and storming the nearby highway to stop trucks. The crowds huddled together, often going without food, their throats hoarse from shrieking angry slogans, displaying a rage that had stunned Kashmiris across the Banihal tunnel, and the rest of India. Curfew would run for two months in the region. Hundreds had courted arrest, including mothers hugging infants. It was a rage that had been simmering for years, stoked by feelings of perceived discrimination of the central and state governments against Jammu, as compared to Kashmir. Further north, hundreds of people had choked the streets of Srinagar. It was 14 August, Pakistan's independence day, and what was unfolding would have seemed unimaginable even a week ago. The protesters were waving Pakistani flags.

In Hiranagar that morning, Khajuria walked out of his home and slunk into the crowd, carrying a folded piece of paper in his pocket. It was a blank letterhead with his qualifications on it. As the crowd outside his house buzzed, discussing the news of the day, Khajuria sat in a corner, writing out a suicide note. Then he folded the paper again and put it back in his pocket, walked unnoticed to a public tap nearby, took out a packet from another pocket and gulped down insecticide tablets. No one noticed him. He went back to where he had been sitting, began shouting slogans with the others and, in a few minutes, collapsed in a heap. The suicide note he had written asked people to oppose the government and 'keep the faith'.

Khajuria had always been an emotional man, but he was not the kind of person who would let his sentiments drive him over the edge. Yet, his anger over the lack of economic opportunities and the uncertain future of his children had proved to be too much. His son, thirty-six-year-old Vivek Khajuria had graduated in agriculture eleven years ago because it was then considered an easy means of getting a job in the state. But he had been jobless since then and he blamed the government's alleged pampering of Kashmir over Jammu for his plight. For the first time in as long as anyone could remember, the citizens of Jammu were raising questions about governance. 'He [Balwant Khajuria] believed that Hindus are minorities in Kashmir and that they are ignored,' said Vivek. 'Employment opportunities go to Kashmiris. If you are against India, you are pampered. If you say "India Zindabad", you are taken for granted.'

Not too far from where Khajuria collapsed, dozens of men sat on a wide sidewalk between a street and a park on a winter afternoon, some wearing khaki clothes, some in their traditional turbans, some holding bamboo truncheons. These were village guards. Alongside them, standing against the blackened stone wall of a shop closed during the protest, was a banner in red announcing the name of their organization, All J&K Low-Paid Government Employees Federation. Their thickly moustached president, seventy-six-year-old Abdul Majeed Khan, stepped aside after announcing to the gathering, 'I will return after giving an interview to a journalist from Delhi.'

The state had committed itself to implementing higher wage levels for the people as mandated by India's Sixth Pay Commission, which had revised government salaries, Khan told us as the protest went into pause mode and everyone looked on. 'But they haven't done it. If you cannot stop inflation, at least raise the wages according to the price hikes. Most of us are village guards. Eighty per cent of our population is in the villages, and they have a critical job. They work for every department but get nothing. Like, when elections are held, all government staff get an allowance except the village guards.'

'Haryana and West Bengal have regularized their village guards. Why shouldn't we?' Khan thundered. 'Every employee should get wages to maintain [their intake of] 2,700 calories a day as laid down under government rules.'

These are the new voices in Kashmir, talking about calories where only Kalashnikovs were the subject of discourse before.

Decades after history visited it, we return to Baramulla. We are at the century-old school, which had faced the ire of marauding tribesmen in 1947.

If, at the time, St Joseph's School was a reflection of Kashmir of then, it is now a reflection of the Kashmir of today – of a people who have not lost touch with their hopes and dreams even in the midst of despair. In Baramulla town, which was once the hub of militancy, down the picturesque highway lined with poplar trees, change is evident. The school's classrooms could compare with the best in the country. Satellite-connected television screens beam lessons to Kashmiri students from professors sitting in Chennai. Students prepare for engineering and medical entrance exams on their LCD screens.

There was a time when students would come to the St Joseph's residency to study from as far away as Rawalpindi, which is now in Pakistan. When the insurgency was at its peak in the state, it was the only school functioning in Baramulla. 'There was always trouble. There was shooting. We didn't know what would happen,' says Sister Rosa, the oldest employee in the school. She had left her home in Kerala's Thrissur district in 1955 to come to Kashmir. Back then, her work included travelling on horseback to faraway villages across the Jhelum as part of the mission's humanitarian programmes. 'Many times, when we were in the market they would start to fire. Earlier, I wasn't scared of dying, but then, suddenly, I was,' she says.

More than twenty-five hundred students come to the school now, walking from mountaintop villages as far as 40 kilometres away. Over the past two decades, in keeping with the churn of the times, several students became militants, while others became engineers, police officers and computer scientists.

'Students do not have much exposure or opportunity to learn. Most leave the valley for medical and engineering studies,' says Father Chacko, the vice-principal of the school, as he offers us tea in quarters on the school campus, the afternoon sunlight filtering in and lighting up the bowl of fruit at the centre of the dining table. 'But the students are becoming more competitive now. They are going out. They are becoming aware of the world outside.'

'We are all studying very hard for the IIT [Indian Institute of Technology] exam ... Other students go for a Bachelor's degree in computer applications or an MBBS,' says Adil Mehraj Wani, eighteen, a twelfth-standard student at St Joseph's.

Today, the children are dreaming bigger, but outside the school, across the state, there are no colleges, no centres of higher learning. The various governments have largely ignored the dreams and aspirations of the students of Jammu and Kashmir. In 1989–90, when the insurgency began, the state had thirty-two colleges. Despite the urgent need to channel the frustration of the youth towards career choices, only six colleges were set up in the next two decades. The total now stands at thirty-eight. This is despite the overwhelming number of students who want to pursue advanced degrees. The number of college students has increased from twenty-one thousand and two hundred, when the insurgency began, to some seventy-three thousand now. No new colleges have been established for special education, and four of the fifteen colleges for professional education that were running in 1989 have actually been shut down. Incredible, when you consider that educational institutions in general have not been known to be a direct target of militants.

Worse, many of the newly established colleges are not really worthy of the name. They are located in rented buildings, sometimes in tin sheds or in government offices. Several establishments are still home to the security forces. Students attend classes on campuses studded with security tents, walk past soldiers to go to the bathrooms, and are frisked every morning as they head to the water taps.

These conditions had prevailed for far too long at a girls' school in Bomai, a village with a population of fifteen thousand in Baramulla district, when the villagers finally decided that they had had enough. But two young men would have to lose their lives for public rage to take the shape of a Gandhian campaign.

High-school teacher Mohammed Sultan, a post-graduate in mathematics, wasn't feeling too well on the evening of 21 February 2009. A friend was urging him to drink some salty tea, a staple in Kashmir, when the phone rang and someone on the other end conveyed the news that Sultan's brother had been shot at.

Apparently, a scuffle had erupted between two groups of youths at a local festival. When soldiers approached one of the groups, then on their way back from the festival, they thought that they were being blocked by their rival gang. Instead of stopping, they began to run away, and the soldiers fired. Sultan's brother, Mohammed Amin Tantray, twenty-three, and his friend Javid Ahmed, twenty, died of bullet injuries. Another student, Nazir Ahmed, was seriously injured. The locals called it cold-blooded murder. A senior police source said it was a 'genuine mistake'.

Sultan rushed to the site and took his bleeding brother to the hospital, where he was declared dead on arrival. 'I still can't believe that he is gone. With his death, my father's backbone has been broken,' Sultan said. Sultan's father sat next to him, silently shedding tears over the loss of his youngest son.

The tragic incident has a remarkable fallout. The villagers began a Gandhian protest, refusing to be swayed by separatist politicians as is the normal drill in Kashmir. They won a decisive battle against the army, the first such example in the twenty-year-long insurgency. It was far bigger than just anger over the deaths. The army camp to which the soldiers had fled to take cover after the firing had been an eyesore for many years. The soldiers had erected bunkers along the boundary wall of the school where Sultan taught. They had made holes in the wall, to instal exhaust pipes, which blew smoke into the classrooms. Sumayya, a student, recalls that some of the soldiers would shine mirrors at the girls and even make obscene gestures at them. Eventually, the villagers decided that enough was enough.

That very night, the residents of Bomai formed a coordination committee to begin an agitation. 'We were very clear that we wouldn't allow any separatist leader to hijack our issue,' says Hakimul Rahman Sultani, the head of the people's committee. The villagers launched a peaceful movement, threatening at one time to vacate the entire village en masse if the army camp was not removed. There was not a single incident of violence during the agitation, which lasted thirteen days.

Ultimately, the authorities were compelled to bow down before the non-violent and apolitical protests. It also helped that the state's young chief minister, Omar Abdullah, who had just come to power, took up the issue with New Delhi. The battle was won. The army camp, which had been set up in 1997, was shifted. No stones were thrown and no pro-Pakistan slogans raised. The people of Bomai did not allow any politician – whether mainstream or separatist – to set foot in their village during the agitation. Since then, the battle has moved into its second phase. 'We will now push for the development of our village through the people's committee,' says Ghulam Hassan Shah, a local resident.

For the families who lost their young members, however, there is little to cheer about. Tantray's young niece, Anika, totters around the house, searching for her dead uncle. Mohammed Sultan sits with the other teachers on the grounds of the school from which the security forces were expelled. He has begun smoking heavily. 'I think I smoke almost five packets a day,' he smiles sadly.

It is recess and a cricket match is going on between two classes. A girl hits the ball hard and, another, who like everyone else wears a headscarf, rushes after it. She picks it up near the wall where the bunkers and the soldiers once stood and triumphantly throws it back towards the pitch. She's managed to save a boundary. It is a victory for cricket – and much else.

All that the government had to do to create jobs was polish the apple.

Sopore town, just 60 square kilometres in area, is located some 10 kilometres southeast of Baramulla. You could call Sopore one of the headquarters of rebellion, for it is the home of the iconic pro-Pakistan separatist leader Syed Ali Shah Geelani, but you can certainly call it the headquarters of the Kashmiri apple.

The people of Sopore have subversion running in their veins, alongside a deep, abiding love for football. This dusty town on the banks of the Jhelum has for a long time been a major trading centre, famous for its spices, bakeries, and fish from the nearby Wular Lake. Wular is one of Asia's largest freshwater lakes and gives Jammu and

Kashmir nearly two-thirds of its fish. But all that fades before the apple, the undisputed star of the state's horticulture industry, the bulwark of its economy. Sopore *is* apple kingdom.

There is the crisp and aromatic Amri (Ambri Kashmiri), which is oblong and conical in shape and hailed as the most popular apple in Kashmir. It matures in autumn, during the last week of September or the first week of October. Then there is the American Trel (American Apirogue), with crisp, juicy, sweet and greenish white flesh. There is also the variety aptly called Delicious (Red Delicious), red and juicy with its trademark five lobes and globally famous. And there is the Maharaji, a white-dotted red apple.

'Tamilians love the Maharaji. They love their apples slightly sour. In Mumbai, they love Delicious; they like it sweet. In Bihar, they want small apples. The Delicious will sell there even for free. They just want small apples,' says Haji Bashir Ahmed Beg, the sixty-year-old president of the fruit growers' association in Sopore.

These and other varieties of Kashmiri apples find glory in Sopore's huge apple market. More than a thousand trucks, each valued at around Rs 2 lakh, leave every day from here to different parts of India, whipping up plumes of dust along the dirt road that leads out of the complex. But the apple market hardly looks like the busy centre of business and export it should have been, Kashmiri apples being globally popular. To an onlooker, it would seem more like a weekly village market. The road is so bumpy, it seems like a steeple chase track. The traders have staged protests, jammed the road and sent numerous letters to the government to have it repaired, but nothing has been done. Invariably, every year, they pool in money and try to get it repaired themselves.

'If the government cannot fix this three-kilometre road, how will it control all of Kashmir?' asks Bashir Ahmed Mir, president of the traders' association here. 'Our life is comfortable, but our minds are locked. It is like this – no one is illiterate here, but it is as if the leaders are just Class-12 pass.'

Horticulture is one of the state's main revenue earners, with a yearly turnover of Rs 1,200 crore, and provides direct and indirect employment to about twenty-three hundred thousand people. But there is no hotel in Sopore, not even a Jammu and Kashmir Tourism facility. More than twenty thousand people come to the market every day, but there is no public facility for drinking water. Nor are there any cold-storage facilities. 'The government is the biggest enemy of horticulture,' Mir thunders. 'Eighty per cent of the population depends on horticulture, and yet look at the conditions.'

It is a quiet winter afternoon. We are sitting in a large, sunlit room, overlooking rows of trucks. Chairs are placed along three walls and Mir sits behind a large table along the fourth wall. Tea is brought in. In the corner of the room, near the door, sits an old man in a Kashmiri *pheran*. He lost his mind four decades ago and now just hangs around the president's office.

'It was Sunday ...' the old man says in a monotonous drawl, in broken English. Everyone looks at him for a second, then returns to the conversation at hand. There are far grimmer things to consider.

For scores of kilometres on all sides of Sopore, the apple is in a crisis. 'Quality pesticides are not available. Our crops are getting destroyed. If we use pesticides today, the results show two months later,' says a trader who stands leaning against a truck. 'The fertilizers we get are substandard ... There is a new disease, it's a mysterious disease. The trees are drying up. We called the (agricultural) university; they said they will send a doctor. They never did.'

Mir adds, 'We have the best quality apples, but the government does not let us dream big. The Indian government does not want to let us prosper. They want to keep us under their boots – that's all.'

The old man by the door gets restless. 'In Srinagar, I went once to Lal Chowk ...'

At Lal Chowk, a few months ago, thousands had gathered at the height of the anti-India agitation. When the demonstrations had spiralled into a violent face-off between the Jammu region and Kashmir, Kashmir's apple traders wondered how their products would reach their destinations. Earlier, the Delicious and Maharaji varieties used to be trucked through the Kashmir valley, along the Banihal tunnel, down the national highway to markets in Jammu, from where they were sent out to destinations across the country. Now, the Srinagar businessmen choked off all traffic at Jammu and refused to take on any business from Kashmir. Decades of business ties, as close as family bonds in many cases, were snapped in one stroke by politics.

So the Kashmiri apple traders demanded, and finally got, permission to trade across the Line of Control, the disputed border between the India-controlled Kashmir and Pakistan-controlled Kashmir. The road was opened on 21 October 2008. The first convoy had eleven trucks. But Kashmiris cannot make phone calls across the border to Pakistan due to security concerns, so as trade progressed traders were not able to get information on buyers for their produce beyond the Pakistani border post of Chakothi. Despite the bravado and threats to only trade with Pakistan, the traders' hearts are in their main market, India.

'We discovered the market in India on our own. The government did not help us,' says Mir, as the other traders around him nod in agreement. 'We had asked people from West Bengal to come. From Rajasthan, they are coming soon. When they come here, they stay with me. When I go out, I stay with them. For twenty years, not a single apple trader has been killed by the militants. Unnecessary fear has been spread that Hindus cannot come here. The image of Kashmir in India is incorrect.'

And voila, as if on cue, a Hindu trader walks in. Bimlesh Kumar Gupta, forty-two, is from faraway Kolkata. This is his first visit to Sopore and he reached Kashmir only the day before. He looks like a tourist, wearing a sweater and jeans in a room full of men in their *pherans*. 'My family was very scared. They refused to let me come,' he says, laughing gently, as he settles down in a chair. 'I just bought a ticket on a whim and came.'

Gupta is distracted for a second – in the corner, the old man is babbling away, mostly incoherent now, but indignantly glaring at all of us.

'Kashmiri apples are so famous. India is incomplete without them,' Gupta continues after the pause, as the others break into big smiles. 'In Kolkata, a lot of people buy them. They have a different taste, look nice, are juicy and scented ... These apples are the bridge between Kashmir and the rest of India.'

Gupta is an 'Indian' in Kashmir. He comes with the political baggage all Indians carry when they come to this part of the country. 'I have been to fifty villages, in remote areas, wherever,' he says, sipping on his tea as his face lights up in the afternoon sun. 'I love the people here. My misconceptions have been cured h-u-n-d-r-e-d per cent. I used to wonder how I would be treated, but I had no problems at all.'

The man who comes in next, also from Kolkata, echoes these sentiments. Fifty-year-old Mohammed Naushad, an apple trader from Bihar who has now settled in Kolkata, has been coming to Sopore since 1984, five years before the insurgency started.

'I am trading in apples from China, the United States, Australia, New Zealand, everywhere,' Naushad says. 'The quality of Sopore apples is the best in the world.'

He was here on a visit in January 1990, when Sopore was in the process of becoming the hub of pro-Pakistan militants. That was a time when the rebels roamed the roads at will and several parts of Kashmir had slipped out of India's control. 'I was stuck in New Light Hotel for twenty-two days,' he says. New Light was the only hotel in Sopore. It burnt down in 2001. Seventeen people died in the fire, mostly apple traders from Uttar Pradesh.

The old man at the door leaps to his feet and walks out. He has had enough.

'If they develop the Kashmiri apple well, it can go all over the world,' Naushad says. 'But traders here have no facilities. No government help. Nothing.'

6

The man opened fire the moment police officer Imtiyaz Mir asked him to identify himself. 'Tu kaun hai?' he shouted out at the man he had spotted sitting under an apple tree in an orchard near Sopore. Mir's eyes were fixed upon the stranger as he waited for a reply, when suddenly he saw a glint of metal in the bright afternoon sun. Instead of revealing who he was, the man, Abu Abdullah, had pulled out his AK-47 rifle. Imtiyaz Mir would have died instantly had it not been for his namesake, Constable Imtiyaz Ahmed, who jumped in front of his boss and took the bullets in his lower abdomen.

Abu Abdullah, Mir says, was no ordinary gunman. He was a hardcore militant of the Pakistan-based militant group, Lashkar-e-Tayyaba (LeT), and he had been sent on a mission to carry out a fidayeen, or suicide, attack in Srinagar. Just hours before Abdullah was to head for Srinagar, Mir, who was then Sopore's police chief, got an intelligence report on his plans. And now they were face to face in an orchard.

Abdullah fought fiercely, so fiercely that he would not let the police party rescue Imtiyaz Ahmed, who now lay wounded in the line of fire. Bits of apple flew everywhere. It took Imtiyaz Mir an hour to crawl and reach close to Abdullah. Then, as the militant tried to ward off the covering fire from Mir's colleagues, the officer swooped in from just a foot away. 'I tilted his rifle away from myself and then shot him with my pistol,' recalls Imtiyaz. But Constable Ahmed could not be saved. He had lost too much blood.

Men of the eighty-thousand-strong Jammu and Kashmir Police, founded in 1873, are at the forefront of the battle against insurgency, but rarely get adequate credit for it, let alone allowances, better wages, or more recruits. In a state where they are hugely outnumbered by the central security forces, six army or paramilitary soldiers for every Jammu and Kashmir Police jawan, the security grid in Kashmir holds out examples of how a local force with intimate knowledge of the local conditions and a superior intelligence-gathering network has not been given its due, an acutely demoralizing aspect in a gritty war.

Mir belongs to the 1999 batch of the Kashmir Police. 'It is called the "fidayeen" batch,' he quips. Mir joined as a deputy superintendent of police in Shopian, in south Kashmir, which was then the hotbed of militancy. But it was in Sopore, from 2006 onwards, that Mir faced the most difficult period of his career.

At that time, Sopore was the hub of the LeT. Most of the fidayeen attacks that took place in Srinagar were orchestrated from Sopore. The security forces and police had changed their strategy in Kashmir by this time. They were no longer pursuing individual militants. They had begun, instead, to kill the commanders of the militant groups, however small they were.

Mir says that containing the LeT was his main objective. He felt that unless the police sent a strong message instilling the fear of death in the militants, it would not be possible to contain them. His moment came when he was successful in bringing down Osama Pehalwan, chief of the militant outfit Al-Mansurian in November 2006. Pehalwan had led a string of attacks against army soldiers. A few months later, acting on inputs received from an informer, Mir came upon senior Lashkar commander Hafiz Nasir, hiding with two Jaish militants, in Rafiabad near Sopore. During the search operation, Mir was accompanied by a colonel from the army. They had heard that the three militants were preparing to carry out a fidayeen attack on the cavalcade of the then chief minister Mufti Mohammed Sayeed.

Mir was instructed by his seniors to move immediately to where Sayeed was supposed to address a public rally. After he left, the militants managed to break through the cordon and kill two soldiers. Hafiz Nasir took refuge in another house. Mir was in favour of blasting the house, but the colonel wanted to be sure. Despite repeated warnings from Mir, the colonel peeped inside and Nasir shot at him. 'He died on the spot,' recalls Mir. In the end, he and his men managed to kill Nasir.

Another informer told Mir that four militants were hiding inside a house in Rafiabad. Mir says he sent a police party three times to search the house, but the militants could not be found. Finally, when the informer called for the fourth time, Mir lost his patience. He shouted at him, accusing him of lying. 'Cut my throat if you don't get them,' the informer whispered. This time, Mir went along with the police party. They searched the entire house, but couldn't find the militants. He was about to call off the search operation when he spotted a black-and-white television set in one corner of the house.

'I don't know ... I had this gut feeling that there was something there,' Mir says. He ordered his men to dig beneath the television set. A couple of feet below, they were still digging up earth. 'Sir, there is nothing here,' one of his men told him. But Mir insisted that they keep on digging. A foot further, and they came upon a layer of concrete. Beneath it, they discovered a bunker, measuring approximately two metres by two and a half metres. And, sure enough, there were four militants inside. Mir asked them to surrender, but they wouldn't. 'Finally, we got the bunker filled with water,' says Mir. Extreme situations call for extreme measures.

Mir and his men used similar tactics in 2008 to eliminate Sajjad Afghani, chief of the militant outfit Harkat-ul-Mujahideen in Kashmir. Afghani had been active for ten years in north Kashmir.

He was hiding inside the false ceiling of the residential quarters of a government hospital employee when Mir trapped him.

'Many Pakistani boys work for us, providing us vital information about militant activities in Kashmir,' says Mir. He has intercepted many calls from across the border directing militants to kill certain people. 'I have saved the lives of at least a hundred people by shifting them to safe places,' says Mir, free for an interview on a Sunday because his bulletproof vehicle has broken down. This means he has to move around without one, putting his life in grave danger.

Mir does not have complaints, although he should. The Jammu and Kashmir Police, who risk their lives every day, get paid a pittance – just Rs 200 a month as risk allowance, for example, as compared to the Rs 5,000 a month an army soldier gets. They are not equipped with the latest weaponry and gadgets. They are not given enough training. In addition, their preoccupation with insurgency operations has created a huge vacuum in the normal policing activities in insurgency-affected areas. 'They have lost sight of professional policing in the areas of police stations for nearly two decades now. The police personnel posted in police stations are busy in law-and-order duties, which has disturbed their concentration in routine crime work,' says an official study commissioned by the force.

Headed by a director general of police, the state is divided into two police zones, Jammu and Kashmir, each headed by a zonal inspector general of police. The two zones are divided into seven ranges that pose a tough task for the police, considering the near-impossible terrain in large parts of the state, from the oxygen-deficient cold desert to the remote mountainous crags. The police force has also been at the receiving end of a collapse of governance. The biggest blank cheque has been the predominantly central government-funded Security Related Expenditure (SRE). In addition to its regular uses, this is what the SRE has been utilized for: repair and renovation of police stations and residential buildings; buying tents, tyres and tubes, furniture, lawn mowers, hard coke, heat convectors, coolers and uniforms; and development of lawns and landscaping. Government officials have used the SRE to carry out woodwork, renovation and repair of kitchens and toilets in government buildings and to install a transformer at an official residence.

Back at his Srinagar residence, Mir's mobile phone rings. His caller tune is a song from *Shaheed*, the 1965 film based on the young freedom-fighter Bhagat Singh's life, '*Ae watan, ae watan, humko teri kasam, teri raahon mein jaan tak luta jaayenge* (O my country, I swear in your name, I shall lay down my life for you).'

Across the proverbial fence in Kashmir's barbed-wire battleground, former militant Mohammed Zameer had also vowed to lay down his life for his dream – a free Kashmir.

We are 150 kilometres north of the state's winter capital of Jammu, in a small cyber cafe in Rajouri town, once a major staging ground for militants trudging in through the remote mountain passes from Pakistan-controlled Kashmir. The man before us is lean, has a thick, uneven stubble on his chin and a rough voice that he lowers as he speaks. It is 8.00 p.m. on a cold winter evening. The cyber cafe is in a narrow lane off the main road and there is no one coming after the man who gave up the gun years ago. But Zameer has worn the low-profile, nervous, fidgety life of anonymity like a *pheran* for years. Strangers have come out of nowhere today – journalists from Delhi – and they want to know his life story. His friend has pulled him away from his shop. The former militant is now a grocer.

Zameer was a fighter in JKLF, then led by Yasin Malik. He was a militant for more than ten years and has served two prison terms –

the last ended in 2005 – but is still dealing with other cases dating back to the 1990s. Zameer emerges from his cocoon once every few weeks when he has to go to court to appear at the trials.

There are an estimated twenty-five thousand former militants who have been released in Jammu and Kashmir, nearly all of them living the same low-profile, stigmatized existence as Zameer. The life of the forty-year-old man, who was twenty when the insurgency began, is a reflection of that of thousands of Kashmiri youth who gave up their lives for a dream sold to them by separatists and got little in return. Even when they gave up the guns, the government continued to view them with suspicion.

Apart from former militants, other youth who take part in public protests, or are even seen as potential troublemakers, can be charged easily by the state police under the Jammu and Kashmir Public Safety Act of 1978, and thrown into prison or prosecuted. This will render them ineligible for government jobs, they will never get a passport and nor will their families, and even a cousin might have to face tough verification procedures for the simplest of dealings with the government. In short, their entire clan will always be under the scanner as far as the government is concerned. It is a humiliating existence, and for a former militant in Kashmir it is like being in a slow-burning hell.

Zameer's name means 'conscience'. Fittingly, he speaks from his heart. 'I regret that I lost at least twenty years of my life. My classmates became police officers, doctors, engineers. And on this side of the movement, everyone made militancy a business after 1994,' he says, his hands shaking a bit as he holds a cup of hot tea in the chilly evening. 'We faced grave injustice from both the leaders of our *tehreek* (movement), as well as India. The militant leaders built big homes, but the thousands who fought for them never even got a job. We can't even get a character certificate from the government.'

He shivers suddenly as a dog barks outside. A vehicle has pulled up. It's only a customer, but we move to another room inside, where Zameer speaks even more softly. He refuses to get photographed. We can take pictures only of his shadow thrown on the wall by the faint light of a bulb that is struggling to stay alive despite the town's low-voltage power supply.

'A friend of mine used to say that Yasin Malik is fighting only for Maisuma's freedom,' he says angrily, referring to the narrow-laned neighbourhood at the entrance to downtown Srinagar, which was once the centre of anti-India rage. 'What did we get? Who supported us?' he asks, raising his voice for the first time during the conversation. 'They had promised they would stand by us, but if they are not supporting us now in dealing with our criminal cases, why did we fight for them then?'

Zameer still faces two cases from fourteen years ago. He has to go to Jammu, the state's summer capital, twice a month to appear before a judge. This costs him Rs 2,000, a large part of his fluctuating monthly income. 'My wife and children have been badly affected. My in-laws have pitched in. Just paying the lawyer has made my financial condition really bad,' he says.

It is one of the least spoken-about areas of governance in Jammu and Kashmir, but the ruthless, unforgiving state machinery has done virtually nothing to rehabilitate the young men who took up a gun or a rock or a separatist banner against the Indian state. Other countries have dealt with former militants in innovative ways. In Saudi Arabia, militants returning from Guantanamo Bay, dreading the thought of living as pariahs in the eyes of the law, have often received an unexpected welcome from the government. Young Saudi men who are handed over by American security officials are forgiven, and then offered a long carrot-and-stick drill, which includes psychological counselling, theological re-education and financial help, including cash, sometimes a car, and expenses for, say, their marriage. The programme, running since 2004, is regulated by a committee that includes different sub-committees of clerics, psychologists and security officials, which determine whether prisoners can be released and monitor the conduct of those who are let off. More than three thousand such people have been rehabilitated.

American authorities in Iraq and the governments of Yemen, Singapore, Algeria and Egypt run similar programmes. Pakistani authorities are using the services of the ulema, a body of Islamic scholars, and psychologists to ease some three thousand imprisoned militants back into mainstream society. In Sri Lanka, former members of the LTTE, including child fighters, are going through life-changing rehabilitation in closely guarded, government-run camps. They are being given vocational training to help them learn English or Sinhalese and become carpenters, plumbers, masons, electrical engineers, tailors and cooks. In Nepal, the United Nations is helping the government give a new life to former Maoist soldiers.

'Did the movement's leadership support us with even Rs 500 a month to fight our cases?' Zameer asks.

Zameer's career as a militant began in 1990, when he was at college pursuing a BSc degree. 'I was a student. Earlier, I didn't know what the movement was about – I just went with the flow. There was no motive,' he says. He went to Pakistan to receive arms training and returned to join active combat. He says he never killed anyone. That was the time when the Kashmiri Pandits were getting death threats from the JKLF, his organization. 'Great injustice was committed against the Pandits, but the government's soft corner for them was probably what set it off,' Zameer says. 'They were killed in large numbers. But many Pandits who migrated to Jammu kept coming back to meet Kashmiri Muslims who were charged with militancy and put in jail. This was a very large-hearted gesture on their part.'

Outside the cyber cafe, the walls are plastered with posters of different political parties. The 2008 state assembly elections are only a week away. It is a critical election – Kashmir and India have never seemed more far apart. Separatist politicians have boycotted the elections and asked the people not to vote.

'I have never voted, but I will this time,' Zameer says. 'But in my heart, I still want independence. Look at the Irish, the Palestinians, the LTTE – they all had a dream. It's not a crime. But I cannot do anything about it now. I am helpless.'

~

Twenty years after Mohammed Zameer, another man is getting ready to cross over into Pakistan. His purpose, however, is far removed from Zameer's.

We are in Poonch, a border town some 200 kilometres northwest of Jammu, which was once the capital of a kingdom of the same name. It included Muzaffarabad, the present-day capital of Pakistan-controlled Kashmir. It had its own currency and its own postal system, and horse-drawn tongas used to ply as far as Rawalpindi, 138 kilometres away and now in Pakistan.

Forty-three-year-old Tufail Hussain is all dressed up when he arrives at the football ground in Poonch. He wears a karakul hat and a white churidar–kurta, and there's kohl lining his eyes.

This is the place from where a bus service connects people on both sides of the border, including thousands of families that have not met or seen each other for decades, many since 1947, when India was partitioned to create Pakistan. Tufail Hussain is headed to Pakistan to meet his sister, who lives there with her husband, for the first time ever. He was an infant when she went away, never to return. 'Finally, I will see her,' he says.

The red-and-white bus travels 55 kilometres – less than the number of years it took to get it running. The nearest Pakistani village, Chakan-da-Bagh, is just 6 kilometres away. When the service was flagged off in 2006, the bus was to run once every two weeks. In September 2008, it became a weekly service, running every Monday. Thousands of people want to use the bus, but the verification process by the state police to get a ticket is long and excruciatingly tedious. Why can the 55-kilometre bus service not get clearance from the central government to run every day – or even twice a day? Security concerns are quoted as the reason.

The restrictions on the bus service are among the many baffling policies imposed in the name of security in Jammu and Kashmir, such as the ban on mobile phones and the Internet. Militants continue to sneak in across the Line of Control, but the security officials who advise the government believe that the buses are the only security risk and starting a regular bus service will mean that militants will board them for a quick ride into India.

The bus is a luxury, since even phone calls to Pakistan are banned in India-controlled Kashmir. That is why Hussain has not seen or heard from his elder sister, Nifa Bi, who went across the border in 1965, when she married a Pakistani. All she could do was write letters, Hussain says he has received four or five. Last summer, Nifa's husband got to come to India. She recorded her voice on an audio-cassette, a message to the brother she had not seen in forty-three years. She put it in the hands of her husband as he boarded the bus to Poonch. 'It's been too long, brother. I am praying that we meet soon,' she said, her voice quivering, in the ten-minute recording. When Nifa's husband was going back to Pakistan, Hussain gave him something for Nifa. It was another audio cassette, his recorded reply to his sister's letter: 'I am waiting for the day when I can get on the bus and see you for the first time.'

Today, he is headed for Pakistan to meet his sister and her family. His eyes are full of tears. He looks away. 'I am taking clothes for my sister, but I have never seen her. I hope they will fit her,' Hussain says, as a young relative who has come to see him off breaks down in tears. 'But why is it so difficult for a brother to see his sister? And why can't these people go as well?'

A ticket to board the bus is virtually a lottery ticket. 'I have been waiting for ten years to come here. And I have been for waiting four years for my application for a bus ticket to be approved,' says flour-mill-owner Mohammed Nazir of Chham village in Pakistan, a fifteen-hour journey by bus from Rawalakote, where he will disembark. 'I stayed here for a month, but I still could not meet everyone I wanted to,' Nazir said, surrounded by his Indian relatives, who are silently shedding tears.

People hug each other, cry, convey last-minute messages, check whether their gifts are packed well enough, and push and lunge at a bus window to get their travel papers in first.

'I am going to see my family although I am going in great pain,' says seventy-year-old Gulshan Begum, tall and well built, sitting on the grass lawn surrounded by her family and awaiting her turn. Gulshan Begum has missed all the birthday and wedding celebrations arranged by her family across the border. In 2005, after the deadly Kashmir earthquake, she also missed all the funerals. The earthquake had killed two of her sisters, a brother and a nephew.

'Many people died. I could not go. I am going for the first time after the earthquake,' she says, and instinctively breaks into a Pahadi song of longing, loss and separation as she weeps along with her daughters and granddaughters.

A few metres away, Ghulam Nabi, eighty-five, of Chhela Dhagri village, clutches half a dozen black umbrellas with gleaming silver handles. Umbrellas from Poonch are famous in Pakistan and make for welcome gifts.

'My brother – my real brother – Ghulam Qadir lives there. He went across in 1965. In the 2005 earthquake we lost ten people in our family there. We can never be there for either weddings or funerals,' he said. 'I had applied for a ticket to go right after the earthquake in 2005, but my verification was done only in 2007 and I am getting to go only now. The ticket costs only Rs 70. I could have gone hundreds of times.'

Hundreds of times – that's how many times young men want to travel on the road that runs southward from their remote mountain village in Poonch. The road is an alternate route into the Kashmir valley, which could change a few thousand lives. The road has been in planning since 1970, but is still nowhere near ready because of the imagined fears of India's security and intelligence honchos.

Not too far from Poonch, we are at Bafliaz, a roadside village that is about to become an important milestone. This is one end of the new Mughal Road, a renovated version of the 90-kilometre medieval mud road that the Mughal emperor Akbar used in 1586 to conquer Kashmir. Later, he and his successors brought opulent caravans down this very road as they travelled for their summer retreats.

The story of this small village, and a few others, showcases the truth that emerges when you peel off the layers from everyday life in Jammu and Kashmir. Beneath the age-old grievances of the valley's residents is a newer discontentment against poor governance, something that has been taken as a given for over two decades.

Abdul Sattar was forty-seven when the Mughal Road project was inaugurated in 1979 by Kashmir's iconic leader Sheikh Muhammad Abdullah. Little happened here after that, however, and the area became a hub of militancy from the late 1980s, totally inaccessible to the security forces and government officials. Not so in 1996, though, when Sheikh Abdullah's son and the then chief minister, Farooq Abdullah, revived the project. There was no fear of militancy then, yet little happened. In June 2005, the Ghulam Nabi Azad government decided to start the reconstruction of the road 'on a war footing', promising to have it ready by March 2007.

In the summer of 2009, Sattar is seventy-seven years old. He has two grandchildren. His skin is shrivelled. He is losing his hearing. But there is still no road. Sattar's eighteen-year-old grandson, Manzoor Ahmed, had to give up on his education after the tenth standard because there was no centre of higher education nearby;

if there had been a road, he could have taken a bus to a college in the Kashmir valley.

The story of the Mughal Road is a snapshot of Kashmir's warped governance. The Mughal Road was to connect the Poonch region to Kashmir, meandering through magnificent valleys on a route overlooking snow-tipped mountains and cutting the travel time from the major towns of Poonch and Rajouri to Srinagar from 588 kilometres and 518 kilometres, respectively, to 126 kilometres. It will also mean that the two million people in the region across the Pir Panjal range, currently out of reach and accessible only through a circuitous mountain route south to Jammu and then northwards, would have access to investment in horticulture and tourism and there would be new opportunities for the youth. The road could transform the economy of the region.

'This road will change our lives. I have waited for it all my life,' says Sattar, his eyebrows arched, eyes half-open in the harsh sunlight. 'It will bring jobs from Delhi and Mumbai. Markets will come up. Cars will come here. Fruit and vegetables from here will go as far as the plains of Punjab.'

The Mughal Road originated in Jhelum town, now in Pakistan's portion of Punjab, approaching Shopian in the Kashmir valley via Kotli in Pakistan-controlled Kashmir, Thanamandi in Rajouri district of Jammu and Kashmir and Chandimarh in the Pir Panjal mountains, from where one branch headed via Heepora to Shopian. The planned road from Bafliaz to Shopian spans some 90 kilometres and traverses across mountains that are 3,500 to 4,000 metres high. There are several Mughal rest houses perched on the mountain peaks, with terraces overlooking waterfalls, and smaller relics and monuments along the route, all of which are expected to attract tourists and revenue.

'Going to Kashmir will really boost our education. There are universities there. And there are many tourist spots along the way. People will forget Gulmarg and Pahalgam when they come here,' says Manzoor Ahmed, Sattar's grandson. 'After we have the road, our whole culture will become Kashmiri. Right now, we are closer to Jammu. We will wear a *pheran*, we will use the *kangri* [the Kashmiri firepot] ... I want to have a *wazwan* – the traditional Kashmiri feast – in Kashmir.'

It seems such eagerness for integration scares officials, a sign of the typical, arrogant, colonial mindset that colours most of New Delhi's dealings with Jammu and Kashmir. Authorities believe that connecting the road will integrate the largely pro-India region with the Kashmir valley and allow the valley's secessionist sentiments to seep into Poonch and Rajouri. On various occasions, this fear has been disguised as lack of funds and concern for the environment. Imaginary fears have been propped up before shortsighted politicians by military and intelligence officers and slothful government officials to deprive people in large parts of the state of their basic rights, schools, health facilities, good roads, trading hubs, and phone and Internet connections.

Such fears are in no way well-founded. Rajouri and Poonch were major strongholds of militancy all through the years of insurgency, but no secessionist sentiment ever took root in these regions.

'Militants used to roam the roads. They would beat us up, they used to ask us to get things from the market – kerosene oil, coconut, dry fruits,' says sunken-cheeked Sattar, who wears a small turban and a brown salwar-kameez. 'The mujahideen came in 1989, but this is India's land.'

Road or no road, Sattar's other grandson, fifteen-year-old Mohammed Shakoor, has already started using it. He says he feels like a Mughal emperor marching in with his army as he walks his buffaloes on it for 80 kilometres, right up to Shopian.

It takes him three days.

7

Dozens of men on horseback are trotting into remote villages every other day, seeking to win over the people, clenching their fists and shouting slogans that pierce the mountain air. It is not the Middle Ages, and the men are not sword-flailing Mughal conquerors in Jammu and Kashmir, but election candidates and their supporters seeking votes in large parts of the state's Kishtwar district.

The horses, which can be hired at Rs 500 each from the point where the road from Kishtwar town ends, are a part of the everyday lives of thousands of people living in areas such as Dachhan, Madwa and Warwan, a black hole of governance. If someone falls ill or a woman goes into labour, people have to walk for up to three days across rocky terrain, past treacherous gorges, carrying the patient on a makeshift stretcher made from two wooden poles. Patients often die on the way and the party returns home, carrying the body across the same jagged rocks. Sometimes, those carrying the bodies fall into gorges or lose their footing on glaciers and die.

'People die for nothing in our area. We are like mad men who have torn their clothes long ago. Nothing affects us any more and nobody cares for us,' said sixty-year-old Ghulam Qadir, a former soldier from Dachhan village, as he sat in Kishtwar's rundown hospital.

Most people here have never seen a battery-charged television set or mobile phone, the two basic indicators of prosperity that are now found in the remotest, most impoverished and worst governed parts of India.

It took Qadir a whole day to get from his village to Kishtwar town, now the headquarters of a district created some years ago out of Doda district in the remote northern reaches of Jammu.

'You tell me, are we even considered part of this country?' he asks.

That is a question a man with henna-dyed hair and a bushy moustache has long stopped asking himself. Fazal Hussain is the head of his clan of Bakarwals, nomadic herdsmen and women, who travel across Jammu and Kashmir, and beyond into the northern plains, with massive herds of sheep and goats. The Bakarwals wade into urban traffic, sleep in the forests and get photographed by curious tourists as they continue to follow the pastoral lifestyle of their ancestors.

Behind this frequently photographed *National Geographic* existence, however, is a sad, hollow life that no government has cared about, although the security forces have often used the staunchly pro-India nomads to gather information about militant movements in high-altitude pastures and inaccessible areas where soldiers cannot reach but the nomads can.

Today, Hussain and his people are on the road that runs from Poonch to Jammu. They have halted for the night. The children are collecting firewood. The women are marking the space where they will set up the hearth. The men rest, tired from carrying heavy sacks with their family belongings on their backs.

'We can't even sign our names. We are living in the dark. People fool us when we want to buy bus tickets,' says Fazal Hussain. He turns around and asks a woman squatting next to a tree, trying to set up a small makeshift stove in the grass if there is milk. Can she make some tea? They have guests.

A large number of the women die here, apparently unable to bear the harsh lifestyle. That is probably why so many among the Bakarwals do not marry. According to the 2001 Census of India, the proportion of 'never married' Bakarwals (57.2 per cent) exceeds that of 'married' ones (39.7 per cent). The average sex ratio for all such tribes under the age of six is nine hundred and seventy-nine women per thousand men – higher than the national average of nine hundred and seventy-eight. The Bakarwals have the lowest sex ratio among Kashmir's tribes – eight hundred and sixty-eight women per thousand men.

These nomadic, mostly Muslim tribes – the Gujjars and the Bakarwals predominant among them – make up about 10 per cent of Jammu and Kashmir's population. And yet, they are just an embellishment, a freak show, a use-and-throw resource for the state's security establishment and for the government.

'We hate this life. We are tired of this life. We want to stop. We don't want to be nomads any more. But nobody has ever done anything for vagabonds, have they?' says Fazal Hussain, his hair and moustache brown with henna, his eyes lined with kohl and a big turban on his head. 'The government gave us nothing. Our children will lead the same primitive life as we have. We are desperate for our children to study, to go to schools. But look at us,' he says, watching a seven-year-old girl as she crosses the highway barefoot, dodging the odd car, to fetch firewood for the night.

The Bakarwals have the lowest percentage of school-going children among all communities – 25 per cent. The literacy level in the community is 22 per cent and only 12 per cent of the women are literate. Only 1 per cent of their community has a graduate degree, not a single member has a technical or non-technical diploma and only 8 per cent have studied till the tenth standard.

Like most other communities in the troubled region, the lives of these nomads have also been turned upside down by the two-decade-old insurgency.

'The militancy changed everything. We used to live in the forests. Now we have to spend much of our time by the roadside,' says Fazal Hussain. 'Still, we are not greedy. We will get our dinner and thank Allah with the reassurance that in the morning, he will do something.'

Civilization is catching up slowly with the Bakarwals, but nowhere as quickly as they would like it to. Some of them have radios. Others have seen television sets in people's houses while spending the summer in Srinagar, where they work temporarily as orchard guards.

A mobile phone rings. Voila, Fazal Hussain whips out a phone from his pocket. The man with no home can still be reached when needed. 'Yes! Just keep looking to your left,' he says, shouting into the phone as he walks away. 'I will give you the address. It's a forest clearing between Chingus and Rajouri!'

In the midst of all the chaos, in a state deeply divided on the basis of regional aspirations, Jammu and Kashmir has a few milestones of pride, which are also probably the bulwark of its future. In a state ripped apart by Islamic insurgency, a jihad fought in the name of religion, no amount of violence and despair has been able to divide certain people on the basis of religion, unlike in many other parts of multicultural India and parts of the state itself.

In the small Kashmiri village of Darhal, which was part of the militant heartland until two years ago, a twenty-four-year-old man shows off his knowledge of Malayalam and Sanskrit to visitors every other day. He is a Kashmiri, wears a skullcap and has a long beard.

Mohammed Asif Mir is a hafiz, or one who knows the Koran by heart. He manages his family-owned madrassa, the Jamia Mohammadiya Rahagul Uloom Madrassa, which has run uninterrupted through the insurgency, even though it teaches comparative religion and holds classes on Hinduism for its five hundred students. Boys in skullcaps and girls in headscarves – perfect fodder for stereotyping the seminary – scamper around and then settle down with a hushed murmur in their classes. The girls have a separate madrassa for themselves and also study with the boys in a school, a triumph achieved after overcoming tough opposition from their parents. Now, half the teachers in the school are women, and some among the madrassa's female alumni have even made it to PhD courses at Jawaharlal Nehru University in New Delhi.

'My experience is that when a boy studies, only he studies. But when a girl studies, the whole world does ... and we don't want to make these boys just imams [clerics],' says Asif Mir, sitting behind a desk in a large office, watching the children playing on the grounds. A car passes outside, a loudspeaker fitted on it belching election slogans in support of a local candidate.

'We are trying to teach them computers, maths, science. If they study only religion, they could become fundamentalists,' he says. 'There is a perception that madrassas produce terrorists. We want to produce good citizens. This has started a movement here. Everyone wants to send their children to school.'

Asif Mir took the leap of faith in 1996 when he left home for theological studies, boarded a train for the first time in his life and landed up at the other end of the country, in the town of Kozhikode in Kerala.

'I had an Egyptian teacher, it was the first time I was seeing an Egyptian. I also saw a computer for the first time. And I was put in a hostel of a hundred and twenty students, all of whom spoke only Malayalam. Everyone except me,' Asif Mir says, to giggles from other teachers sitting along the long cream-coloured wall. 'I learnt Malayalam from my teachers and friends. Slowly, I widened my horizons. I wanted to understand Hinduism.' He missed Kashmiri food terribly, but acquired a taste for south Indian food. Then, Asif Mir started an interesting study of comparative religions. He once stunned a Hindu family on a train journey by telling them the meaning of several shlokas from the Rig Veda.

The young man brought the same sensibility back to his village and it is changing the worldview of hundreds of students every year. That is not unusual in a state that has witnessed traditionally close relations between Hindus and Muslims – between Kashmiri Muslims and Pandits in the valley, and between members of the two faiths in the Jammu region.

'That is the way ahead. It takes very little to break up people. The situation in Kashmir might have ruined everything over twenty years and the government might have done very little for Kashmir, but its strength is us, its people,' Asif Mir says, speaking slowly as the others listen in silence. 'We are unbreakable.'

Postscript

In 2010, New Delhi is yet again committing the same mistakes in the Kashmir valley. After an incident of human-rights violation by the army surfaced in north Kashmir, thousands of angry young men assembled on the roads and resorted to stone-throwing. The protests soon spread across the valley.

Amidst what could be called a political void, India's youngest chief minister, Omar Abdullah, looked completely inept at handling the situation. As usual, the centre had no blueprint ready to tackle the chaos that followed. As the nation watched a relatively calm period in the troubled state come to a shattering close, more than fifty men died as the police and the CRPF retaliated with gunfire. But that did not deter more young men, some of them with professional degrees, from coming out on the streets and engaging the security personnel in fierce battles. These battles, as the authorities realized, were harder to handle than gunning down armed militants. As more civilians were killed or wounded, the violence only escalated further.

The home ministry did not help matters by continuing to issue statements about the situation rather than let Omar Abdullah talk about it. This further established that the chief minister was not in the driver's seat. That impression, as Kashmir-watchers will tell you, can be very dangerous.

Part Three

The Collapse of the Northeast

'THERE IS A PARALLEL GOVERNMENT RUNNING BECAUSE PEOPLE ARE NOT GETTING WHAT THEY EXPECTED FROM THE GOVERNMENT'

1

The car stopped right in front of Camp Hebron, the headquarters of the National Socialist Council of Nagaland (Isak-Muivah) (NSCN-IM), the insurgent group that leads India's oldest secessionist movement. A man had come visiting from New Delhi, from India's premier investigating agency, the Central Bureau of Investigation (CBI).

Perched on a hillock 40 kilometres south of Nagaland's business hub, Dimapur, Camp Hebron covers a sprawling forest area overlooking the Dhansiri river. Flanked by trees guarding muddy tracks, the camp is a craggy expanse that shares its boundary wall with the Intangki National Park. Rebel soldiers in battle fatigues are swarming all over the camp. The NSCN-IM is perpetually in readiness for battle, and clashes with rival factions are frequent, although, currently, the group has agreed on a ceasefire with New Delhi.

The CBI official, one of the organization's leading investigators, had arrived in a civilian vehicle. That was one of the preconditions of his visit. The other was that he would not carry any weapons. He was frisked at the gate, near a wall where the name of the camp was written in bold bright green letters. The officer had been compelled to undertake this journey because the police machinery of Manipur had pleaded helplessness in a case and had advised him to seek the help of the very rebel group they had been fighting.

The CBI official was led into the camp along a road that passed by a church with a giant cross above its entrance. The guards accompanying him stopped near a building and he was taken inside a room. A few minutes later, the military chief of the group arrived, and the two shook hands. Two traditional Naga spears were displayed crisscrossed on the wall facing him, the officer noticed. He started to speak. It was about a little girl.

When they found her body, Lungnila Elizabeth's hand was still gripping her handkerchief. Her green and white school uniform was intact on her small body, as was the ribbon in her hair. Had it not been for her school badge, however, it would have been difficult to recognize Elizabeth. A week ago, eight-year-old Lungnila Elizabeth, a student in the third grade in Imphal's Little Flower School, had been abducted by unidentified men. Now her body lay in a gunny bag, decomposed beyond recognition.

Abductions are a daily routine in Manipur as well, the state bordering Nagaland. Every week, government officials or their families are kidnapped by underground insurgents known locally as Undergrounds or UGs. Some of them return with bullet wounds in their knees, inflicted as a warning. Others, who are not so lucky, end up with a bullet in their hearts or their heads. Sometimes it takes weeks for corpses to be found, as they lie rotting on a deserted road or thickly forested area. Elizabeth's was one such body.

In a state where nothing – no amount of farcical governance and no amount of pain – seems to move anyone any longer, Elizabeth's death brought a lump to people's throats. Francis Ngazokpa, the education minister of Manipur, and Elizabeth's father, had reportedly paid a ransom of Rs 10 lakh for her safe return, but it could not save Elizabeth.

In encounters between the insurgents and the armed forces, young children often become victims, but this was perhaps the first time that such a young child had been killed in a planned and gruesome manner. Elizabeth's murder highlighted the sorry state of affairs in Manipur. The state, whose name means 'jewelled land', was now a piece of rusting iron. Decades of insurgency, coupled with political apathy and total administrative collapse, had brought Manipur to the brink of disintegration.

Manipur's saga is, in turn, a reflection of what is perhaps the world's most complex and oldest-running web of ethnic insurgencies. The crisis in the northeastern states of India is grave; militancy in this region is deeply intertwined with the establishment and people have had to come to terms with it. Thousands have died. Successive governments have looked the other way as rebels ruled the state. Many government leaders are, security officials say, just a phone call away for the militant chiefs, ready to do their bidding.

Investigations have revealed that of the estimated Rs 3,000 crore that is sent as central government aid every year to Manipur, barely a fifth is utilized.

There are some twenty-five insurgent groups in Manipur, belonging to various ethnic communities such as the Meiteis, Nagas and Kukis, and their objectives range from 'restoring the sovereignty' of the region to protecting the interests of their respective communities. But, as a government official puts it, belonging to one of these groups is not a prerequisite for turning into an extortionist. Four young people can get together, get a letterhead printed and form an insurgent group, which will then send out extortion notices to individuals and government departments. According to a recent estimate by the police, there are around fifteen thousand people involved in militant activities in Manipur. The government has long collapsed and militancy has become just another job option – the highest-paying source of employment in the midst of a massive job crisis.

When Elizabeth died, the police groped in the dark for a long time to find out who among these fifteen thousand people was responsible for killing her. No insurgent group claimed responsibility, perhaps due to widespread public outrage, and the police gave up on the case. It was then that a local insurgent group, the United National Liberation Front (UNLF), disclosed that Elizabeth was kidnapped and killed by a man belonging to a Kuki outfit. The UNLF's revelation was based upon the confessions of Nameirakpam Rome, who was later handed over by the insurgents to a women's group. The Kuki man who committed the crime was identified as James Kuki and it was revealed that he lived in Imphal, the capital of Manipur. But by the time an angry mob could lay its hands on him, James and his wife had fled their hometown.

James Kuki, the police found out, had escaped to Nagaland. It was clear now that the man who had killed Elizabeth could not be nabbed – he was out of the hands of law enforcers in Manipur, since there is hardly any coordination between the police of the two states. Moreover, the police in Nagaland, very much like their counterparts in Manipur, have very little control over their own turf, insurgency in Nagaland being as old as independent India itself.

Months after he allegedly killed the little girl, James Kuki was finally nabbed, but not by any police agency. Across the Northeast, the rules are clear. There might be democratically elected governments in the states, and regular police forces guided by the law of the land, but, in reality, it is the insurgents who are in control. It was the NSCN-IM that caught James Kuki. They tracked him down and kept him in detention. Later a spokesperson of the group claimed that he had been let out on 'parole'.

Four years passed. In February 2007, while speaking to a local newspaper, the information and publicity minister of the NSCN-IM said that handing over James to the Manipur government was a 'matter of serious concern ... [as] the organization has doubts [whether] the investigation would be carried out effectively'. When the rebel spokesperson's statement became public knowledge, sentiments ran high in Manipur once again. The police said it was trying to catch James Kuki, but months passed and no breakthrough was achieved. Finally, the case was handed over to the CBI.

'The police expressed its helplessness and advised us to instead take the NSCN-IM's help,' the CBI officer would later recall. He established contact with the NSCN-IM military chief and, after agreeing to the conditions the chief laid down, travelled to Dimapur and onwards to Camp Hebron. At first, the chief refused to provide any assistance in the case. But after hours of persuasion and the investigator telling him about the grisly nature of the crime, he finally relented. 'He said, "We will not hand him over to you, but we will tell you where he is. You coordinate with the police and launch a joint operation to nab him",' the investigator revealed.

Finally, James Kuki was arrested. A charge sheet has been filed against him and he is being tried for murder.

The forty-five-year-old man sitting on the sofa refuses our offer of a cup of tea and keeps looking towards the door of the hotel room at every sound in the corridor outside.

'Governments in Manipur are run by two opposing parties – the government itself and the underground,' he says softly. Then he changes his mind: 'In fact, there is no government. All government contracts are issued by the Underground. Government officials are just rubber stamps.'

For his safety, we shall refer to the man by his first name, Peter. He wears a cream shirt and brown trousers. He makes small-talk, trying to assess which side of the power divide we might belong to, and opens up after half an hour.

He has had quite a run over the past year. In 2008, he got a Rs 1 crore contract to build a school and a two-storey building to be used as government staff quarters and hostels. 'Before the work order was given, the executive engineer took his share of 10 per cent. Then the assistant engineer. Then the section officer. We negotiated with them. But we still had to give them money from time to time.

Every time they had to pass a bill, they took a share. If I finished the first floor and the bill came to Rs 20 lakhs, they deducted 10 per cent.'

This could have happened anywhere in corruption-ridden India, but not what followed thereafter. For he now had to pay the insurgents their 'taxes'. Groups in the Imphal valley – dominated by the Meitei community – deducted 9 per cent at source from the money paid to the government. In the Naga-dominated hills, 5 per cent tax was charged by the finance department of the NSCN-IM. Another regional department of the NSCN-IM deducted 2 per cent on that. 'That left no money for construction, so we were forced to use substandard material. If we were supposed to use three bags of concrete in one pillar, we used one and a half,' Peter said.

'After paying all this, I thought I was free.' Not quite. Peter still had not paid the insurgents belonging to the Kuki community, the third major ethnic group in the state. He had been ordered by them to pay Rs 3 lakh, but had been unable to make the payment.

On a Sunday morning, at around 11.30 a.m., Peter was driving on the highway that connects Manipur's plains to the hills. He slowed down as he approached a culvert that was being repaired. Three trucks stood by. 'Suddenly they came running from all sides,' Peter said. 'One of them had a pistol. He said: "Come out!"' He was abducted by members of the Kuki Revolutionary Army (KRA). 'They knew who I was. They took me to a small town called Kampupi, and said I would have to wait there. Their boss had gone to the neighbouring district and would be back in two or three days.' They took away his mobile phone. The village headman was asked to inform Peter's brother.

At night, the rebels took Peter to a forest to sleep. Armed guards stood by as Peter slept in a conical hut they had made out of a plastic sheet, with wooden planks and straw laid on the ground for him. During the day, he was brought into town.

'After three days, they demanded Rs 10 lakh. My family members negotiated for five,' Peter said, getting restless and keen to go home as evening set in.

On the day of his release, his family paid the KRA militants Rs 3 lakh in cash, promising to pay the remaining amount later. His mobile phone had been put to good use by the rebels. 'Long after my release, their friends and relatives were calling me back,' Peter said, smiling wistfully.

Peter wanted to complain about his abduction, but he knew it was useless going to the police. So he went to the Underground, as most people do in the Northeast, for redressal. 'Once I was out, the whole tribe contacted the NSCN-IM which had groomed the KRA ... The NSCN-IM forced the KRA to return the three lakh,' Peter said, with a feeling of salvaged pride.

The parallel government ruling the Northeast works on some principles, after all. 'The chief of the KRA – a man everyone called Chongloi – came to apologize,' Peter said. 'He said, "There will be chances when I can help you."'

As we travel through Imphal, past bustling markets selling contraband goods, the general sense of neglect is overwhelming. Just a few metres away from where the state's ministers live amidst high security, kerosene oil is being sold in the black market at Rs 35 a litre, instead of Rs 9. Power and water supply in Manipur are both abysmal. People living in the heart of Imphal do not get more than a few hours of electricity in a day. In some areas, water is available in taps just once or twice a week. Add to that the potholed roads, a rickety public transport system, dilapidated buildings – everything seems to mourn the idea of Manipur being a state.

In September 2007, while the Indian government was conducting the Northeast India Trade and Investment Week in Bangkok,

Thailand, four elderly men from Manipur were doing the rounds of Raisina Hill, India's political corridor, where decisions are taken on the fate of the nation. The men had come to petition the prime minister and political leaders of India to do something about the 'total breakdown of law and order in Manipur'.

'The prevailing law and order situation amply reflects the inefficiency and ineffectiveness of the present state government in tackling the ever increasing crime rate in Manipur. It seems there is no administration and governance in the state today,' said their memorandum. It highlighted the fact that strikes, bandhs and blockades had become a norm for the Manipuris; between 2004 and 2006, the total financial loss due to bandhs and blockades was a hefty Rs 1300 crore. 'Manipur is now in a state of chaos and anarchy. If the present state of affairs is allowed to continue unchecked, ultimate doom is not far off,' it stated.

The memorandum also brought to the prime minister's notice the rampant corruption in the state. 'Siphoning of public money by unscrupulous public servants, fraudulent withdrawals of taxpayers' money without executing public works, irregular/fake appointments in government departments, and bribery in appointments, transfers and postings of government servants have become the order of the day. Merit and talent are no longer the sole criteria for government appointments, and every government job has a price tag in Manipur.' Drawing attention to the unbridled unemployment in the state, the memorandum cautioned that 'until and unless these frustrated, hungry and angry young people are provided gainful employment and engaged in constructive activities, there will be no end to the troubles in Manipur.'

More than 6 lakh educated people are unemployed in Manipur. That is a quarter of the state's population. They find a ready source of employment in the militant groups, where they get guns, drugs, power, and attention from women. On the streets of Imphal, many of those frustrated, hungry and angry faces pull cycle-rickshaws.

Most of the rickshaw pullers are graduates, yet they earn their living by transporting people from one corner of Imphal to another because they have no option. When they ply their rickshaws in their neighbourhood or in busy marketplaces, they cover their faces to avoid being recognized by relatives or friends. Outside Imphal's Jawaharlal Nehru Hospital, Y. Sharma blows out rings of smoke from his cigarette, smuggled in from neighbouring Myanmar. He is a post-graduate from the prestigious Delhi University. 'And yet when I came back,' he says, 'only an underground outfit offered me a job.' Sharma belongs to a well-off family, so he was lucky. 'I was able to start my own business, but most can't,' he says, pointing to a rickshaw puller passing by, his face covered with a scarf.

Most militant groups have turned contractors themselves, and if they do not get contracts to build schools or government buildings or roads and bridges, they use guns to get their way. Residents sometimes hold protest rallies and sit-downs, opposing 'unreasonable demands' from militants - which is to say that most demands from them are considered reasonable. 'The lives of the people here are a series of compromises,' says a senior army officer.

At the border, it is, as another officer puts it, 'a problem beyond imagination'. Manipur's border with Myanmar is open and unfenced, and there are no roads. Thousands of people cross over every day, walking along forest tracks in the dense vegetation. Under bilateral treaties, Myanmarese people living in the region can enter 24 kilometres into India without a visa and Indians can go 16 kilometres into Myanmar without one. This had been initiated with the intention of spurring local economies and helping people to get vegetables and food items from each other's markets, but it has become a convenient passageway for gun-running and drug cartels that have intimate links with militant groups. Myanmar has long opposed the construction of a fence along the border due to an on-going border dispute.

According to an estimate, 10 per cent of the central government's funding, including 5 per cent of employees' salaries, go into the coffers of insurgent groups. Even government departments have to comply with the extortion demands. Extortion, which is rampant in the state, is termed as fund drives. In recent years, the state's tourism, industries and agriculture offices have reportedly been threatened with closure by insurgent groups after they failed to meet the incessant demands.

In January 2008, insurgents threatened senior officials of the United Bank of India with dire consequences if the bank did not pay the money they demanded. This led to the indefinite closure of the bank's fifteen branches. Many other banks, including the Manipur Rural Bank, were forced to shut down their services after receiving extortion threats from various insurgent groups. In the past, government-owned agencies, such as the Life Insurance Corporation have had to shut shop in Imphal after extortion demands were made to them. Many other insurance companies have closed down their offices as well. It was only after several assurances from the police that they resumed their services.

To an outsider, the ease with which militants operate in the state is astonishing. The NSCN-IM is in total control of National Highway 39, which serves as the lifeline of Manipur, connecting it to the other states. There is absolutely no sign of the state's authority on the highway; in fact, the government checkposts on the highway are not manned by government representatives, but by rebels. The insurgents collect taxes at some two dozen collection points from vehicles that traverse the highway. One estimate puts the amount of money collected from every commercial vehicle at Rs 4,000. For other vehicles, there are tax receipts of Rs 200 and Rs 500. Many truckers and drivers who have failed to comply in the past have been beaten up and their vehicles burnt.

In August 2009, due to long spells of curfew and highway blockades, Manipur faced an acute shortage of oxygen cylinders, crucial to healthcare centres across the state. 'If we don't get a supply in the next few days, we will be forced to close down the emergency department,' said a senior doctor in the government hospital in Imphal.

In 2007, pharmaceutical companies stopped sending medicines to Manipur after the insurgents slapped an extortion demand of Rs 100 lakh on pharmaceutical associations. Within days, this caused an acute shortage of lifesaving drugs in the market. Many imperative medical operations had to be postponed. In a state where HIV infections are among the highest, in the country stocks of antiretroviral drugs began to dry up. A majority of the people living with HIV and AIDS are dependent on the market for these drugs and, many had to risk their lives and go without them for days. (Antiretroviral therapy, once started, cannot be stopped for fear of mutation of the HIV.)

In the AIDS hub of India we meet Soman Keishing, thirty-eight, infected with the HIV virus.

'The HIV problem is very severe, but we cannot do tests, because there is no power supply,' he tells us. The wiry, calm-faced Keishing speaks slowly, smiles occasionally, and sits in a room lit by shafts of sunlight in the district hospital in Ukhrul town straddling the Myanmar border. Keishing sits with two other HIV-positive youth who have no problem being mentioned by name, Biswajit Sagolsem, forty-one, and thirty-year-old Anand. All three are members of the Manipur Network of Positive People. 'We want to reach people in remote areas but there is no vehicle. People cannot come here to get their blood tested. We go as far as we can by bus, but then we have to walk. And that is difficult for us,' says Keishing.

'Earlier, people said the Underground will kill you, because you are HIV-positive,' says Sagolsem. 'So we went to their office and they then had some understanding.'

'UGs (Underground) do not touch the AIDS money,' Sagolsem claims, though they are widely believed to be seizing stakes in most other development funds.

One can hear loud groans from the ward next door. A stocky man in uniform is lying on the bed, surrounded by armed paramilitary soldiers. The man on the bed is the local commanding officer of Manipur Rifles, who needs urgent medical care to survive. His men prepare a jeep to take him to the state capital of Manipur. The HIV room hears such groans every other day. Its occupants barely flinch. It is just a slice of life in Manipur.

'We are not getting any financial help from the state government. All the government schemes are being run by the Underground,' says Anand. 'That is why I came here.'

Economic blockades are not the only cause for healthcare facilities in the state being in a shambles. A team of investigators put together by the centre visited a government hospital in Imphal in August 2009 and found that the operation theatre had been shut down. It took the hospital administration some time to even find the key to the operation theatre when the officials insisted on inspecting it. When it was opened, the officials noticed that the surgery table had been in disuse for eight months. There were no surgeons present and the mobile medical units, on which millions of taxpayers' rupees had been spent, lay rusting in a corner. The outpatient department, the officials were told, functioned only twice a week, so most of the patients were forced to go to private doctors.

What are the politicians doing while ordinary Manipuris are, sometimes quite literally, struggling for oxygen? Well, among other things, they are harbouring militants.

On 17 August 2007, three members of the legislative assembly of Manipur, who belong to the Congress Party, received unexpected guests at their official residences. A Manipur Police team had come visiting, or rather on a raid, acting on an intelligence input. While searching their houses, the police nabbed twelve militants belonging to various underground groups. Several weapons, including an

M-16 rifle, were recovered. As the police officers continued their raid, they were in for a further surprise. From the residence of one of the MLAs, the police recovered extortion notes meant to be sent to various people and private companies.

The former governor of Manipur, Ved Marwah, an ex-police officer himself, does not find this surprising at all. 'There are hardly any politicians [in Manipur] who do not have links with one insurgent group or the other,' he says.

Similar allegations have been levelled against Manipur's current chief minister, Okram Ibobi Singh. In 2005, the then chief of the Indian Army, General J.J. Singh, claimed that Ibobi Singh had paid a donation of Rs 50 lakh to one insurgent group and Rs 1 crore to another. A senior state politician, H. Nabashyam, wrote an open letter dated 6 August 2009 to Ibobi Singh, with a copy to Prime Minister Manmohan Singh, condemning the chief minister's statement on the floor of the state assembly after a man was killed in an encounter that had clearly been faked in Imphal on 23 July 2009. Ibobi Singh had said, '[I am] not telling [the security forces] to kill them all [the Underground elements], but there is no other option ...,' leading to accusations that he was openly supporting extrajudicial killings.

In the letter, Nabashyam wrote, 'Is it not true that the Honourable Chief Minister, one of the richest men in Manipur today, was a middle-class contractor cum politician before he became the chief minister in March 2002, for which achievement he has earned the title. "Hon'ble 10% Ibobi"?'

'The chief minister is a part of the problem,' Nabashyam told us in an interview. 'He can speak to any underground outfit at any time; in fact, he often uses them as disposable syringes for furthering his own agenda.'

It was probably allegations like these that prompted the prime minister to express concern over the developments in Manipur during the Chief Ministers' Conference on Internal Security in

August 2009. 'Assam and Manipur account for a disproportionately large number of violent incidents reported from the Northeast, with the latter's share being as high as 30 per cent,' Manmohan Singh said. In an apparent reference to Manipur, the Home Minister P. Chidambaram is reported to have said: 'At times, we find that some state governments have allowed themselves to bend before insurgent groups, making the fight against insurgency that much more difficult.'

At the same conference, all Ibobi Singh asked for was the central government's help in banning prepaid phones as a measure against the insurgency in the state. That was the only suggestion he had to fight the collapse of his state.

Manipur constitutes a little more than 8 per cent of northeastern India and just above 6 per cent of its total population, but it accounted for 47 per cent of all insurgency related deaths in the region in 2008. In the first six months of 2009, the state had seen around seven hundred and fifty-two violent incidents and accounted for close to one-third of the total casualties of unrest in the Northeast.

Public outrage is rising. In the eighteen months since January 2008, there were more than three hundred major public protests against insurgents in the state. But Prime Minister Manmohan Singh's Congress Party, which also runs Manipur, has mostly looked away thus far.

In the past, successive governments in New Delhi did make some attempts to break the politician–militant nexus in Manipur. In 1997, during I.K. Gujral's prime ministership, the home ministry had drawn up an elaborate action plan to break the nexus. Years later, Prime Minister Atal Behari Vajpayee decided to set up a judicial inquiry into the nexus. Both efforts bore no results.

In November 2000, in a report, the then joint secretary of the home ministry, G.K. Pillai, said that 'deterioration' had taken place in Manipur with 'active connivance of the political leadership'. The report further said that only eighteen of the state's fifty-seven police stations were functional. Of Manipur's three hundred and sixty-eight intelligence gatherers, only eleven actually did what they were supposed to. The rest, the report said, functioned as bodyguards, on 'security duty'.

A central intelligence official, who is not a Manipuri, puts it plainly: 'One turns cynical quite early in the Northeast. And there has never been a sincere effort from mainstream India to understand it.'

2

On a cold and extremely foggy night in January 2003, a large gathering of young Naga men and women stood outside Delhi's Indira Gandhi International Airport. Wearing their traditional tribal costumes and colourful Naga shawls, they waited to welcome two elderly men who were setting foot on Indian soil for the first time in thirty-six years. While they waited, braving the wet chill, they sang a song that has become an anthem for protesters all over the world: 'We shall overcome, some day.'

The plane from Amsterdam landed at around midnight, and the two men finally appeared in the arrivals lounge. Some among the waiting group let out tribal war cries upon seeing their leaders. One of these men was rebel leader Thuingaleng Muivah, who could be mistaken for a Harvard professor in his formal suit, complete with a tie. But this was not what he wore decades ago when he undertook a long and treacherous journey to China from Nagaland, along with a group of followers, to receive ideological training and carry back arms. Accompanying him was his old comrade, Isak Chisi Swu. Together, they headed the Isak–Muivah group of the National Socialist Council of Nagaland, often simply called IM after it split from the NSCN to form NSCN-IM in April 1988.

From the dream of self-determination, the Nagas had moved directly to insurgency and the region, where the British had fought a fierce battle with the Japanese during the Second World War, had turned into a bloody theatre of war.

In 1997, thirty years after the group's failed in talks 1967 with the then prime minister, Indira Gandhi, the NSCN-IM signed a ceasefire agreement with New Delhi. And now, seven years after signing the agreement, Muivah and Swu were back in India.

Since the 1997 agreement, more than sixty rounds of talks have taken place between the NSCN-IM and the central government in places as diverse as Amsterdam, Bangkok, Davos and Paris. The discussions have always proved to be difficult. Sometimes, the meetings would continue day and night and, suddenly, as New Delhi's emissaries recall, Muivah would get up from his chair and announce that he was done with the talks. Sometimes nothing would come out of meetings that extended over two days and then an agreement would be signed minutes before New Delhi's emissary was required to board a plane home.

Ironically, when the two rebel leaders arrived in India, one of the first items on their itinerary was a visit to Raj Ghat. This gesture was not without reason. First, the Naga rebels wanted to send out a signal that they were all for peace. There was also some history behind the visit. During all their years of running a secessionist movement against India, the Naga leaders would often refer to a meeting between Angami Zapu Phizo, the man who first dreamt of a separate Nagaland and Muivah's mentor, and Mahatma Gandhi at the Bhangi Colony ashram in Delhi before India's Independence. Gandhi had reportedly told Phizo at the time that the Nagas were 'family' as far as India was concerned, but they could stay separately if they so desired.

Over a period of time, the demand for a separate state had softened. Muivah and Swu were now ready to settle for much less – greater autonomy for 'Nagalim' or Greater Nagaland. But what they called Nagalim extended much beyond the territorial limits of the current state of Nagaland and included parts of Assam, Arunachal Pradesh and Manipur.

'If New Delhi respected the reality of Nagaland, the Nagas would respect the reality of India ten times more,' Swu said after Muivah and he met the then prime minister, Atal Behari Vajpayee, at the latter's official residence. It was a great moment, as the peaceniks called it. The two leaders were all over the national dailies and on primetime television for the next few days, their fingers raised in a 'victory' sign.

But beyond the photo ops there lay a complexity of which New Delhi had already had a taste. Carving out portions from the other states would undoubtedly be a tricky issue. In 2001, the home ministry decided to extend the ceasefire with the NSCN-IM in Nagaland to its neighbouring states, including Manipur.

Of Manipur's population of twenty-five lakhs, some eighteen lakh people belong to the ethnic Meitei community that lives in the Imphal valley. The Nagas number about three lakhs and occupy the hill districts of Manipur – Ukhrul, Chandel, Senapati and Tamenglong – which the NSCN-IM considered to be part of Greater Nagaland. Muivah himself belongs to Ukhrul. To the Manipuris, the government's decision to extend the ceasefire was seen as a clear attempt to redraw Manipur's territorial boundaries. A sixty-six-hour bandh was jointly called by dozens of local groups.

The Meiteis decided to act. It was drizzling on 18 June 2001, a damp Monday morning, when as many as a hundred thousand protesters stormed on to the streets of Imphal, burning effigies of Muivah and the then home minister, Lal Krishna Advani. As the crowd surged towards the VIP area, the CRPF soldiers on guard opened fire. Thirteen protesters died and hundreds were injured. The angry crowd set the Manipur state assembly on fire. Several leaders had a narrow escape, some of them sustaining severe burn injuries.

In 2003, when the news of Muivah and Swu returning to India reached the chief minister of Manipur, Okram Ibobi Singh, he reacted with great bitterness, saying, 'He (Muivah) will not be let off if he comes to Manipur.'

But the upheaval in Manipur was not an immediate concern for the A.B. Vajpayee-led union government. They had scored a major victory by bringing Muivah and Swu back to India. Manipur's bridge could be crossed later. And that is precisely where the talks got stuck within days. After the initial euphoria was over, it was back to square one. The Naga leaders wouldn't budge from their stated demand for Greater Nagaland. Emerging from Vajpayee's official residence on Race Course Road in Delhi, Muivah and Swu made it clear that for them the issue of Greater Nagaland was not negotiable.

'There is no small or greater Nagaland. Nagaland is Nagaland,' Muivah told the battery of journalists waiting outside. One of us asked him, 'Mr Muivah, do you consider Ukhrul to be a part of Nagaland?' 'Yes, of course,' he shot back, 'I was born there.' It was clear now. There would be no solution to the Naga problem in the near future. From that time until now, it has been a turbulent ride, with both the government and the NSCN-IM accusing each other of breaking the terms and conditions of the ceasefire.

This has been a win-win situation for the NSCN-IM. On the one hand, its cadres move around freely, without the risk of getting arrested. As a part of the ceasefire agreement, they can appear unarmed only outside Camp Hebron. But they are everywhere, running a mega extortion racket, earning billions of rupees every year. According to some estimates, the NSCN-IM and two other factions had extracted Rs 2 billion from Dimapur alone in the first seven months of 2008, and Dimapur is only a small territory in their area of influence. Central intelligence agencies say that the NSCN-IM has an annual budget of between Rs 20 crore and Rs 25 crore. The NSCN-IM has also used the ceasefire to acquire more arms and strengthen its cadre. According to a survey carried out in early 2008, the NSCN-IM's cadre had almost doubled from the original three thousand. It has also nearly doubled its weaponry since 1997.

In May 2009, In Assam's Dhemaji district, which borders Arunachal Pradesh, a senior army officer received a tip-off. There was no time to spare. The officer immediately rang up his equivalent in the Assam Police. Together, they set out for the forest area near a village called Subahi.

Two cadres of the NSCN-IM were arrested swiftly. Upon interrogation, the rebels revealed that the NSCN-IM and its other faction, the Khaplang group - named after S.S. Khaplang, who broke away from Muivah in 1988 - had managed to create a base in Arunachal Pradesh and launch a major extortion drive there. Confirming the increasing activities of the NSCN-IM in Arunachal Pradesh, Inspector General of Police Deepak Mishra says that the police had come across many cases where both factions had extorted money from local businessmen. 'They are also on a recruitment drive, providing a stipend of Rs 1,000 to every recruit,' he adds.

Police sources reveal that the insurgent groups have jointly set up large bases in the Tirap and Changlang districts, which border Myanmar. A senior police officer in Assam says that the NSCN-IM had been able to lure youth from Arunachal Pradesh's West Siang district and many bordering villages of Assam into joining them. It is believed that some of the new recruits are being trained at Camp Hebron in Dimapur.

The situation is alarming in Arunachal Pradesh because the terrain provides a natural sanctuary for insurgents. 'The inhospitable terrain makes it difficult for the police to control the movement of the insurgents,' says Mishra.

When the NSCN-IM wants more money it urges its cadres to loot banks. One such attempt was foiled in the West Siang district of Arunachal Pradesh after the police caught a 'sergeant major' of the NSCN-IM in Dhemaji in May 2009. The rebel revealed that he and four other men had been planning to rob the Manipur Rural Bank branch near Aalo, the district headquarters of West Siang. Police investigations revealed that the arrested rebel and his accomplices were responsible for an attack on security personnel in Dhemaji a few months ago and had also been supervising the outfit's recruitment drive in West Siang.

Perhaps more alarming than the NSCN-IM's recruitment drive across the northeastern states are intelligence reports that Islamic extremists are establishing sleeper cells in Nagaland with the help of the NSCN-IM. Nagaland's chief minister, Neiphiu Rio, believes that some Muslim members of the outfit, who are a part of its extortion cell, have been playing a major role in establishing links with Islamic extremist groups such as the Harkat-ul-Jehad-i-Islami. He identified one such member as 'Lieutenant' Halal-uddin of the NSCN-IM's armed wing. The claims, however, could not be independently verified.

A recent confidential report sent to the home ministry by the CRPF says that insurgent groups in the Northeast supported by Bangladesh have been trying to set up bases for Islamic extremists in the region. It mentions that the insurgent groups are working on a long-term plan to create a separate homeland for Muslims in Northeast India. Recently, posters and banners stating such demands have surfaced in a few areas.

The Northeast has already witnessed decades of trouble as one ethnic insurgent group after another has surfaced in the region. Now with the fear of Islamic extremism also looming large over it, and New Delhi's commitment limited to sending funds and emissaries, the Northeast, as one intelligence officer puts it, has the potential of turning into 'India's migraine'.

3

Wherever you go in Manipur, the Undergrounds or UGs have an address. There it is, the office of the Undergrounds, behind the row of shops in the main market in the mountain town of Ukhrul. Hidden behind grocery, meat and stationery shops, the small tin-roofed structure that houses the office is both inconspicuous and anonymous. This is where the rebel administration's chief administrative officer sits. We cannot meet him because he is away on 'official duty', we are told.

The militants' office is more powerful than any government office in town. When a road called Circular Road had to be built in the area a while ago, contractors were unable to get the land cleared. Then the Undergrounds stepped in, the locals say, and forced people to give up part of their land to widen the road.

'If people go to the police or courts, it will take ten years, so they go to the UGs. It is very quick – takes a month, or even just a day. But justice is sometimes not done because it is very hurried,' says L.M. Ngaranmi, a community elder and president of the Tangkhul Long, a powerful Naga tribe.

Far away from national attention, far away from the gleaming malls and industries and wide avenues and the information technology boom, another universe has been functioning for years in Manipur.

Directly or indirectly, every citizen of Manipur pays taxes to the militants. A tax of about 5 to 10 per cent is deducted every payday from the salary of every government employee over and above the income tax paid to the government of India – for the Undergrounds, no questions asked. The extortion business has been running for decades. Manipur really doesn't care now, for it has learnt to live with it. New Delhi never cared anyway.

'It is an open secret. There is a parallel government running because people are not getting what they expected from the government,' said Ngaranmi.

Though they are called Undergrounds, the militants seldom operate underground. The rebels have swooped in to fill the massive vacuum of governance in the state. They have all the trappings of a real government. They arrest motorcycle thieves, treat patients, investigate rapes and murders, punish students cheating in examinations and help build roads. The appointment of a new chief administrative officer in Tamenglong by the rebel administration was a front page story in the *Imphal Free Press*, the region's leading daily newspaper.

> **New NSCN-IM CAO takes charge in Zeliangrong region**
> From Daniel Kamei
>
> TAMENGLONG, June 22: L. Gonmei took over the charge of central administrative office, CAO, of the Government of People's Republic of Nagalim, Zeliangrong region, today from the outgoing Z.T. Bohn, who has been deputed as a member of the steering committee of the outfit, NSCN-IM.
>
> The Zeliangrong Union, Tamenglong zone, has in the meantime hailed the new CAO and expressed hope that he will bring peace, harmony and development in the region.
>
> The handing over and taking over of the charge was done in a simple function held somewhere in Tamenglong district, which was attended by leaders of several Zeliangrong based social organizations, pastors and village authority chiefs.
>
> Speaking on the occasion, the new CAO said that his first duty is to build up peace and unity and bring development in Nagalim in general, and particularly in the Zeliangrong region.

The militant stranglehold on Manipur is so tight that rebel groups openly announce the names of its officers who should be paid taxes by government officials. Stories like the one below from the *Sangai Express* newspaper are routinely carried by local newspapers as regular news reports:

> The Kuki Liberation Army has appointed Elwin/Hangsai Kuki as its finance secretary and Milan/Jack Meitei as its project officer, said its information and publicity secretary, Malsawm Kuki, in a statement.
>
> The outfit said that all financial matters will be dealt with by its finance secretary and project matters will be under the charge of the project officer.
>
> The outfit also warned all not to misuse its name and added that all individuals and government departments should deal with the said officials respectively.

Corruption edges on the farcical. City sidewalks, and areas covering manholes and even sewage drains, have been sold to people. These include local judges and police officials who have built their homes on that land, a top official said on condition of anonymity. An official who was once the administrator of Ukhrul district said, 'I had assigned work on a culvert for Rs 3 lakh, for a check dam on a stream. I kept insisting to the contractor that I would go and inspect whether he had actually built it on the stream. He kept saying it was too far, I should not go.'

Regardless, he went one day.

'I found some ten to fifteen bricks, that was all,' the official said. 'So we duly paid him not Rs 3 lakh, but just the cost of the bricks – nineteen rupees and ten paise.'

In another instance, Manipur's Public Works Department had claimed in official documents that it had executed a hill-cutting job worth Rs 42 lakh in Ukhrul in just eight days, an extraordinarily short period of time for such a complex task. But when enquiries followed, PWD officials could not produce any evidence before government auditors to show that the work had actually been done on the ground.

Between 2005 and 2007, thousands of government employees in Manipur did not get salaries. Until 2007, the state government had no idea how many people worked for it. It was assumed that eighty thousand people worked for the government because that was the number on the rolls, but a tedious headcount revealed that the government had only sixty-one thousand employees. The rest were 'fake appointments', drawing salaries with the connivance of superiors without actually being employed by the government. In the education department alone, seventeen thousand people had been earning salaries, whereas only twelve thousand were actually employed in the department, the official said. Five thousand people who were said to be drawing pensions had been dead for a long time. The revenue department had seventy-six lower-division clerks on paper, though there were only fifteen posts.

A multipurpose project to generate electricity and water for irrigation, the Khuga project, commissioned in 1980 by the Planning Commission of India, is still not ready. New equipment is being bought now because the electrical and mechanical equipment bought fourteen years ago has rusted away; other equipment has been stolen.

Vigilante justice is common. The UNLF asked the alleged abductor of a valley student called J. Rengwin Lamkang to release him and surrender within five days. Otherwise the abductor, his family and his friends would be given 'befitting punishment'. Lamkang was released within two days. When students were found to be cheating in the state examinations and using knives to threaten the teachers, members of the Meitei militant group KYKL shot the students in their legs. Another rebel group made unproven charges of corruption in appointments against the vice-chancellor of Manipur University and shot him in the leg. The Imphal valley-based militant group UNLF recovered Rs 47 lakh from government engineers, which, it said, they had taken as bribes. The UNLF kept the money. 'They said they were going to use it for development work. They build roads and all,' a security official said.

Much of the dispensation of justice also takes the form of kangaroo courts.

'The people who are in the insurgent groups are high-school dropouts. They don't know what is the law, what is their responsibility. They just hold the guns. Sometimes, they don't even follow the orders of their superiors,' said Ngaranmi, the Naga community leader in Ukhrul.

Not too far away from where Ngaranmi stood outside the district collector's office, is the office of a political wing of the NSCN-IM. It is a large space, its walls plastered with the flags of an independent Naga nation, which is the aim of the rebel organization. Yang Maso Raising, vice-president of the Tangkhul Naga Long, leans back authoritatively in his chair and speaks with pride about the rebels' government. 'They have their own administration, their education and health and finance departments and so on. They are powerful. They also have their own MPs and MLAs, but with different titles,' he says nonchalantly.

In Imphal, afternoon is setting in. Cycle-rickshaw pullers laze in their vehicles, waiting for customers, all of them with their faces masked in large scarves. Paramilitary soldiers stand in the markets, idly watching the movements of passers-by and refusing to be photographed. At a busy flea market in the centre of the city, old grandmothers selling clay pots take a break for some ice cream. Shoppers looking for fish and vegetables – mostly brought illegally across the border from Myanmar – walk under long stretches of jute hung high above them like latticed ceilings, creating tiny squares of sunlight across the narrow corridor.

Half an hour later, a few kilometres away in a large building guarded by policemen, a senior security official leans forward and picks up a cup of tea. It is a relaxed day. Chief Minister Ibobi Singh is away yet again in New Delhi. His absence makes little difference to the functioning of the state.

'There is a vested interest in keeping the insurgency moving. This state is slipping away ... Some biscuits?' says the security official. 'People get bullets and grenades in the mail when they are threatened. Every militant group is leading a luxurious lifestyle.'

Yet, the official says, in their need, people turn only to the Undergrounds. 'Rape cases are not attended to. So people go to the insurgents. The Undergrounds listen to the complainants. 'Ninety-nine per cent of the time they are bang on. In the first instance, offenders are shot in the leg. In the second, they are killed.'

But when three bodies were found in Ukhrul in February 2009, they were not those of rapists. One of the bodies was of a doctor, who had been killed because he did not pay up. Dr Thingnam Kishan Singh was a whistleblower, and Manipur, a state where the government and the Undergrounds often seem to be on the same side, was not a good place to be a whistleblower. Kishan Singh, who was also a sub-divisional officer (a senior local administrator), was the face of the new Manipur – a cheerful, optimistic man who had dared to give up his comfortable urban life in New Delhi, return to his roots and look optimistically beyond a life shrouded by insurgency.

On 13 February 2009, he and five of his colleagues stepped out of the office of the district commissioner after a meeting. They walked down the dimly lit corridors, damp and cold, officials absent from most rooms, and ambled past the sandbagged bunker at the entrance of the building, where two guards watched them. Before they could get into Kishan Singh's official Maruti Gypsy, militants rushed in, and the six men were bundled into their own vehicle and abducted. For the next three days, no one knew their whereabouts. The superintendent of police said he had no information about the abduction. The district collector went on a day's casual leave. Senior government officials washed their hands off the matter.

Shortly after dawn on 17 February, villagers found three bludgeoned bodies near Taphou Kuki village of Senapati district, to the west of Ukhrul. A spade and a bloodstained stone were found nearby. The bodies were identified as belonging to Kishan Singh, his aide, Yumnam Token Singh, and his driver, Aribam Rajen Sharma. The other three men who had been abducted were Nagas and were let off.

In July 2008, a letter had arrived for Kishan Singh, who was then looking after a project under the NREGS, bearing a simple and direct demand. It was an official letter from the NSCN-IM, dated 9 July 2008 and signed by Th. Rainam. It even had an official reference number for correspondence: No. 02-03/RCM/NCA/GPRN/2008. Rainam was in charge of the NSCN-IM's finances in the area.

'The NSCN-IM had asked our beloved Kishan to hand over 7 per cent of the fund allocated for the implementation of the NREGS in Kasom Khullen sub-division ... The same letter also threatened our Kishan in case he refused to comply with the diktat,' his family said in a statement released after his death. 'The NSCN-IM called this the "royalty tax of the GPRN (Government of the People's Republic of Nagaland) from the NREGS". Our beloved Kishan believed that the money rightfully belonged to the villagers of Kasom Khullen.'

Kishan Singh was bludgeoned to death with a spade perhaps because he had asked the headmen of seventy-eight villages to clarify how much of the government funds that they had received for the NREGS had been diverted to the NSCN-IM; this involved a major scandal in the sale of spades. He was also found to have been starved before his gruesome killing. Kishan Singh was, in fact, killed in a manner apparently aimed at setting off ethnic riots.

Nagas, Meiteis and Kukis are often in face-offs with each other, and Singh's killing was made to look like murder for ransom. The rebels removed the licence plates from Kishan Singh's government-allotted Maruti Gypsy, plunged it down a hillside, and then moved the captives from village to village for four days before killing the doctor in the neighbouring Senapati district, uncannily near a Kuki village.

Singh was educated at the Don Bosco School in Imphal, where he had friends of many ethnicities and where he dived early with his friends into rock 'n' roll and sang songs by the Doors, Jethro Tull and Led Zeppelin. Grand Funk Railroad's *Closer to Home* was one of his favourite songs, his classmates remember. He later moved to New Delhi, where he obtained his graduation and post-graduation degrees from the Jamia Millia Islamia University. He was good in his studies and regularly topped his class. 'We tried to unravel the mysteries of *Das Kapital*, dissect the enigma that surrounds Che Guevara and Mao Tse-Tung, and hum the edgy lines of Bob Dylan,' his classmates wrote in his memory. He completed his MPhil and got a job at Delhi University, but gave it up to return home.

For some time, Singh taught English at an Imphal school and is remembered by his students for the evocative way in which he taught Saratchandra Chatterjee's *The Drought*. He also alerted them to the fact that Bob Marley's popular reggae song '*No woman, no cry*' wasn't a romantic song at all – it was the story of Jamaica's suffering during French colonial rule. Later, he got a job as a government official. The down-to-earth officer stunned villagers by scolding them for not sending their children to school and for not going to government doctors when they fell ill.

The young doctor's life was a reflection of the aspirations, dreams and extreme challenges that lie before the young men and women of the northeastern states, who face the fallout of insurgency back home and racial stereotyping in every other part of India.

When the doctor's battered body was found, thousands of people rose in anger, uncharacteristic in a state where dissent has frightening consequences, and it is neither fashionable nor safe to mourn the death of a government official. There were massive street protests cutting across ethnic lines demanding to know the identity of the killers of the young doctor. The people's demands were not directed at the police, a force that has long been ineffective in tackling insurgency and extortion in the state. The angry demands were, instead, directed at the rebels, who are looked upon as the principal crime fighters in the state.

Under pressure from the raging public, the NSCN-IM, which had earlier said it had no connection to the killings, was forced to identify the alleged killers within its ranks: Lieutenant Colonel Hopson Ningsen, Ukhrul town commander Apho Sibo, and Major Ashang. The three men were declared to be in the custody of the NSCN-IM and the people were promised they would be dealt with according to their law. Ningsen has now been arrested by the CBI as the prime accused in Kishan Singh's murder and is being tried.

The region may have forgotten to feel pain after learning to live with it, but Kishan Singh's former students remember him in a poem amidst a swell of support for his cause.

'It was some time after spring
you and me were mourning
with smile, you and me were crying,
  remembering
how we would miss the burning flame
that [was] ceased by the rain of bullets.
We knew such heroism lasts only in literature
it will last only in hearts
the hearts of the weakest of the weak
And now today they have taken you in my heart,
the weak heart of mine.'

We are sitting with a portly, chubby-cheeked man who appears to have a long list of complaints.

'Money comes from the various departments of Manipur ... And the NSCN-IM is taking annual taxes – transport tax, godown tax, and so on. It is becoming quite unbearable. The biggest problem is the tax being collected at Dimapur [the trading hub of the neighbouring Nagaland],' he says. 'There is such a big difference in prices of things between Guwahati [the region's largest city] and Imphal. The same things cost much more in Imphal. In government offices, people do not take calls on their landlines or mobile phones because they call could be from UGs.'

Yumnam Joykumar Singh is no helpless citizen whining about the state of affairs in Manipur. He is the state's police chief.

'People are going to the Underground to resolve disputes. It is like this in most parts of the state,' Joykumar says, playing with a glass paperweight on his table. 'The UG elements can give you instant justice – whether correct or not. The Indian judicial system is time-consuming. It takes years to pursue cases, with most of them loaded against the prosecution.' When the director general of police complains helplessly about militants extorting tax, little more needs to be said about the role of the government or the police in protecting the people from militants.

'The boys are roaming around. Any vehicle not carrying receipts is burnt or damaged,' says Joykumar, referring to the official receipts given by the rebels to the people from whom 'tax' is collected. He quickly clarifies, 'The police do not pay the rebels.' The DGP's assertion is part of the farce at play in Manipur.

'Nah,' says Ukhrul-based Naga community leader Ngaranmi. 'People give them [the militants] shelter and money. Even uniformed persons give donations. It is an open secret.'

It is not possible to verify whether the police pay taxes to the rebels, but one thing is certain: Joykumar's men are among the most trigger-happy in India, though they are also the most irrelevant in the insurgency situation as compared to other rebel-affected states in the country.

An abnormally high number of deaths has been reported from Manipur, many of them allegedly extrajudicial killings, like that of twenty-three-year-old former militant Chungkham Sanjit by Manipur police commandoes, which was photographed and evoked national outrage. The mad rush for kills seems to be linked to the national gallantry awards. Out of the two hundred and twelve gallantry medals announced by the central home ministry in 2009, seventy-four went to policemen serving in Manipur – almost three times the number they were awarded in 2008.

Despite the large proportion of policemen deployed in the state, the police force in Manipur has made little contribution towards easing the insurgency. Manipur has six hundred and twenty-seven policemen per hundred thousand people, as compared to the Indian average of a hundred and twenty-five. It has more than seventy-three policemen per hundred square kilometres of area, as compared to the national average of forty-five.

At the local hospital in Ukhrul, young men open up in a rare moment to talk about the Undergrounds. 'Here, the police department is of no use. Any case, whether rape or murder, goes to the UGs either directly or indirectly,' said Tuithing Zingkhai, twenty-seven, of the Young Raphei Conference, a youth body that has sometimes opposed the rebels on issues. 'The UGs have their own reason and mission. But they should stick to their objective rather than interfere with us.'

The daily extortion demands by the militants have become Manipur's only thriving industry. An innocuous letter arrives first, on a printed letterhead, requesting financial assistance for the revolution. A live bullet could follow in the mail.

In February 2009, the managing director of the S. Kumar Hospital in Imphal's Porompat neighbourhood was sitting in his office when he received one of those infamous bullets. The militants had forced a patient to deliver the envelope to him. Students and teachers at the S. Kumar Hospital, which provides acupressure treatment and trains paramedics, stopped work and classes soon after to protest against the demand for Rs 50,000 per year from a local rebel group called the People's Revolutionary Party of Kangleipak (PREPAK).

In January 2009, cooking gas carriers shut down work at the Sekmai Bottling Plant in Manipur after the NSCN-IM demanded that they pay an annual 'godown tax' of Rs 13 lakh. In the past, pharmacies have closed down in protest after militants demanded Rs 1 crore from them and surgeries have had to be stopped for the duration of the strike at the Imphal-based Regional Institute of Medical Sciences, the region's largest hospital.

This is the hospital where Superintendent Y. Mohen was examining patients in 2007 when a young man walked in with a note. It was from an unheard of militant group, written in poor English, demanding Rs 10 lakh for the 'sanitization of the organization'. Mohen was furious and told the boy to get lost. Two nights later, during a power cut, Mohen was sitting at a tea shop across the street from his house when two young men on a motorcycle drove up to his ground floor home and rang the bell. Mohen's daughter answered the door. 'In the darkness, they probably assumed it was me. One of them hurled a grenade at her and fled,' Mohen told us. 'Fortunately, the grenade was of poor quality – it didn't explode.' In May 2009, the militants threw a grenade into the hospital campus to scare the patients. Again, luckily, no one was injured.

'The government of India is funding the insurgency in Manipur,' said cultural and human rights activist Yamben Laba. 'Ten per cent of the plan budget is going straight to the coffers of insurgent groups. Plus five per cent of the salary of all government employees. It's become a way of life.'

Here is an example of the farce that rules the lives in these states: two fringe militant groups are fighting Indian security forces in

Manipur, but their main demand is a separate state in neighbouring Myanmar!

'The government is not there to protect those who want to speak out. There is no government, in fact. All government appointments go to the Undergrounds and their families. Manipur is a completely failed state,' said Peter, the businessman who had been abducted. 'If India is really serious about Manipur, they should impose President's Rule for ten or fifteen years. Let there be no parties, no elected government. Maybe, then, things will heal.'

Postscript

In 2010 the situation in Manipur remained critical, with complications created once again by the centre.

New Delhi granted Muivah permission to travel to his village in Manipur's Ukhrul district. The move was, however, resisted by Manipur's chief minister who opposed Muivah's visit given the tension between the Nagas and Meiteis over the issue of Greater Nagaland. This led to rebels from Nagaland blocking the crucial highway to Manipur which serves as its lifeline, a blockade that continued for sixty-nine days. Nothing reached Manipur in that extended period of time, not even essential items like drugs, food and fuel. LPG cylinders were sold for Rs 2000 in the black market and prices of most food items rose by 500 per cent.

During those days, Manipur became a hangnail state, almost severed from India. The signs of healing, which Peter had hoped for, are yet to surface.

Gaaon chhodab nahi,
Jungle chhodab nahi,
Mai maati chhodab nahi,
Ladai chhodab nahi ...

Baandh banaye, gaaon duboye,
Karkhaana banaye,
Jungle kaate, khadaan khode,
Sanctuary banaye.
Jal, jungle, zameen chhod hum
Kahan kahan jaaye?
Vikas ke bhagwaan bata
Hum kaise jaan bachaye.

Mantri bane company ke dalaal
Humse zameen chheeni,
Unko bachane lekar aaye
Saath mein paltani.
Afsar bane hein raja
Thekedar bane dhani,
Gaanv humare ban gaye hein
Unki colony.

(Excerpts from a song inspired by Bhagwaan Maaji, leader of the adivasi struggle against bauxite mining in Kashipur, Orissa)

We won't leave our village,
We won't leave our forests,
We won't leave our mother Earth,
We will not give up our fight ...

They build dams, submerge villages,
They build factories,
They destroy jungles, dig mines,
They create sanctuaries.
If we leave our water, forest and land
Where do we go?
O God of development
Tell us how to save our lives.

Ministers have become the company's middlemen
They have snatched away our land,
To protect themselves
They also bring in platoons [of police].
Officials are now kings
Contractors have become rich,
And our village has
Become their colony.

Acknowledgements

A book can never be written just by its authors.

We wish to thank numerous friends, some who can be named, some who cannot, without whose help this book, a three-year effort with reportage spanning 40,000 kilometres of travel, would not have been possible.

Akshay Kumar of the *Hindustan Times* in Ranchi provided us invaluable support and insight. Tragically, Akshay passed away in a fatal car accident last year.

B. Vijay Murty in Jamshedpur shared our bravado and madness, and helped us in innumerable ways.

Dharish Chandra Singh of *Prabhat Khabar*, based in Ghatsila, Suresh Mahapatra in Dantewada in Chhattisgarh and Karimuddin in Jagdalpur.

In Kashmir, our friends and fellow journalists Aijaz Hussain, Suhail Bukhari, Zubair Dar and Parvaiz Bukhari, who broke bread and shared wisdom with us subversive kinds.

In Chhattisgarh, Jharkhand and West Bengal, the many Maoist leaders, activists and police officers who cannot be named. Thank you, Hartosh Singh Bal, for your 'scientific' clarity on life and beyond, Sandipan Deb for the absolute freedom to chase stories in conflict areas, and Kasauli Regency owners Preetie and Rajesh Dogar for those wonderful evenings in misty Kasauli where the final touches were given to this book.

We wish to thank our friend Krishan Chopra for handholding us for part of this journey.

Our gratitude to our colleagues and superiors at *Hindustan Times*, where Neelesh works, and the *Open* magazine, which Rahul writes for, for indulging us, supporting us and encouraging long-form writing.

Neelesh thanks Nidhi Razdan for her support and encouragement over the past four years. Rahul thanks Pinky Maikota for enduring long spells of silence.

Last, and most definitely not the least, thank you Nandita Aggarwal, Anurima Roy and Poulomi Chatterjee at Hachette India for chiselling the book into what it is. All the credit shall henceforth be ours, and all the blame yours!